THE
MAZ FILES

Mazhar Farooqui, also known as Maz, is a Dubai-based journalist currently serving as Senior Editor at *Khaleej Times*. He has previously worked for publications such as *Gulf News*, *The Times of India*, *Hindustan Times* and *The Pioneer*, among others. Maz has received numerous national and international awards for his investigative work. Additionally, he is the founder and president of Aaghaz Foundation, an educational charity organisation based in India.

THE MAZ FILES

SCOOPS, SCAMS AND SHOWDOWNS

MAZHAR FAROOQUI

Published by Westland Non-Fiction, an imprint of Westland Books, a division of Nasadiya Technologies Private Limited, in 2024

No. 269/2B, First Floor, 'Irai Arul', Vimalraj Street, Nethaji Nagar, Alapakkam Main Road, Maduravoyal, Chennai 600095

Westland, the Westland logo, Westland Non-Fiction and the Westland Non-Fiction logo are the trademarks of Nasadiya Technologies Private Limited, or its affiliates.

ISBN: 9789360450373

10 9 8 7 6 5 4 3 2 1

Typeset by Ashutosh Jha

Printed at Thomson Press India Ltd, New Delhi

To Eram, my rock and my joy

Contents

Part 2: Evil Geniuses

Part 3: Intriguing Scoops and Exposés

Introduction

Why did I write this book? To tell the truth and get a weight off my chest. But, in some measure, it's also because of a promise I made to a public prosecutor in Dubai as I sat in his chamber on a balmy September afternoon in 2018 facing defamation charges that could have put me in jail for a year and resulted in a fine of Dh2,50,000 ($68,000), which I didn't have then and still don't.

The swivel chair behind the prosecutor's desk creaked as he leaned back, fixing his gaze on me. His deep voice cut through the stifling air. 'This is your last chance, Mr Mazhar,' he said. 'Accept that what you did was wrong, and we will not press charges. You know what that means, right? You could be jailed.'

In the United Arab Emirates (UAE), defamation is a criminal offence, unlike in most other countries. The prosecutor seemed to relish the moment, his hand slicing the air like an aeroplane taking off. 'And when you complete your jail term, Mr Mazhar,' he said, 'we will deport you. Your career, job, all this fame—gone.'

As the weight of his words bore down on me, he thrust a bunch of A4-sized papers in Arabic at me. 'Your confessional statement,' he said. 'Sign it, and we will spare you.'

The translators, both locals, nodded knowingly. 'Sit straight,' one of them commanded. 'You are an accused.'

I uncrossed my legs and leaned forward, gently resting my palms on the wooden table that separated us. 'I am afraid, Mr Public

Prosecutor, I cannot sign any statement,' I said firmly. 'I will not apologise. *Maafi mushkil.*'

Anyone who has lived in the Gulf would be familiar with this Arabic term. Loosely translated into English, it means 'No problem'. But in my Urdu-speaking Indian hometown, 'maafi' means sorry and 'mushkil' difficulty. What I meant that day was that I would not apologise for doing my job. 'You may press charges,' I said. 'We will fight it out in court.'

I had already suffered a night in a dingy Sharjah police lock-up alongside petty thieves and loan defaulters. I wouldn't let this Arab prosecutor browbeat me into submission. After nearly two hours of negotiations, the prosecutor let me go. As I prepared to leave, he asked via the translator, 'Are you going to write about all this?'

'You mean in our newspaper?'

'Yes, your newspaper or a book.'

I looked at him and smiled as a kernel of an idea began to form in my mind. 'Yes, I promise, someday inshallah.'

We won that case. But more followed, until a time came when my mornings were spent in courts and afternoons in police stations. We even had a lame office joke: our legal team at *Gulf News* would be jobless without me.

From notorious drug lords, ruthless killers and dreaded gangsters to serial scammers, forex fraudsters and sex predators, my stories have rubbed a great many people the wrong way.

If someone were to bump me off, it would be difficult to determine who it was, which is slightly disturbing.

By a conservative estimate, my stories have resulted in legal action against over 250 individuals, some of whom are still serving time in prison. These reports have also brought me recognition in the form of awards, and a fair bit of fame. An anonymous reader once sent me a T-shirt emblazoned with the words 'The King of

Sting'. Montegrappa gave me a pen with my name inscribed on it. But the accolades didn't come easy.

Investigative journalism is hard anyway, and in the UAE, a country ranked 145 on the press freedom index, it can be nerve-wracking.

There are hurdles at every step. The lack of resources, the reluctance of editors, the interests of advertisers, the legal implications of going undercover, the ever-lurking danger of expensive lawsuits, and the never-ending threats.

Yes, the intimidation never stops. Every few days, I get threatening calls from computer-generated numbers. Recently, I got twenty in one night from the same man. What I did to antagonise him, he didn't tell, and I didn't ask.

'I will kill you,' he said one evening. 'You know that, don't you?'

'Yes,' I replied, 'but could you call back? I am driving.'

'You think it's some joke? Is that what you think it is? Wait, you just wait.'

'I know you are dead serious,' I said, 'but right now I really can't talk.

'Okay, so when shall I call?'

'Hmm, maybe after an hour.'

'Why does it always happen to you?' asked Abdul Hamid, my editor at *Gulf News*, once after the umpteenth legal notice landed on his desk. 'There are other journalists who have been working for much longer. They never get into trouble.'

'Right, sir,' I replied, 'but who was ever threatened or sued for writing about the benefits of eating dates?'

He never questioned me again. But I think he secretly held a grudge.

Even before celebs had turned Dubai into the planet's influencer capital that it is now, local journalists and bloggers rarely discussed anything other than food, fashion and beauty. The front pages of newspapers often featured the top ten brunch spots in town. Crime stories were primarily based on police handouts, and the mere mention of investigative journalism would cause editors to roll their eyes in disbelief. 'This is the UAE, Maz. You can't do that kind of thing here,' I was repeatedly told, and am still told today.

Looking back, I believe this disapproval, or what I may call self-censorship, was not so much about fearing government repercussions as it was about a culture of lazy journalism.

I am proud to say that I laid the groundwork for investigative journalism in this part of the world. I did it while managing teams, planning content, designing pages, rewriting and editing stories by other reporters, and running an educational charity in India.

To this day, I remain the UAE's only investigative journalist. Whether it's a woman whose child has been abducted, a girl who has been trafficked, a man who has lost his life savings to a scam, a blue-collar worker facing exploitation or an uber-rich tycoon cheated by his business partner, I am the go-to person for anyone with a problem. One day, a representative of a Marvel Superhero reached out to me with proof, detailing how the Superhero got duped out of over a million by a local big shot. When I called the man for a comment, he started dropping names and insisted that I kill the story, claiming it would be detrimental to Dubai's image. But I stood my ground. Frustrated, he asked angrily, 'Where do you get your bread?' He meant livelihood, but I cheekily responded, 'Multigrain from Carrefour and regular from Safestway.'

People seek me out in the hope that their issues will be addressed. More often than not, they are.

On another occasion, during Eid celebrations with guests, my youngest daughter, Zara, innocently inquired, 'Abba, are these people your friends or scam victims?'

I did not take this career path to give voice to the voiceless—to say that would be a lie. I was drawn to it as it was an uncharted territory in the UAE. Now it is second nature to me.

I'm often asked if I'm inspired by Mazher Mahmood, the famous British investigative journalist known as Maz or the Fake Sheikh. The similarities between our names and monikers are purely coincidental. While he did some commendable work, I don't approve of his tactics. Entrapment is one thing; investigative journalism is another. If I had the resources he had at *News of the World* or operated in a country with a free press, unlike the UAE, I might have tackled even more significant stories.

But do these threats and lawsuits rattle me? At times, yes. Do they waver my resolve? Hell, no.

That said, I'm not just about scam-busting. People are at the heart of everything I do. My stories have reunited families, helped patients with unpaid bills, provided shelter for the homeless and led to landmark reforms.

For every major story I've published, though, there have been many that never saw the light of day. Some were killed at the last minute, while others were never pursued. In this book, I'll reveal some of those untold stories. Additionally, I'll take you behind the scenes of audacious scams I've reported on and recount some truly bizarre incidents from my journalism days in India. You'll also find bits on newsroom politics. Didn't someone say, 'Don't mess with a writer; they will kill you in their book?'

THE EARLY DAYS

In the introductory chapter of *The Maz Files*, I shared my reasons for writing it, but the story of my becoming a journalist is a more gripping tale that began on a frigid wintry morning during the height of the Ram Janmabhoomi–Babri Masjid movement in the early 1990s.

It was 17 January 1991, and news of the US attack on Iraq was just beginning to flood the airwaves, serving as a stark reminder that the safety and security we take for granted could be shattered in the blink of an eye.

What I couldn't have foreseen was that the events of that very morning would have a similarly profound impact on my life. The wave of communal violence that began in India with a chariot journey by the Bharatiya Janata Party (BJP) president Lal Krishna Advani showed no sign of letting up.

Called Ram Rath Yatra, the chariot journey was a political and religious rally to support the agitation by right-wing Hindu organisations like the Vishva Hindu Parishad (VHP) and the Rashtriya Swayamsevak Sangh (RSS) to build a temple for the Hindu God, Lord Ram, on the site of the Babri Masjid mosque in Ayodhya. The mosque was constructed in 1528 after the Mughal conquest, but some Hindus believed it was built over a temple dedicated to Ram, marking his birthplace.

In the 1980s, the VHP and other Sangh Parivar affiliates initiated a movement to construct a Ram temple at the site. The BJP provided political support to this cause. In 1990, the government led by Prime Minister V.P. Singh announced the implementation of the Mandal Commission recommendations, reserving 27 per cent of government jobs for Other Backward Classes. The announcement threatened the BJP's electoral base, prompting them to exploit the Ayodhya dispute to consolidate the Hindu vote through anti-Muslim sentiment.

To advance this movement, the BJP launched a rath yatra to Ayodhya.

The rath, with its symbolic chariot-like appearance, was a Toyota pickup truck, complete with mounted loudspeakers. Led by Advani, the procession included thousands of kar sevaks, or volunteers, from the Sangh Parivar. Advani addressed up to six public rallies in a day as the yatra covered 300 kilometres daily. It sparked intense religious and militant fervour among Hindus and became one of India's largest mass movements.

But when the Yatra was stopped in Bihar, and frenzied kar sevaks tried to break into the Babri Masjid on 30 October 1990, Uttar Pradesh chief minister Mulayam Singh Yadav ordered police firing to repulse them, resulting in sixteen deaths. The incident sparked riots in Lucknow, which has always remained known for its unique composite culture called Ganga–Jamuni tehzeeb.

On 17 January 1991, as the first light of dawn began to illuminate our Muslim-dominated Qasaibada locality in Lucknow, chaos descended upon us. Nearly two dozen policemen, including personnel of the notorious Provincial Armed Constabulary (PAC), stormed into the neighbourhood.

Their mission was to apprehend a man suspected of arson the previous evening. As the police entered the narrow streets, the residents fought back, hurling brickbats and petrol bombs.

To subdue the fierce resistance, the policemen retreated to the top floor of the nearby three-storeyed St. James Mission school building. From there, they raised the infamous slogan of 'Jai Shri Ram', a rallying war cry of the Hindu nationalist movement, and unleashed a hail of bullets on the homes below, shattering windows and tearing through flesh and walls with deadly force.

The consequences of their actions were devastating.

Within minutes, four innocent Muslim men lost their lives. Several others lay injured. The men who were killed were all in their homes. One of them was an affable young man who had recently got married. He was shot in the head by a .303 bullet as he stumbled out of bed and opened his bedroom window to look out.

When the guns fell silent, the cops broke into homes and rounded up any young Muslim they could get their hands on. Shaukat, the blind muezzin of our mosque, was dragged out onto the street and shot in the palm of his hand in full public view.

The police also gatecrashed into my cousin Zubair's house, a mere 200 metres from my own. They forcefully took two other cousins, Javed and Farid, to the Aminabad Police Station where they endured a day of brutal beatings and relentless pressure to chant 'Jai Shri Ram'. The officers jeered at them with derogatory slurs, shouting, *'Katwe, yeh lo Javed Miandad ka chakka,'* while mercilessly pounding Javed.

For those unfamiliar with the context, *'Javed Miandad ka chakka'* holds a significant meaning in the world of cricket. It refers to a historic moment during the Austral-Asia Cup final in Sharjah in 1986 when Pakistani cricketer Javed Miandad hit a six off the last ball, leading his team to a stunning victory over India. The moment became etched in the annals of cricketing history, but it made Javed Miandad a villain. My cousin's name was anathema to the cops.

Now, allow me to elucidate the term 'katwa', which serves as a derogatory slur frequently used in India to belittle Muslim males. Derived from the Hindi word 'kat' meaning 'cut' in English, it alludes to the circumcision practised among Muslim males. The offensive term aims to marginalise and demean Muslims solely based on their religious practices.

In hindsight, I think Javed and Farid were arrested because they were dressed in Pathani suits.

Zubair was spared because he had the presence of mind to hurriedly pull over a pair of jeans.

Later that evening, a few of us visited the Aminabad police station with the help of an influential neighbour to deliver warm clothes and blankets to Javed and Farid who were still behind bars and shivering in the cold. As we were handing the blankets, a police inspector with a handlebar moustache looked at me with scorn and asked: '*Saaley katwe, bhainsa khaatey ho, phir bhi sardi lag rahi hai?*' (You eat buffalo meat, but you still feel cold?)

I was not at home when the police firing started. Minutes earlier, my dad and I had left for the Charbagh railway station in our family's blue Ambassador car to pick up my dad's elder brother and his son who were coming back from Delhi via an overnight train. And since there were no cell phones those days, we remained unaware of the carnage until we drove back.

We had no clue even when a posse of policemen, who had set up a barricade in the middle of the Latouche Road, stopped us and asked us to step out of the car.

As we hesitantly revealed our names, the policemen's expressions twisted into scowls, and they began raining brutal blows upon us with their lathis. Even though we were all well-dressed, with my father even sporting a flashy necktie, we were not spared. It was clear that their hatred towards us was based on our mere identities as Muslims.

The police officers also rummaged through the car. 'They could be hiding guns and bombs,' declared one of them. From the corner of my eye, I recognised a familiar face. She sat on a plastic chair on the road in the distance surrounded by about a dozen policemen. It was an officer who went to the same school as me. As a child I had grown up listening to how she had risen through the ranks to assume a position of authority. 'Do you want to be like her?' our class teacher at Christ Church School would ask when we were in grade five. 'Yes, ma'am,' we would shout back in unison.

At that moment I hated her more than anyone.

My father's attempts to show the cops railway tickets as proof of our innocence fell on deaf ears. The police continued to hit us with rifle butts and lathis.

A Provincial Armed Constabulary (PAC) constable even took aim at me with his rifle, asking his superior in a matter-of-fact tone if he should shoot me down. When we finally made it back home, I was horrified to learn that a policeman had pointed a gun at my mum too. She had opened a window in the veranda on hearing the cries of a young man on the rooftop of an adjacent house convulsing in his last moments. He had been shot in the neck.

News reports about the incident shook me to my core. A leading Hindi daily reported how my heavily armed cousins had attacked the police with sophisticated weapons. They had not even thrown a pebble, let alone opened a volley of gunfire. Zubair didn't even own an airgun and would borrow one from me to get rid of house lizards.

My disbelief turned into amusement when I came across another report claiming that the blind-as-a-bat muezzin, Shaukat, had been injured by a crude bomb exploding in his hand. I mean, how could a blind man be throwing bombs? None of the journalists had bothered to visit us, instead relying on press handouts given to them by the police.

A marvel of red-brick architecture, my twenty-eight–room ancestral house is a conspicuous landmark in the neighbourhood. In times of riots, the fortified walls of Lal Kothi or Bada Ghar stood tall as a refuge for both poor and rich Muslims seeking safety and solace. We sheltered something like seventy people that night. As we huddled together in the darkness, with no electricity and the ominous curfew outside, I made a vow to myself. I would become a journalist, but not just any journalist. I would pursue the truth with unwavering dedication. That I would never settle for mere stenography or half-truths.

Foray into Journalism

I was born and raised in Lucknow, the culinary gem of India, a city steeped in history and culture. It's also where my journey in journalism began, a journey that took me through a maze of publications and eventually led me to Dubai in 2005, where I joined the Al Nisr Group, publishers of the English daily *Gulf News*.

Newspapers in the UAE at that time were hefty beasts, weighing up to a whopping two kilograms. Classifieds alone spanned 104 pages, while the business and sports sections each ran a formidable twelve pages. Glossy, colourful pages adorned the entire newspaper, which included weekly magazines and supplements on anything from property and cars to showbiz and fashion. Advertisements practically leaped off the pages, often requiring you to flip through fifty pages before reaching the content panel of *Friday*, a lifestyle magazine published by *Gulf News*.

This spectacle was unlike anything I had ever witnessed in India, and I wasn't alone in this sentiment. My colleagues, hailing from various corners of the globe, had never seen anything quite like it either. We had all been recruited to spearhead a unique project: a fast-read multicultural community newspaper. Given the cut-throat competition, we had to keep the project under wraps. We even gave it a codename: 'Project X'. We toiled away in a secret bunker-like setting, a team of sixty-four, with only a select few in the building privy to our mission.

The culmination of our hard work, *XPRESS* burst onto the scene in 2008, quickly earning its reputation as the nation's most captivating and beloved read. By 2015, I had climbed the ranks to become its editor. But as often happens in the ever-evolving world of journalism, staff numbers dwindled to just five, and the print landscape underwent an irrevocable transformation. Following the closure of *XPRESS*, I found myself at *Gulf News* until late 2020, when I embarked on a new adventure at *Khaleej Times*.

However, my journey into the world of mainstream publications had actually begun back in my schooldays in India. I cut my teeth writing light-hearted features for the lifestyle section. One piece that stands out in my memory was an imaginative article for *The Times of India*. It envisioned the changes in Lucknow through the eyes of a fictional character, Nawab Achkan, should he revisit the city after 300 years.

While I pursued my college education, I simultaneously enrolled in a journalism diploma programme at a now-defunct institute located in Hazratganj. Sadly, it turned out to be a rather fruitless endeavour, teaching me little beyond the history of the printing press and similarly insignificant topics that added no real value.

As part of my diploma requirements, I joined *The Times of India* as an intern. Initially, it felt like an exercise in futility, as my presence went largely unnoticed. The plight of interns, it seems, hasn't changed much over the years. However, my persistence paid off when I stumbled upon a story of how members of the paramilitary force PAC used to store their weapons in a temple while encamped near old Lucknow. Equipped with my father's trusty Yashica camera, I even managed to capture photographic evidence. The story carried my name, with a joint byline with my friend Tariq Khan, who had provided the tip and collaborated with me on the article. It was prominently featured under the captivating headline 'Gods, guards, and guns'.

After completing my diploma, I stepped into the world of journalism, starting at *Lucknow City Magazine*, a monthly local publication. There, I wore many hats, simultaneously working as a reporter, subeditor and page designer. In fact, I handled nearly everything, from content to sales. My initial salary was a humble Rs 800, but the experience was invaluable.

Unfortunately, in July 1993, *Lucknow City Magazine* abruptly ceased publication, leaving me in professional limbo. Yet, as I grappled with this unexpected career setback, an even deeper family tragedy unfolded—the brutal murder of my cousin Zeenat's British husband, Yusuf Gordon Carr.

Yusuf, who had embraced Islam five years prior, tragically lost his life at the age of twenty-six in his farmhouse in Jehangirabad, a small hamlet in Barabanki, about thirty kilometres from my home. This shocking murder resonated not only in India but also in the UK. Within days of the incident, international journalists arrived in Barabanki, and the UK Foreign Office became actively involved due to Yusuf's British nationality.

Zeenat and I shared cherished childhood memories, and Yusuf was a man of remarkable character. His friendly demeanour and genuine warmth endeared him to all who crossed his path. His fusion of British heritage with traditional attire, such as the shalwar kameez or kandura, along with a striking green turban, made him stand out.

Yusuf had created an idyllic world in Jehangirabad, reminiscent of the rolling countryside of a British county. He had built a picturesque farmhouse where he personally operated a tractor, tending to the fields for vegetables, and maintained a pond for fisheries.

Yusuf, who came from a distinguished and wealthy English family, had embraced Islam during his travels after meeting members of the Tablighi Jamaat, a missionary and reformist organisation.

Renowned Islamic scholars of the time, such as Syed Abul Hasan Ali Hasani Nadwi, sought Zeenat's hand for Yusuf, a union that was wholeheartedly embraced by both families. Their marriage seemed destined and a match made in heaven.

However, fate took a dark turn. Initial investigations unveiled a gruesome reality: Yusuf had met his untimely demise at the hands of armed assailants in his farmhouse, as Zeenat and their two children, then eighteen months old and just twenty-five days old, slept nearby. The twenty-acre plot of land Yusuf had acquired from one of Lucknow's most famous personalities, Raja Jamal Rasool, for his farmhouse could not be legally registered, as it had been commandeered by the government under the Indian Ceiling Act. In response, Yusuf had vowed to pursue legal action against Raja Jehangirabad for fraudulent dealings

As the investigation deepened, Raja Jehangirabad and his manager Ram Avtar were arrested and charged with murder, fraud and conspiracy. In the initial stages, the case was handed over to the Crime Branch of the Criminal Investigation Department (CID), and Advocate Mridul Rakesh was appointed as the special counsel to represent the case.

I distinctly remember contributing to CID's investigative efforts. I accompanied a team of their officials to Nizamuddin Markaz, a mosque located in Nizamuddin West in South Delhi. This mosque holds a special place as the birthplace and global centre of the Tablighi Jamaat. At that time, Yusuf's family had flown in from the UK, and the CID enlisted my assistance in talking to the then-global head of the Tablighi Jamaat, Hazrat-ji. Posing as a young CID officer, I engaged in candid conversations, even asking probing questions about a Muslim cleric who had fallen out of favour with Yusuf.

For years, Zeenat waged a lone court battle, fervently hoping that someday the killers of her husband would be brought to book. In 2023, three decades after the murder, the Fast Track Court delivered the verdict, an anomaly considering the significant passage of time, discharging all accused.

First Sting Operation

My first big sting operation came in July 1995 when I was an ambitious reporter at *Newslead*, a local daily published in Allahabad (now renamed as Prayagraj).

I was out for an early morning stroll when I overheard a group of men discussing a mob attack that had taken place in Dilerganj hours earlier. It was a Muslim-dominated village near Kunda MLA Raghuraj Pratap Singh's native Beti, some sixty-five kilometres from the city.

The urgency of the situation struck me, and I immediately alerted my editor Vicky Bhargava. Soon our photographer and I were off to the place in a Maruti Omni van to investigate.

The scene that awaited us at the village was beyond catastrophic. The air was thick with smoke and the stench of burning flesh as over two dozen houses smouldered in ruins. The cries of the wounded pierced through the chaos. As I stood there, the first journalist to reach the spot, I couldn't believe the utter savagery. Three girls as young as eight had been raped, shot and dismembered with swords and hatchets, their lifeless bodies dumped into a nearby river.

The gut-wrenching accounts of the survivors left me shaken. They claimed that the attack had been carried out at the behest of Raja Bhaiya. After speaking to multiple eyewitnesses and taking pictures we hurried back to piece together our story.

We splashed it on the front page. Inside, a full page was dedicated to pictures and the accounts of survivors. The story had an immediate impact. It shook the country to its core and was a hot topic in the Uttar Pradesh Assembly.

I was catapulted to fame overnight.

However, my moment of glory was short-lived as the Director General of Police in Allahabad held a press conference a few days later to refute my report, claiming that the victims had died of drowning while fleeing from the fight. To my shock, he even presented a post-mortem report that supported his claim.

My credibility as a journalist was questioned, leaving me embarrassed.

Raja Bhaiya wielded immense power. I was certain that the drowning theory was a mere cover-up as the victims were shot, hacked and thrown into the river. To prove the post-mortem was compromised, I had to do something. My simple premise was that if the hospital could falsify the report once, they could do it again. So, I took a chance and sneaked into the Allahabad hospital with a small micro-cassette recorder hidden in my breast pocket.

To blend in, I dressed in an old kurta, worn-out trousers and bathroom slippers. While in the mortuary, I discovered the body of a farmer who had died by suicide. I collected his personal details from a ward boy and approached the chief medical officer, pretending to be the younger brother of the deceased.

'I need a report saying that my brother's death was an accident, not a suicide,' I said, my heart pounding.

The medical officer eyed me sceptically. 'You seem to be educated. Is this about insurance claims?'

I nodded. 'It will be denied if you say it is suicide.'

'Rs 4,000 it will cost,' he said. 'Do you have the money?'

'Not right away but I can get it quickly. I don't live far from here.'

'Good,' he said. 'Get the money, and you will have it.'

I recorded the conversation.

The next day, we questioned the post-mortem report arguing that if a chief medical officer could turn a suicide into an accident for Rs 4,000, he could just as easily manipulate a murder case to appear as drowning. The article created a stir. While investigating further, I found an inquest report at a police station where the bodies were fished out from the river. It unequivocally stated that the victims had been shot. We published the gaping hole in the official version of the events.

My articles had clearly hit a nerve with Raja Bhaiya's supporters. I knew I had taken on a powerful politician known for his ruthlessness and vindictiveness. Raja Bhaiya even kept a pond full of crocodiles. There were rumours that those who crossed him risked being fed to his pets. Even the family I was staying with in Allahabad grew increasingly anxious and expressed concern for my safety.

A few days later, we received a chilling anonymous handwritten letter in Hindi. The editor's secretary, Vibha, read it to me. The letter warned that if the newspaper did not rein me in, there would be serious consequences. There was reference to a crocodile pond. The threat was undeniably real.

Concerned for my safety, my editor advised me to go on vacation. It was a tough decision but I knew I couldn't take any chances and left for Lucknow until things settled down.

Raja Bhaiya and I bumped into each other several times in subsequent years. He went on to become a minister while I moved back to Lucknow, leap-frogging from *The Pioneer, Hindustan Times* and then *The Times of India*. In November 2002, I found myself reporting on Raja Bhaiya when he was arrested for making menacing threats, going so far as to plot the kidnapping and potential assassination of a prominent politician. Raja Bhaiya was officially designated as a terrorist, leading to his prosecution under the stringent Prevention of Terrorism Act (POTA). The trajectory of Raja Bhaiya's fate took an unexpected turn in 2003 when the state government dropped all POTA charges against him within twenty-five minutes of assuming power in Uttar Pradesh.

After his release from prison, Raja Bhaiya went on to become a cabinet minister. However, his controversial journey took another dark detour in 2013 when he found himself embroiled in the murder of a police officer named Zia-ul-Haque. No surprise by now, Raja Bhaiya was ultimately absolved of all charges, receiving a clean chit and being reinstated in the cabinet. In September 2023, the Supreme Court directed the Central Bureau of Investigation (CBI) to further investigate Raja Bhaiya's alleged role in Haque's murder. Around the same time, his wife Bhanvi Kumari Singh submitted an affidavit before a family court, wherein she alleged that she was subjected to domestic violence, abuse and extramarital affairs spanning nearly three decades, dating back to their marriage in 1994. Coincidentally, Bhanvi Kumari Singh happens to be my wife's college mate.

A Friend's Betrayal

s a journalist, I have had my fair share of experiences conducting sting operations early on in my career. It was a necessary aspect of my job, albeit one that often left me questioning the ethical boundaries of my profession. However, there was one particular incident that stands out.

During my career, I mentored a colleague, giving him his first break in the industry. We worked closely together, sharing stories and building a strong professional relationship. I saw potential in him and believed in his abilities. But he betrayed my trust in a way that was truly unforgivable. Although I cannot disclose his name due to his passing in 2023, the impact of his actions lingered.

In 2006, while covering the inaugural flight from Sharjah to Jaipur, I found myself immersed in an eventful two-day trip. I reported on a variety of stories, ranging from the tale of a 115-year-old man to a mass child marriage ceremony, hoping to receive the recognition I felt I deserved upon my return.

My expectations were shattered when I was summoned by my editor, Nirmala Jansen, and our editor-at-large, Francis Matthew, to a meeting room the very day I returned. Their expressions were stern as they questioned me. 'Who did you meet in Jaipur?' Nirmala asked flatly.

'Lots of people, why?'

She didn't answer directly. Instead, she handed me a plastic folder containing a bunch of papers. 'Can you explain this?' she asked. I read the contents in disbelief.

The papers included printouts of an email sent to them by a man who claimed that I had offered to sell my stories to him and had been secretly working for him for years. The email even referenced my story on Michael Jackson and alleged that I had offered to sell it as well. Attached was the child marriage story that I had mailed the previous day.

Shocked, I realised that someone had hacked into my email and was using it to make false allegations against me. I denied the accusations and requested time to prove my innocence.

'You have one day,' Nirmala said.

As I returned home, I sat down to gather my thoughts and investigate the situation properly. I created a flow chart and list of suspects, employing the process of elimination to narrow down the possibilities.

After several cigarettes and cups of Turkish coffee, deep into the night, three key points emerged. First, the perpetrator must have known my password to gain unauthorised access. Second, he seemed to harbour a grudge against me and my success. And last, he knew who to precisely target with the malicious emails.

Only one person matched all these criteria—my dearest colleague. Back at *The Times of India*, we often used each other's passwords. I would routinely use his password, 'dinocrisis', to access stock pictures of Hollywood celebrities from his desktop, while he would use mine, 'Anthony Gonsalves', named after Amitabh Bachchan's character in the movie *Amar Akbar Anthony*, to access pictures of Bollywood stars.

I found myself repeatedly reading the damaging email that had been sent to my bosses. It was evident that my colleague was the culprit behind this elaborate and targeted hacking.

I knew I had to act carefully and decisively to protect myself. But first, I needed to ensure I had all the evidence in place. Just as a musician recognises the composition of his disciples, I recognised the familiar language used in the email. It bore the stamp of this colleague. A particular detail caught my attention in the email—the spelling of the word 'grammar' was incorrectly written as 'grammer.' While many people make this mistake, the chances of an editor making it are very little. So the next day, as this colleague and I sat in the smoking room of *Gulf News*, I executed my plan.

I had prearranged with a friend to call me at a specific time. Pretending it was an urgent matter, I took the opportunity to make it seem like the call was from Eram and she wanted me to buy some schoolbooks on the way back. I was supposed to jot down their names, so I asked my colleague to do it for me. With bated breath, I read out the names of the books as if following my wife's instructions: 'Elementary Maths, Islamic Studies, English Grammar'. My heart raced as my colleague noted down the names and handed the slip of paper back to me.

There it was—my colleague had misspelt 'grammar' as 'grammer'. The evidence I needed to confirm my suspicions was now in my hands. It broke my heart. I didn't speak to him for years, but eventually I forgave him and stood by him in his darkest hours.

Sadly the colleague lost his job, then his wife and child, his home, and finally his life after being diagnosed with cancer.

Joining *The Times of India* in the Middle of the Night

I joined *The Times of India* in extraordinary circumstances. Before I made the leap, I was a key part of the team that had launched *Hindustan Times* in Lucknow. Sure enough, my connection with the newspaper ran deeper than ink on paper. As the sole male member in the features section, I brought a unique perspective to our storytelling. Nevertheless, when a more promising role and a heftier salary beckoned, I joined *The Times of India*.

If only *Hindustan Times* had not declined my promotion, I might have lingered contentedly within my comfort zone.

After bidding farewell to *Hindustan Times*, I took a brief respite to utilise my accrued holidays, which served to cover my notice period.

It was during this hiatus that a friend extended an invitation to her kathak performance at Lucknow's Taj Hotel, which coincided with an annual gathering of esteemed doctors. This event marked the city's inaugural hosting of this prestigious affair, drawing luminaries such as filmmaker Muzaffar Ali and politician Amar Singh. The evening's agenda featured a fashion show and presentation on Lucknow's cherished tehzeeb, exemplifying courtesy and decorum.

Accompanied by my cousin Zubair, I attended the event. However, the evening's tranquillity was shattered when a dispute between an inebriated doctor and a hotel staff member escalated into a fierce fight rallying scores of doctors to one side and an equal number of hotel staff to the other.

The confrontation grew so intense that many ended up falling into the swimming pool, where they continued to grapple in the waters. Terrified guests, who had gathered to witness a night of culture, were suddenly caught unawares. Plates, cutlery, and even pieces of furniture turned into unexpected projectiles. Chandeliers crashed to the ground, and guests scrambled for cover under tables, their laughter from moments before replaced by terrified screams.

Ironically, all of this unfolded mere minutes after a presentation on Lucknow's renowned tehzeeb and hospitality.

After an hour of pandemonium, the police arrived, quelling the turmoil.

I knew I had a scoop in my hands as I was the only journalist present at the scene. The aftermath of the fight was akin to a devastating storm. It was a front page story. It was 9.30 p.m. I could still file a story report before the press roared to life.

I found Dr Chandravati, the event's host, engrossed in a conversation with a police officer in the hotel's lobby. I excused myself and extended my business card to her. 'I'm a journalist from *Hindustan Times*, and I need to speak with you,' I stated. Turning to the officer, I added, 'I'll need to speak with you as well.'

'Certainly,' responded the officer, but Dr Chandravati's reaction was one of disdain. She arched an eyebrow, sizing me up before she replied, 'We didn't invite the media, so why are you here?'

'Well, ma'am,' I began, 'the media found its way here, as they often do. We're preparing a story for tomorrow's edition, and I would appreciate your insights.'

She smiled at me dismissively. 'Don't trouble yourself with that. I'll discuss it with your editor. There will be no story.'

I was taken aback. 'We'll see about that,' I retorted, gesturing to the broken chandelier, shattered chairs and smashed vases. 'A police complaint has been filed, extensive damage has occurred and injuries are widespread. This story won't be silenced, not even by the editor.'

I dashed out, hopped onto my trusty LML Vespa scooter, and sped towards my office. As Zubair and I made our way to the newspaper's Ashok Marg office, he looked at me with concern and asked, 'Do you think you'll be able to get the report published?'

As soon as I reached my desk, I powered up my computer and began typing. I was halfway through when a senior editor strolled over. 'What brings you here at this hour?' he asked.

'Filing a scoop,' I responded, recounting the chaotic events at the hotel. He listened intently. 'But aren't you on leave?' he inquired.

'Yes, I am, but I'm not incapacitated,' I replied curtly. 'I'm still on your payroll, and this story—'

He cut me off. 'I'm afraid, Mazhar, you have to give it a pass.'

I couldn't believe what I was hearing. 'Give it a pass? I thought you'd put this on the front page.'

He hesitated. 'Well, we still don't know what happened, so let's not rush it.'

I jumped from my chair. 'I was on the spot. I saw what happened. It was a war out there. I have a comment from the police and testimonies from the hotel staff, so what is the problem?'

But the senior editor stuck to his guns. 'That's an order. You can't file the story. Period.'

As I stormed out of *Hindustan Times* office in disgust, Dr Chandravati's words rang in my ears. 'What will you do now?' Zubair asked.

I knew exactly what I had to do.

It was 11 p.m., and *The Times of India* office was less than two kilometres away. I rushed to their office, charging down the stairs. The late-night staff gaped at me as I burst into the newsroom.

'Good Lord, Maz, what brings you here at this time?' the night editor asked. I had heard the same question a few minutes before.

'I'm joining you,' I declared, settling at a workstation.

He blinked at me.

'Now?' he exclaimed. 'Can you not wait until tomorrow?'

'I can, but not the story I have for you,' I replied. 'Now, could you get someone to open a Word document for me?'

A senior reporter, sensing the gravity of the moment, quickly switched on the computer and entered his password. I wasted no time.

The Times of India published the story prominently in the morning newspaper. I didn't use my byline. It went as a staff report.

I can picture the astonishment on Dr Chandravati's face on reading the report. I'm sure she must have pondered how she had encountered a journalist from *Hindustan Times*, only for the story to mysteriously appear in *The Times of India*.

As for the senior editor at *Hindustan Times*, I can only imagine the mix of disbelief and regret that may have washed over him. Perhaps, in the morning meeting, he might have said, 'So, *Times of India* was there too … ' little realising that it was me who had filed that report.

Nights with Cannibals

I was covering Kumbh Mela in Allahabad when I encountered a world so bizarre and unsettling that it would forever alter my perspective on life and spirituality.

I was working for a lifestyle magazine at the time, and an intriguing lead had drawn me to the sandy embankments of the Ganges in Jhunsi (formerly called Puri), a small town about fifteen kilometres from my office. It was here that I would come face-to-face with the aghoris—a nomadic cult that follows a small and highly controversial sect of Hinduism, most renowned for their taboo practice of feasting on human corpses.

Cannibalism remains legal in numerous countries, including India, where some states have passed Acts against it but failed to enforce them. Globally, nine locations, including the Ganges in India, still allow and legally permit this practice. Surprisingly, even in highly developed nations like the USA, there is no specific law against cannibalism.

The Ganges, revered by millions as a sacred river, plays a pivotal role in Kumbh Mela. It is here, on its hallowed banks, that millions of devotees gather to cleanse their souls and seek spiritual enlightenment. The river's significance was palpable in the air, as if every drop of its water held the essence of salvation.

Ascetic Hindu monks of the Shaiva sect, aghoris revere the Bhairav manifestation of Shiva. According to their beliefs, attaining moksha (freedom from suffering) involves fully abandoning one's personal identity. In this transformative journey, individuals confront the realities of the human body, including interactions with excrement, urine, mucus and other bodily fluids.

My pulse quickened as I approached their hutment. The cold February night had cast an eerie glow on the surroundings. There were about eight aghoris, their lean bodies smeared with ash as they stood naked under the moon's watchful gaze. Their wiry, thin leader, a man in his forties, with bloodshot eyes and hair matted like a rope, commanded attention.

The aghoris are in a perpetual state of drunken trance, thanks to the charas (marijuana) they smoke continuously. Huge trishuls, symbolising Lord Shiva's divine power, lay planted in the sands around their hut. I attempted to engage the head aghori but he was too intoxicated to hold a coherent dialogue.

His deputy assured me that if I returned past midnight, I would witness them in their true element. The knowledge that aghoris were cannibals weighed on my mind. A few years earlier, they had reportedly killed a policeman in Uttarakhand and consumed his flesh. The idea of visiting them in a deserted cremation ground made my nerves tingle.

But I gathered my courage and enlisted the company of my colleague Suresh Paul. Together, we returned to the aghoris at 1 a.m. As we reached their hutment, a family arrived in a battered hearse car to perform the last rites of a relative. The atmosphere was thick with grief as we observed the ritual from a distance. The family placed the deceased on the funeral pyre and set it ablaze. However, just as the ritual started, it began to rain.

Caught in the deluge, the family abandoned the cremation and drove away.

As the hearse car disappeared, the aghoris emerged from their huts and leaped into the smouldering pyre. We watched in horror as they pulled the half-burnt body from the fire and began eating it. Limbs were torn asunder, flesh was devoured.

The sight was akin to a pack of hyenas tearing into their prey.

One of the aghoris managed to sever the skull. This set off a mad frenzy as they fought over the prized brain meat, known as maghaz, believed to bestow superhuman powers. It was a nightmarish scene—moonlight bathing the sandy banks of the Ganges, distant city lights flickering, and the frenzied dance and growls of the cannibalistic aghoris.

The morning after, I shared my experience with my editor, Vicky Bhargava. He arranged for a photographer and a car, and the very next night, we ventured back to the aghoris.

I cautiously edged close to an aghori, who seemed grounded in reality, and asked the question that had been haunting me: 'Why do you eat dead bodies?' His gaze locked onto mine. 'Not just bodies,' he replied, scraping bits from a human skull. 'We consume four things with the letter "m"—mal (human excrement), mutra (urine), madira (liquor) and murda (dead bodies),' he explained. I couldn't help but inwardly smile, finding an odd solace in the fact that my name, starting with an 'M', was not on their list.

This time, I observed that the aghoris had descended even further into their trance. Consumption of human flesh had exacted a toll on their sanity. While we maintained our vigil, a pack of nearly twenty stray dogs lingered. In Hinduism, dogs are revered as they are believed to be the divine vehicle of Lord Kalabhairava, an incarnation of Lord Shiva.

Visiting the aghoris was risky and unpredictable. They were as changeable as the monsoon winds along the riverbanks. One moment they would converse, albeit cryptically, but the next, they could become violently chaotic. Their leader seemed disinterested in materialistic possessions. However, his subordinates, the aghori lackeys, were driven by earthly desires. Money and mutton were their demands, and they made no secret of their intent to extract whatever they could from us.

On the third day of our encounters, the undertaker, our intermediary with the aghoris, conveyed an unusual request. The aghoris wanted vermilion, sandalwood paste, joss sticks, betel leaves and nuts, a red silk scarf, and even a bottle of whisky. We were told that they wanted to perform shava sadhana, a tantric ritual of meditation involving a corpse, timed to coincide with the new moon day.

This shava sadhana was shrouded in dark mysticism, a ritual that held secrets and power known only to the initiated. The corpse they sought had to meet stringent criteria—it had to be fresh and undamaged, with no missing or deformed parts. The most preferred, known as maha-shava or great corpse, was a Chandala, a child of a Shudra father and a Brahmin mother, who had met a specific, unusual demise.

As we approached the aghoris' secluded spot, a ghastly sight greeted my eyes. The corpse of a young woman was bound to a stake by silken threads. A protective circle had been drawn around her, a sort of makeshift barrier to keep malevolent spirits at bay. The aghoris, chanting mantras, had gathered around the body.

One of them reached for the bag I carried, which held the requested items. I watched in morbid fascination as the head aghori tied the hair of the corpse, applying vermilion and sandalwood paste to her face while invoking cryptic incantations. Then he straddled the lifeless form and began to meditate. The dead woman's distended belly had ballooned, yet, the head aghori balanced himself on it as if riding a horse, proceeding to perform one ritual after another.

Sesame seeds, scattered around the corpse, formed a spectral mosaic as the rituals continued. It was a macabre spectacle. I was told that during this ritual, the woman might open her eyes. I stared, unable to look away, as the aghori placed a betel nut in the corpse's mouth and then turned it onto its back, smearing the body with sandalwood paste. The cameraman captured the scene.

But if we thought we had seen everything, we were mistaken. Soon, an aghori began to engage in intercourse with the corpse. I recoiled, my stomach churning with revulsion. The aghoris, incensed by our presence, started shouting. 'Go away from here. Go away, or we will eat you up,' their leader ordered, taking swigs from a whisky bottle.

On each of those nights, I wore a rugged leather jacket that my dad had got me from the US. When I returned home during those Ramadan nights, the clock had usually already ticked into the suhoor hours, yet any trace of appetite had abandoned me. In the shower, I would scrub vigorously, but the mark those experiences had etched upon my soul remained. The leather jacket seemed to carry a reminder of those nights, soaked with the acrid scent of burnt flesh and the thick haze of marijuana smoke.

Vicky Bhargava told us that it was no longer safe to meet the aghoris. We already got the story we wanted.

But fate, with its capricious nature, had different designs for us. Just a week later, our intermediary conveyed an eerie message—a body had become ensnared beneath the river embankment, and the aghoris aimed to recover it. It presented an opportunity we couldn't ignore.

We returned, our anticipation taut as a drawn bowstring. Javed bhai, our elderly driver, manoeuvred the office Jeep as close to the embankment as he dared. Around 2 a.m., the aghoris emerged from the veil of darkness, their bony forms wading into the knee-deep river waters. We shadowed them, maintaining a safe distance. The idea was to click a few pictures and head back. Our photographer, senses sharpened by dread, fixed a zoom lens to his camera.

In that silence, punctuated only by the murmurs of the Ganges, our presence betrayed us. Suddenly the aghoris, like hunting predators detecting intruders, turned their attention towards us. One of them bellowed, '*Pakdo, jaaney na paaye* (Catch them, don't let them go)!' In an instant, the aghoris transformed from the mystic seekers of the macabre to a relentless force pursuing our doom.

Trishuls, glinting in the moonlight, quivered in their grasp as they surged towards us. For a frozen moment, terror held us in its vice-like grip. Then, at last, I found my voice. '*Bhaago* (run)!' I yelled. The photographer shoved his camera into his jacket and we fled, burdened by water-soaked jeans and our shoes stuck in the clinging mud.

'Javed bhai,' I shouted, 'start the engine.' By some miracle, my plea pierced the stillness of the night. I heard the engine of the 1975 Willys' thunder to life.

The aghoris, mere metres behind us, brandished their trishuls. One of the lethal weapons whizzed past my head and buried itself in the sand.

We sprinted for our lives. Then, a lifeline appeared on the horizon—the silhouette of the open-air Jeep emerged from the shadows.

We leaped into the moving vehicle as Javed bhai shifted gears and hit the accelerator. Yet, in the throes of our frantic flight, the Jeep momentarily succumbed to the clutch of the sand, its rear wheel churning for grip. We panicked, but Javed bhai's resolve prevailed. '*Allah Hu Akbar, Ya Ali, madad!*' he screamed, invoking a higher power, and with one final surge of effort, the Jeep broke free from the mire.

We hurtled away from the aghoris, thankful we hadn't met the gruesome fate of becoming their meal.

That night, as the first light of dawn broke, I reflected on those experiences. They had left an indelible mark on me, blurring the boundaries between the living and the dead, the sacred and the profane. For months, the thought of eating meat turned my stomach.

Pranks That Made Headlines

The cricketing world was still reeling from India's loss to Australia in the 2002-03 ICC Cricket World Cup Final but our newspaper saw an opportunity to inject a little humour into the sombre mood.

The plan involved a front page spoof in *The Times of India* on April Fools' Day with a headline that declared, 'ICC Disqualifies Australia—World Cup Handed to India!' The reason? Shane Warne and a handful of Aussie cricketers had supposedly tested positive for banned substances.

Of course, we added a disclaimer at the end to ensure nobody took our jest seriously. Most readers and fellow journalists chuckled at the clever prank, understanding it for what it was—a light-hearted April Fools' Day joke.

However, not everyone possessed the same discernment. In Allahabad, a senior journalist, at the rival *Hindustan Times*, took the bait hook, line and sinker. He decided to make up for his 'missed scoop' by publishing a reaction story the very next day.

He reported how Allahabad was awash with joy, celebrating the ICC's supposed decision. The story even featured quotes from local, obscure cricketers who condemned Australia for their alleged cheating.

The real kicker was that the city edition of the rival newspaper was solely published in Allahabad back then, and its Lucknow headquarters had no inkling of what had transpired. As a result, the incredulous story made it to print, unvetted.

The prank had worked far too well, and the aftermath was as hilarious as it was unexpected.

A few years earlier, I pulled off a memorable April Fools' Day prank at *Newslead*, the newspaper where I worked in Allahabad. I fabricated a story claiming that giant whales had appeared in the sacred Ganges river. To bolster its believability, I included details about scientists from an oceanography institute in Australia who were supposedly en route to conduct an investigation of the phenomenon. A disclaimer was placed within the story, but it was cleverly woven into the narrative.

Little did I know that the managing editor of the newspaper decided to make his rounds that evening, somewhere around midnight. He stumbled upon my bogus tale and it appeared so convincing that he took it for the truth. He was so convinced, in fact, that he summoned one of our photographers and asked him to rent a boat, acquire battery-powered lights, and venture out onto the river in search of the whales. 'Your photos will make you famous,' he exclaimed.

Thankfully, the lateness of the hour and the photographer's sound judgement prevented him from embarking on this fantastical quest right away. Instead, he wisely chose to wait until morning.

In another April Fools' hoax, I wrote a story for the lifestyle section of *Hindustan Times*. This article claimed that a certain Dr Bhaskar Ranade had discovered a revolutionary cure for longevity, enabling people to live up to 150 years. To add an air of authenticity, I convinced my uncle, Shahid Farooqui, to pose as the fictional Dr Ranade, donning a white coat and brandishing test tubes and beakers. We included a disclaimer at the end, just as we had with the whales' prank, but the story appeared so credible that many readers couldn't help but believe it.

A few days later, I visited a scientific research institute and was dumbfounded to find the newspaper prominently displayed in a glass frame alongside important notices.

Lights, Camera, Corruption:
A Bollywood Villain in
Government Attire

In early 2004, an unlikely figure in the heart of Uttar Pradesh boasted a repertoire of movies that could rival even the portfolios of Shah Rukh Khan, Aamir Khan and Akshay Kumar. This character was Avdesh Narain Dubey, the man steering the ship at the Uttar Pradesh Film Bandhu. For those unfamiliar, the Film Bandhu was essentially the government's wing dedicated to giving the film and entertainment industry in the region a little boost—financially, logistically and atmospherically.

Now, Mr Dubey may not have possessed the striking looks or acting talent of a Bollywood star, but he did possess something else—a firm grip on the purse strings. So, when directors came seeking Bandhu's support, they often found themselves casting Mr Dubey in their movies.

My journey into this cinematic drama began while working for *The Times of India* in Lucknow. As I delved deeper into the story, I found that Mr Dubey had secured roles in at least five movies shot in Lucknow. Each of these cinematic ventures had been showered with generous grants by Mr Dubey himself. I decided to pay Mr Dubey a visit at Film Bandhu's Park Road office. When I questioned him about his sudden fascination with greasepaint and the camera, he looked aghast. 'You see, I'm a helpful soul. There were emergencies, directors needed someone pronto, and I just decided to step in,' he said.

How could there be emergencies on five separate occasions? And even if we were to entertain that idea, why didn't he recommend any local artist, as stipulated by the film policy?

'The list of local artists is a work in progress. We're still in the process of tabulating it,' Dubey replied, nodding towards an operator typing away at a computer. 'And as for why directors want me in their films, that's a rather personal question.'

'Won't this send the wrong signals to filmmakers who were promised the moon by Chief Minister Mayawati during her visit to Mumbai sometime back?' I asked.

'No, I don't think so. What I am doing in my personal capacity shouldn't be anybody's concern.'

I was stunned, so I approached the Director of Information, Rohit Nandan, but even he didn't provide much clarity. 'I don't think anybody should have any problem with what Dubey is doing. Neither should one jump to conclusions and draw any inference from the fact that a government officer is acting in movies. I guess he is getting all these roles because he is readily available to the filmmakers. Or it could be just a coincidence,' he stated.

We slapped the story on the front page of *Lucknow Times*, the lifestyle supplement of *The Times of India*. The aftermath? Lightning fast. The government suspended Mr Dubey and ordered a probe. Investigations revealed that Mr Dubey had dabbled in more than just bit parts—forgery and a misappropriation of nearly Rs 10 million. I fired off another story, this time exposing how Film Bandhu had bled millions, thanks to Dubey's cinematic duds. It was the final straw. Looking back, it's clear that Dubey's theatrics had all the makings of a star turn as the real-life villain in a rollicking blockbuster. His escapades could have been the stuff of Netflix legend!

Towards the end of this story, I must emphasise the crucial role journalists play in holding government officers accountable for their actions. It is the duty of journalists to uncover the truth, especially when it involves public servants who are entrusted with taxpayers' money and government resources. However, in today's media landscape, there is a concerning trend where many journalists rely heavily on press releases handed to them, either due to laziness or because they have vested interests that compromise their objectivity.

It is common knowledge that journalists covering government beats, such as the Public Works Department (PWD), health, education and even crime, sometimes benefit from their relationships with government officials. Those covering PWD, for instance, may receive monthly pay packets, while others may secure ad hoc job postings for their spouses and family members. Some journalists even have their private cars leased to government offices, creating a situation where their independence and integrity are compromised.

This compromise in journalistic integrity is why there is rarely any in-depth investigation into the actions of government officers. When journalists are entangled in a web of favours and benefits, their ability to report objectively and fearlessly is severely undermined.

Driving Home the Point: Security Lapses at the State Secretariat

On 13 December 2001, India was put on red alert following a brazen attack on the Parliament House in Delhi, where five terrorists had driven in an Ambassador car to unleash a devastating assault. As a journalist at *The Times of India* at the time, I was compelled to investigate the security situation at the Uttar Pradesh Secretariat in Lucknow, a place that had long been a potential target.

Behind the wheel of my old Maruti 800, I boldly drove inside. To my astonishment, the security personnel, expected to be vigilant after the Delhi tragedy, were nowhere to be found. One guard leisurely munched on groundnuts at a gate.

In this lax environment, it seemed anyone could waltz in or, in my case, drive their car without a care. Exiting the secretariat precinct was as effortless as my initial entry. Before unveiling my exposé on this glaring security lapse, I sought an audience with the principal secretary of the Secretariat Administration Department (SAD). Unfortunately, her response was far from reassuring. 'We're entrenched in high-level meetings to comprehensively reassess our security measures,' she offered cryptically. 'An intricate security plan is in place, but I'm afraid I can't disclose specifics; it's classified, you understand.'

My exposé the following day left government officials scrambling. Subsequently, SAD tightened its security measures, making it abundantly clear that gaining access to the state secretariat and the adjoining state annexe building would no longer be a walk in the park. They issued a statement outlining how these highly sensitive locations were to become impregnable fortresses. The media was informed of the security procedures one would now have to undergo to gain entry. Government officials took great pains to explain the extensive brainstorming sessions that had culminated in a foolproof plan to prohibit unauthorised cars from entering the premises.

On the second anniversary of the Parliament attack, a red alert echoed across the nation once more. Amidst whispers of a potential suicide attack at the Uttar Pradesh State Secretariat, security measures were cranked up to the max. Yet, for all the grandiose plans, security protocols and a vehicular ban, there I was, breezing into the State Secretariat like it was a drive-through. No gate pass. No security checkpoint. No questions asked. It was like I had found the VIP entrance to a government theme park.

I drove in and out multiple times, my Maruti car becoming a regular fixture inside the building, and still, no one gave me even a second glance. Feeling like a secret agent in a Bollywood flick, I decided to dig deeper and approached the Officer on Special Duty (OSD) responsible for security. With a sense of pride, he assured me their security measures were so airtight that not even a bird could penetrate them. '*Yahan koi parinda par nahin maar sakta* (Not even a bird can enter here),' he declared with unwavering confidence.

Stepping out of the OSD's office and entering the main hall of the Assembly building, my gaze was drawn to the timeless wisdom etched on the walls. Among them, one quote stood out: '*Galti karna bura nahin hai, baar baar galti karna bura hai*', which translates to: Making a mistake is not bad; making the same mistake repeatedly is.

The Ishrat Jahan Enigma

This story dates back to June 2004. During my time as a correspondent for *The Times of India* in Lucknow, I came across a striking incident. In Ahmedabad, the Gujarat Police had shot and killed a nineteen-year-old Muslim girl named Ishrat Jahan, along with three others, in a predawn firefight. The narrative we were given was that Ishrat and her companions were Lashkar terrorists on a mission from Mumbai to assassinate Narendra Modi, the chief minister of Gujarat at the time.

What particularly caught my attention were reports suggesting that Ishrat and her deceased accomplice Javed Sheikh had visited Lucknow multiple times in the two weeks before their fatal encounter, staying at Hotel Mezbaan, which was just down the road from my place. Familiar with the area, the notion of alleged terrorists seeking refuge there sparked my interest.

The question that troubled me was straightforward: why would they choose to visit Lucknow if their supposed mission were to eliminate Modi, who lived in Gujarat? It simply didn't add up.

I decided to reach out to the Gujarat Police headquarters. My call connected me to the then Ahmedabad additional commissioner of police, D.G. Vanzara. He stated unequivocally, 'Javed and Ishrat went to Lucknow to procure weapons from Lashkar modules.'

The notion of travelling over 1,300 kilometres from Mumbai to Lucknow for weapons seemed as absurd as carrying coal to Newcastle. I remained sceptical.

'But couldn't they obtain weapons elsewhere? Why choose Lucknow of all places?' I probed.

'We are still trying to figure that out,' Vanzara replied. 'In Lucknow, they met Lashkar terrorist Salim alias Amjad Ali, who was nursing a gunshot injury. I believe they initially planned a major operation in Lucknow but later changed their plans,' Vanzara explained, emphasising the state capital's proximity to Ayodhya, the birthplace of Lord Ram, making it a potential terrorist target.

So, we had three terrorists, one of them wounded, criss-crossing the country with no clear mission, frequently visiting a city where weapons were unlikely to be found. It stretched incredulity but, at that time, I had no grounds to suspect Vanzara, who had yet to emerge as a key figure in the case.

Curiosity gnawed at me. I decided to visit the hotel myself. Mezbaan, a short walk away from my house, would hold the answers I sought. However, the hotel staff didn't appear certain.

'I've seen the photographs of Javed and Ishrat in newspapers and on TV,' Urfi, a Mezbaan receptionist, said. 'The woman who checked in under the name of Ayesha did bear a slight resemblance to Ishrat, but I cannot say that with 100 per cent certainty. Maybe she was Ishrat, or perhaps my mind is playing tricks on me.' Another staff member couldn't recall anything.

In the end, there was no conclusive evidence that the couple who checked in as Ayesha and Abdul Rahman on 7 May 2004 were indeed Ishrat and Javed, let alone any connections to dubious activities.

Yet, an Intelligence Bureau officer supported Vanzara's claims, and like many other journalists, I was led to believe that Ishrat and her associates were scouting for weapons and targets in Lucknow. We realised we had been led down the garden path when Vanzara was arrested for his alleged involvement in the killing of a criminal gangster, Sohrabuddin Sheikh.

Later, he was also made an accused in the Ishrat Jahan case, which was declared as staged by an Ahmedabad Metropolitan Court. The decision was challenged by the state government and taken to the Gujarat High Court. After further investigation, in 2011, a Special Investigation Team (SIT) told the High Court that the story peddled by the police was fake. In July 2013, India's premiere investigative agency, the Central Bureau of Investigation (CBI) filed its first chargesheet, saying that the shooting was staged and carried out in cold blood.

I watched from the sidelines as Vanzara was imprisoned, serving eight years, from 2007 to 2015. During his time in custody, he composed a letter to the CBI, fiercely defending himself and thirty-one other police officers, all facing allegations of conducting extra-judicial killings. Vanzara argued that they had simply carried out their duties as part of a deliberate policy orchestrated by the Narendra Modi government in response to the growing threat of jihadist terrorism. He emphasised that this 'pro-active policy of zero tolerance for terrorism' was a directive from the highest echelons of the Gujarat government.

The letter set off speculation about whether the jailed officer, who appeared to be smarting under the feeling of having been abandoned by the Gujarat government, was planning to implicate his political bosses. That he attacked Modi's closest aide, Amit Shah, who was also a co-accused in two extra judicial killings cases. This only heightened the interest in what Vanzara, a self-confessed acolyte of Modi until he dropped the letter bomb, might do next.

But then in 2014, the Narendra Modi government came to power, and Vanzara was released on bail. Shortly after that, he was discharged in both the Ishrat Jahan and Sohrabuddin cases. If this was not enough, he was given a post-retirement promotion as the Inspector General of Police (IGP) by the Gujarat government, six years after he retired from service. Vanzara went on to launch a right-wing political party, Praja Vijay Paksh, with a view to merge dharmsatta (theocracy) with rajsatta (political power).

Looking back, I realise how we, as journalists, can inadvertently become instruments of the establishment's narrative. We operate within a web of information, often handed to us by those in authority, and must make critical decisions with limited time and resources.

Ishrat Jahan's unlawful killing wasn't an isolated case; it was part of a perplexing series of killings in Uttar Pradesh during the regime of the BJP chief minister Rajnath Singh, a staunch supporter of Narendra Modi. One particular event still stands out. In April 2001, we were told that 'three dreaded terrorists' were intercepted and shot dead in Lucknow's Gomti Nagar suburb. They were supposedly making a 125-kilometre trek to Ayodhya, carrying a conspicuously marked bag labelled 'PAKISTAN' and purportedly armed with assault rifles. I couldn't help but find it absurd for these supposed terrorists to be so blatantly marked.

What added to this bizarre narrative was the uncanny resemblance in the names and ages of these 'Jaish-e-Mohammad terrorists' to three Muslim youths arrested by the police from different cities just a few days prior. These arrests had even made headlines in local newspapers.

In my article, I posed a simple query: assuming this was a one-in-a-million coincidence, where were the terrorists' namesakes arrested by the police? Over two decades later, this question, like many others, remains unanswered.

As these events unfolded, and with the police seemingly getting away with these acts, instances of Muslims being arrested on trumped-up charges increased alarmingly. The aftermath of the 9/11 attacks only fuelled Islamophobia further. I recall government billboards across the city featuring Osama bin Laden's image, warning against any form of support for him. Ironically, this served as significant publicity for the terrorist.

Against this backdrop, the Special Task Force (STF) and the Intelligence Bureau arrested two Jordanians and a Palestinian from their rented apartment in Lucknow in early 2002, labelling them as Hamas militants. The police also confiscated their computer. An officer told local media that these men used to engage in online chats with girls in Western countries: 'I believe their plan was to marry these girls, travel to Western countries, and carry out 9/11 type attacks.' There was no concrete evidence to substantiate this claim, yet the media eagerly sensationalised it, reporting on how a major international attack had been thwarted by the police. When the three men were produced in court, they were even attacked by lawyers.

Nobody seemed interested in fact-checking. No journalist bothered to investigate further. It was during this time that Faiz Siddiqui, my colleague at *The Times of India*, and I decided to visit the house in Indiranagar from where the men were arrested. After a prolonged wait, a young woman from the Northeast opened the door, fear in her eyes. 'I thought no journalist would come,' she said, relieved. She then shared her story. The three men, she informed us, were not terrorists but students at Lucknow University who had simply overstayed their visas. 'What about the other incriminating documents recovered from them?' I asked. 'Those so-called incriminating documents are forged academic certificates,' she clarified. 'One of them had failed his exam, and his parents were pressuring him for results, so he made a fake certificate.' She asserted that she had known the men for several months and they had no connection to any radical group.

She agreed to be quoted in the story, but when I reported this back to my editor, he turned down the story. I was told that officers in the STF were already unhappy with my report on the Gomti Nagar killing, and it wouldn't be wise to raise questions about this arrest.

I felt disappointed, but my vindication came when the Palestinian embassy raised the matter with India's Ministry of External Affairs, leading to the release of the men. The ministry clarified that not only were they found to have no connections with Hamas but also that membership in Hamas was not something the Indian government was acting against. However, the damage had already been done. Parents of numerous Palestinian students living in India wrote to their embassies, with at least twenty-five of them suggesting their children be brought back from India.

Allahabad: The Good Old Days

I forged some of my fondest memories at an unlikely media house in Allahabad, called BPPL. It was kick-started by a young visionary named Vicky Bhargava, who founded the enterprise in the early 1990s with the winnings from a card game on Diwali night.

Vicky's venture began with an adult magazine named *Fantasy*. It wasted no time sinking its claws into the minds of countless Indian readers, their hunger for sex education and alluring pin-ups insatiable.

Priced at just Rs 60, it defied all odds, selling close to 1,00,000 copies each month. Riding high on *Fantasy*'s success, Vicky introduced *Fantasy Fun* for a younger crowd and a women's magazine, à la *Cosmopolitan* and *Femina*, named *Faces*. All three were instant hits, vanishing from the stands as soon as they arrived. Readers even sent cash in envelopes, requesting specific issues. Flush with funds, we could afford some of India's top writers and columnists, including the likes of Khushwant Singh and Rahul Singh, further fuelling our meteoric rise.

Our readers' responses flooded in, literally, in bags of letters. It was a whirlwind. We started in a humble first-floor office on Sarojini Naidu Marg, but as we expanded, we moved to a more impressive space within a disused cinema hall named Payal, owned by Vicky's partner, Bunty.

I fondly recollect sitting alone in the cinema hall's balcony, pondering and brainstorming or simply writing stories. The focal point of our magazines were their covers. Hours were dedicated to scrutinising countless pictures to select the finest one. We were a bunch of youngsters who were disrupting the media landscape of India.

Looking back, I can confidently say that among the editors I've worked with, Vicky stood out as the best. He wasn't just an exceptionally gifted writer; he possessed astute business acumen.

I joined *Fantasy* as a senior subeditor and rapidly ascended the ranks, becoming a pivotal member of the team, alongside subeditor Suresh Paul, graphic artists Mukesh Sah and Satish Dhiman, and chief designer Shantanu Mukherjee. Yet, running an adult magazine from a holy city presented its share of challenges. Self-proclaimed guardians of virtue raised their voices, clamouring for our shutdown. Vicky's clever solution to silence these protests was to launch a newspaper and wield influence. And so, *Newslead*, the English daily, came into existence. It was an exceptional newspaper, and I assumed control of its lifestyle supplement, *Break*, in addition to my responsibilities for *Fantasy*, *Fantasy Fun* and *Faces*. While the newspaper grappled with financial difficulties, our magazines thrived.

At *Newslead*, I had the privilege of collaborating with some of journalism's unsung heroes. One such character was Prakash Shukla, a seasoned journalist who once worked with the UNI news agency. I recall a specific day when our deadlines were slipping away, and Prakash Shukla's editorial had yet to arrive. I found him in the office cafeteria, casually sipping tea and puffing on a Capstan cigarette. 'Mr Shukla,' I implored, 'we need your edit; it's nearly 7 p.m. We were supposed to have it by 4 p.m.'

He lounged in his rickety plastic chair, took a leisurely drag from his cigarette, and grinned, addressing me with an enigmatic nickname. 'Relax, Robin Hood. You want the edit now?'

'Yes,' I pleaded, 'the pages are at a standstill, and—'

Prakash Shukla cut me off, asking, 'Do you have a pen and paper?' My heart plummeted. 'Jesus, are you going to write it now? Don't tell me you haven't written it,' I blurted in panic.

'I'm not going to write it; you will,' he calmly declared. As my confusion deepened, he signalled to the cafeteria staff to fetch his cash register, tore out a page, and handed it to me. 'Write,' he commanded. With that, he shut his eyes, interlaced his fingers behind his head, and reclined further into his chair, recounting the entire editorial in a seamless flow. He even provided instructions on where to place commas, dashes and paragraph breaks. I've never encountered anyone quite like Prakash Shukla since that remarkable day.

Among our spirited bunch at BPPL, there lurked another captivating character, Shital Mukerjee. A former *Times of India* cast-off, he was a walking oddity, a frail, thin man with a shock of white hair that defied his tattered appearance. He sported faded, betel-stained kurtas and shabby, worn-out slippers. One day, he probed the security guards about the functionality of their double-barrelled guns. Unconvinced by their assurances, he insisted they fire into the air. When they declined, he impulsively snatched the weapon from a guard's grasp and pulled the trigger. A deafening blast tore through the air, leaving a gaping hole in a neighbouring balcony and sending shards of debris into power lines, causing an immediate blackout. He was swiftly dispatched to Delhi. Suffice it to say, he wasn't a crowd favourite.

Yet, from Shital, I learned the art of storytelling, the knack for crafting snappy headlines, and the skill of writing compelling captions.

The camaraderie within our team was incredible. Vicky Bhargava was not just a boss; he was a friend. His hospitality and unforgettable parties fostered an atmosphere of true togetherness.

As our publishing house continued to soar, Vicky expanded operations to Mumbai and Delhi. From a rank outsider, he had become a media baron. Lifestyle magazines featured him on their covers, and he wasn't even twenty-six. We basked in the glow of our success. But then, a storm broke loose. The nude photographs of a girl we had prominently featured across four pages in the magazine turned out to depict a minor. These photos had been peddled to us by a freelance photographer who had lured the girl with promises that they would appear in a foreign magazine, and she had agreed, signing a contract. Unbeknownst to us, the photographer sold the pictures to our publication. This incident provided the perfect opportunity for those who had been critical of us, and they descended upon us like hungry wolves.

The debate on obscenity and its clash with Indian values became central to our predicament. In a nation that exalted the art of Khajuraho paintings, we found ourselves under siege. Vicky was apprehended, and our office was summarily locked down. The police swept in, confiscating all our computers, while Rita Bahuguna, a local politician and advocate for women's rights, mounted a campaign outside our besieged fortress. Even the newspaper was coerced into shuttering. The livelihoods of hundreds hung in the balance, their salaries tethered to the fates of our magazines. We had been gearing up for a special anniversary issue that week, and the market had been eagerly awaiting its release. Though there was no official ban on the magazines, we found ourselves unable to deliver. Recall, this was in an era long before the advent of cloud storage and internet servers. Communication with Vicky, incarcerated in the infamous Tihar Jail in Delhi, was nigh on impossible. In the face of this dire predicament, Suresh Paul, Satish Dhiman, Mukesh and I felt compelled to take charge.

Using a discarded desktop computer that had been sent for repairs, we painstakingly pieced together the entire anniversary edition. We worked tirelessly, sometimes for up to eighteen hours a day, in Satish Dhiman's small house, which suffered frequent power outages. Since *Fantasy* had become a topic of national conversation, that single anniversary issue became a massive hit. We sold a record number of copies. The proceeds not only saved the company but also funded the legal battle ahead. When Vicky was released from jail, he treated us to an all-expenses-paid trip to Kathmandu, Nepal. It was an unforgettable experience, filled with adventures, including my comical mishap of ordering a Bloody Mary, mistakenly thinking it was a harmless mocktail, and my daring choice of attire—a blue silk dressing gown with Chinese dragon prints—at a Kathmandu casino. I thought it was cool.

With things slowly falling back into place, I approached Vicky Bhargava with a daring proposition: let's launch *Newslead* as an English evening tabloid in Lucknow. Armed with a well-thought-out plan in a notebook, I outlined every detail, from selecting the printing press to hiring the staff and securing an office space. Vicky was intrigued, and he gave me the green light to put the plan into action. Starting from scratch, I brought this vision to fruition. I secured a rented space on Jopling Road and assembled a dedicated team. Many of those who kick-started their careers at that small newspaper went on to achieve remarkable success in journalism. For instance, Tanya Chaitanya later rose to become the editor of *Femina*. I negotiated contracts with printing presses, syndicates and agencies, furnished the office, and even set up an office canteen. My optimism about the success of *Newslead* was well placed. We had a wealth of distinctive content from our other publications that we seamlessly integrated into the evening daily. When *Newslead* made its debut in October 1995, it caused quite a commotion. Suddenly, journalists began to take notice of this group of young upstarts challenging established brands. The late Chandan Mitra, the editor-in-chief of *The Pioneer*, was one such senior journalist who paid attention. He sent a message to me offering to meet me. The next day I found myself at the Taj Hotel lobby, where Mitra sat with a copy of *Newslead* in front of him, a wry smile on his lips and thick-framed glasses framing his gaze. 'How soon can you join us?' he inquired. His disbelief was evident when I responded, 'In a few months. We have just launched this newspaper. Once it stabilises, I might consider,' I told him.

He agreed. As soon as *Newslead* found its footing, I accepted Chandan Mitra's offer.

Leaving the familiar comfort and family-like atmosphere of BPPL was an agonising decision, but new opportunities beckoned. Sadly, *Newslead*, which had begun with such promise, folded not long after I departed. The reason? Alleged misappropriation of funds by an advertising manager. Although I had moved on to *The Pioneer*, the closure of *Newslead* felt like a personal loss, akin to losing a dear friend. Vicky Bhargava's media empire, too, met a similar fate. One by one, all his publications shuttered. Perhaps he was ahead of his time, and had he ventured beyond Allahabad back then, who knows what the future might have held for him.

The Day I Tasted Gandhi

When people speak of Gandhian principles, my mind drifts back to an extraordinary incident from my days as a journalist with *The Pioneer* in the late 1990s. One that involved the revered Mahatma's ashes, a long-forgotten bank vault and a taste of history.

Following his assassination by Nathuram Godse on 30 January 1948, Gandhi was cremated with full state honours in New Delhi.

Respecting the wishes of the man revered as the apostle of non-violence, his devotees scooped his ashes from the burning funeral pyre and poured it into urns so that they could be sent across various states in the country for immersion in holy rivers as per Hindu custom.

Call it carelessness, covetousness or what you may, but by a strange turn of events, the ashes meant for the Eastern Indian state of Odisha (then Orissa) were never given back to nature and somehow ended up in a bank vault in the city of Cuttack.

Apparently, they were kept aside for use in a monument, but were forgotten and remained sealed and locked in a wooden box in the bank's strong room for nearly fifty years.

After a prolonged legal battle, Gandhi's grandson Tushar Gandhi got possession of the urn and was now on his way to the North Indian city of Allahabad to immerse the ashes in Sangam, the confluence of three of India's holiest rivers—Ganges, Yamuna and the mythical Saraswati.

As a budding reporter, my job was to accompany Tushar on a nineteen-hour train journey and report on the historic event, which had drawn journalists from all over the world to Allahabad, once regarded as the 'Oxford of the East' for its famous university.

Also on board were armed police personnel, the registrar of the Orissa High Court and a senior official of the State Bank of India, in accordance with the court order.

Slogans like 'Long Live the Mahatma' rent the air as the train carrying the last remains of Gandhi chugged into the Allahabad railway station, its final destination, at 9.30 p.m.—nearly two hours behind schedule—on 29 January 1997. I watched in awe as thousands of Gandhi supporters jostled with each other to catch a glimpse of the red wooden box containing the ashes.

Around midnight, the box was transported by a police convoy to a nearby government guest house, where musicians and preachers of different faiths sang hymns once sung by Gandhi.

Huge crowds thronged the guest house the following morning as people from various parts of the city turned up to pay their tributes to the great leader.

Later that afternoon, we boarded a motorboat to reach a wooden platform specially erected for the media in the middle of the river. Bang opposite us was another, much bigger stage, featuring Tushar Gandhi, Hindu priests, and dignitaries including, if memory serves me right, the then Uttar Pradesh governor Romesh Bhandari and federal ministers Chaturanan Mishra and Jnaneshwar Mishra.

Barely a few metres separated the two stages. At the anointed hour, Tushar, his wife Sonal, and their two children stood up with the blackened copper urn that had remained sealed since 1948.

It was the moment we had been waiting for. As we stiffened to attention and the photographers readied their cameras, Tushar opened the urn amid chanting of shlokas from the Vedas and other Hindu scriptures. Just then, a gale of wind swept across the river and Gandhi's ashes flew right in our faces.

I was standing in front and swallowed a fair bit of it. As I doubled over coughing, a visiting foreign journalist remarked in jest: 'Mate, you just tasted Gandhi.'

PART 2

EVIL GENIUSES

Let's be honest, deep down, we all admire con artists. Who hasn't secretly rooted for Frank Abagnale in *Catch Me If You Can* or Anna Delvey in *Inventing Anna*?

The UAE, the land of opportunity and excess, is no stranger to the cunning ways of con artists. Over the course of my career, I have crossed paths with countless slippery characters, like the Syrian sorcerer I reported about in July 2023. This mystic claimed to possess supernatural powers and wove a spell so compelling that it coerced an Emirati woman, Alia, into parting with Dh4 million ($1.23 million). But that was just an opening act. The sorcerer went on to manipulate Alia into writing post-dated cheques and debt acknowledgments totalling over Dh100 million ($27.3 million). Alia was deluded into believing that these astronomical sums were needed as ransom for the release of the sorcerer's husband supposedly kidnapped by the terrorist group ISIS in Syria. The sorcerer promised that the post-dated cheques would merely serve as negotiation tools with the kidnappers and wouldn't be presented at the bank. However, she betrayed Alia's trust and filed a case when the cheques bounced. The poor woman spent several days in jail.

If you find this tale bizarre, consider the late Foutanga Babani Sissoko, also known as Baba Sorra. Hailing from a humble village in Mali, Africa, with no formal education, Sissoko pulled off one of history's most remarkable bank heists, relying solely on black magic and tribal voodoo. His target? Dubai Islamic Bank (DIB), from which he managed to pilfer over $240 million.

Sissoko went on to become a prominent politician and entrepreneur in Mali, even launching his own airline, Al Dabiia, although I think 'Al Dubai' might have been a more fitting name. Ironically, when Sissoko strolled into the DIB head office on an

August afternoon in 1995, he didn't even have the funds to purchase a car and sought a loan instead.

Inside the bank, he met the manager, Mohammad Ayoub. What transpired between the two remains unknown, but what we do know is that Sissoko extended an invitation to Ayoub for dinner at his house. During the meal, Sissoko made a bizarre claim: he possessed magical powers to double any amount of money. To prove his assertion, he performed a demonstration, supposedly summoning a djinn and using some cheap tricks that caused lights to flicker and filled the room with smoke. The voices of spirits seemed to echo, and then, in a moment of silence, the money Ayoub had given him miraculously doubled.

It's still baffling how a senior banker would fall for something so banal, but Ayoub did. Over the next three years, he remitted $242 million (Dh888.89 million) into Sissoko's accounts in 183 transactions, clinging to the hope that it would return to him exponentially increased.

Ayoub's foolishness brought the bank to the brink of financial ruin, while Sissoko revelled in opulence, going so far as to acquire two Boeing 727s to realise his ambition of launching an airline for West Africa.

In addition to his extravagant pursuits, Sissoko entered into multiple marriages and secured a seat in parliament. He retained this influential position for an uninterrupted twelve years, from 2002 to 2014, shielding himself with legal immunity.

But any courtroom drama around black magic and supernatural powers that the Sissoko case would have provided was supplied when the case of a Yemeni trader, Qasim, went to trial in Dubai for fraud. The dad of six was caught peddling a 'bulletproof' stone at Dubai's biggest cultural showpiece, the Global Village, for Dh1.8 billion, a figure he arrived at through a draw of notes, each bearing different amounts.

In the courtroom, the man spun his extraordinary tale. He told the jury that the clove-shaped onyx stone had the ability to immune its wearer to bullets. Qasim then went on to describe how he wrapped the stone around a sheep's neck and fired four shots from an arm's length, and each time the bullet obediently bounced off, leaving the sheep unharmed.

Qasim stayed strong throughout the trial. He even offered to test the stone on himself, ready to face any consequences, even the death penalty, if his claims proved false. His attorney suggested using a puppet for the test and recommended involving government-approved laboratories, along with three international scientific experts, for a thorough assessment of the stone. The lawyer argued that the Dubai Municipality lacked the expertise and technical resources for such an extraordinary examination.

As for Sissoko, he passed away in March 2021 at the age of seventy-nine, never having faced trial for the DIB fraud.

Although I did not have the chance to write about Sissoko due to the bank's reluctance to speak about the case, I did report on hundreds of other crooks who were just as brilliant.

One of them was the Russian diplomat Valentin Lysi. In a con job straight out of a movie, he sold 15,000 square feet of land belonging to the Russian embassy in Mumbai to a Dubai businessman for $10 million.

The scam was carried out with such ingenuity that it wasn't uncovered until the Russian Consul General went to visit the property, known as Marine House, and was stopped by security guards.

At least Marine House was a real property, unlike the grandiose Islamic City promised by an Indian conman I reported about in Dubai. In January 2018, the wily smooth talker held a press conference at the Burj Al Arab Hotel to announce a Dh7 billion Islamic City in the heart of Dubai. We were told the development would reflect the traditional lifestyles of three prominent Islamic eras—the Ottoman, Mamluk and Umayyad.

Investors were promised a utopian city where residents could move around in carts pulled by donkeys and horses, taking them back to the days of ancient Islamic civilisation. In reality, they had been taken for a ride of monumental deception and shattered dreams.

The city never materialised. It couldn't have. It was a pipe dream. The conman's wife tried to pull a fast one on me when I rang her up after his arrest in October 2018.

'Who told you my husband has been arrested?' she said when I introduced myself.

'I understand that this is a difficult time for you,' I began.

However, she remained undaunted, attempting to navigate the conversation through sheer confidence. 'I don't know what you are talking about. My husband is sleeping,' she said, 'and he doesn't want to be disturbed.'

Then, there was this developer who amassed a fortune by selling plots in the sea. His multi-billion-dollar project lacked approvals and had neither been registered nor regulated by any government authority in the UAE. In 2018, when I exposed this racket, the man attempted to buy my silence with Dh1 million in bribes and a job offer, doubling my current salary. I vividly recall meeting his emissary at a coffee shop opposite the previous office of *Gulf News* at Holiday Inn in Al Safa.

When these attempts failed, he resorted to filing a case against me. It was a classic case of shooting the messenger. Strangely, the same lawyer who had purchased an underwater property, and initially approached me as the developer's victim, ended up representing him in court.

I will never forget the day when an officer at the Port Rashid police station called me for questioning following the complaint.

The lawyer was there too, sitting across from me with a smug look on his face. I recognised him instantly and greeted him by his name. The exchange left the police officer puzzled. 'How do you know each other?' he inquired.

I smiled at the lawyer and said, 'Shall I explain, or would you prefer to do the honours?' The lawyer stumbled over his words. 'I, uh, well, you see.'

I filled the gaps recounting how I had uncovered the racket with evidence provided by the very lawyer now seated beside me.

The officer listened intently, and when I was finished, he turned to the lawyer and asked for a response.

The lawyer sputtered and stuttered, unable to come up with a coherent argument. The complaint against me was dropped.

It's impractical to chronicle every single tale of deceit and trickery that I have uncovered. Therefore, I have carefully curated the stories of the top thirteen devious and insidious scammers, some of whom I encountered in person and others that I wrote about. Each was slyer and more manipulative than the last. Their schemes range from the unbelievable resurrection of a deceased man to the devastating fraud committed by a footballer. You will also discover the story of a fugitive woman who created a false identity to execute a deceitful plan. Their stories will astound you. So buckle up and get ready to explore the treacherous terrain of con artists who were either based in the UAE or preyed on victims there.

Ajay Kolla: World's Biggest Recruitment Thug

I don't know much about cooking other than bringing people to a boil. However, in the winter of 2018, something unexpected happened. Five-star hotels in Dubai were falling over each other to hire me. Their human resources (HR) managers told me they were so impressed by my credentials that they wanted me to join their teams immediately. It was crazy, because my bogus CV categorically stated that I 'develop unpalatable menus' and 'pass off recycled scrap as healthy nibbles'. But why did I do it? To expose a recruitment racket run by one of the world's biggest job portals—Wisdom Jobs.

Headquartered in the Indian city of Hyderabad, Wisdom Jobs was a one-stop shop for job hunters worldwide. With a staggering 33 million registered users, their reach rivalled the entire populations of Canada and Malaysia. The company's founder and CEO, Ajay Kolla, served as a shining role model for aspiring entrepreneurs.

Wisdom Jobs garnered accolades from esteemed trade associations and tech magazines. In 2016, India's most prominent apex trade association, the Associated Chambers of Commerce & Industry of India (ASSOCHAM), not only placed Wisdom Jobs in the country's top SME 50 Index but also bestowed upon it a Certificate of Excellence. Simultaneously, a renowned tech magazine crowned it as the 'Company of the Year'.

But when I delved deeper, I discovered that Wisdom Jobs had no real jobs. The employment opportunities listed on the portal were either fake or stolen from other recruitment websites. And worse, the phone interviews arranged by them didn't have prospective employers at the other end of the line, but call centre agents operating from the company's head office at Cyber Tower in Hyderabad. Very little about Wisdom Jobs was real—except for the money it was making from the well-knit racket that extended beyond Indian shores, spanning Canada, USA, South Africa, New Zealand, Italy, Malaysia, Singapore and their favourite hunting ground, the Middle East.

The company's success was fuelled by its lucrative business model that promised guaranteed job placements for a fee. Thousands of people worldwide fell for it every day.

The process was simple. Job seekers would apply through Wisdom Jobs's website and were directed to a login screen where they filled in their personal details and uploaded their CV. Shortly after, they received an email from a 'career service adviser' stating that their CV had been shortlisted by multiple companies. The candidates were reassured that they were dealing with a reputable placement firm that fulfilled the recruitment needs of 35,000 'top-notch companies'. To make things even more tempting, an overview of the 'guaranteed' job was emailed, complete with details of the salary and perks.

But there was a catch. Candidates had to first pay a resume forwarding fee of $150. It didn't stop there. Job seekers were then tricked into shelling out more and more money towards a series of bogus fees and charges, leaving them trapped in a vicious cycle. By the time they realised what was happening, they would have spent up to $2,000.

The bulk of the ill-gotten money came from the resume forwarding fee. At $150 per client, it may not seem like much, but for a portal with 33 million registered users, it was a hell of a lot. To allay clients' fears, Kolla's company would email them a letter titled 'Why Should You Pay?' that justified the fee by stating that the jobs were not in the public domain but were rather exclusive. The letter would also list the many 'benefits' of paying, such as 100 per cent 'guaranteed placement assistance' and 'immediate hiring'.

The scam fooled the most discerning job seekers. I remember the day I received that call from Nikhat Shah, a Dubai-based teacher with a story that piqued my interest. It was a typical day filled with meetings, deadlines and the constant buzz of my phone. But this call, this voice on the other end, held the promise of a scoop.

Nikhat's voice was filled with indignation as she recounted her experience with Wisdom Jobs. In November 2018, she had willingly parted with $150, believing that this payment would unlock the gateway to the high-paying job she had dreamed of. In those initial days, Nikhat genuinely thought it was a small price to pay for the promising future that lay ahead. She was told that a staggering forty-eight different organisations were eager to snatch her up. Shortly after remitting the money, she was offered an assistant professor's job at the prestigious American University of Sharjah (AUS) with an attractive salary and perks.

A few days later, she found herself on a conference call with a woman who identified herself as Ms Emma Cowan, senior HR manager at AUS. Now, AUS did have an HR manager by that name, but neither she nor anyone at the university had ever contacted Nikhat.

The person who conducted the interview posing as Cowan was a call centre agent reading from a script in Hyderabad. The bogus interviewer carried out the charade for nearly forty-five minutes, covering a variety of topics from qualitative research to differential learning, classroom engagement and lesson plans. At the end of the interview, the impostor asked Nikhat to wire $150 more towards a 'certification fee', and she readily obliged.

The extent of Wisdom Jobs's deception knew no bounds, and soon I found myself immersed in the depths of their fraudulent practices. K. Sarthi, a hopeful candidate, shared damning evidence of how he was coerced into paying $1,750 after a job interview with a man claiming to be the head of an IT company in Dubai. Anis Khan had a similar tale. He handed over $800 under the mistaken belief that he was in direct correspondence with the HR manager of a distinguished British bank in Dubai. Gurtej Singh, seeking a managerial role at a real estate company, ended up giving away $1,700 to a man who spoke with a heavy Arabic accent, attempting to lend authenticity with phrases like 'wallah habibi' and 'marhaba'. The same modus operandi was used to extort money from Pakistani Qamar Ahmed and Indian Roohi Shaista for non-existent positions in Dubai.

I was shocked to learn from a former Wisdom Jobs staffer that they were provided with an Excel sheet containing the contact details of HR managers from hundreds of organisations worldwide. The list was systematically used to arrange interviews and gain the trust of potential victims. Despite paying large sums of money, job seekers who fell for this trap never heard back from Wisdom Jobs. Phone calls went unanswered, and emails remained ignored.

I knew there was only one way to expose the racket—a sting operation.

Eight years earlier, I had used a similar approach to uncover a job racket in Sharjah. I created a deliberately ridiculous CV that said, 'I am a dim-witted moron', and sent it to multiple recruitment firms in the Emirate. The audacious plan worked.

Within twenty-four hours, I was hired by a company that offered me a $5,000 salary and accommodation for a sales position. My absurd CV, which claimed I would bring about 'a steady erosion of values and company ethics' had been 'forwarded' to the employer by the recruiting agency. Astonishingly, my employer had no qualms about hiring me.

Similarly, the fact that I made 'perilous graphics and inconsistent logos' did not put off a British company from taking me on board as a graphic designer.

'They [the client] are very happy with your CV. Actually we forwarded them seven candidates but out of seven they shortlisted your CV,' [sic] I was told over the phone. But to secure the job I had to visit them with my photographs and $150 towards a 'refundable' processing fee.

I played along and visited the agency's office where I was promptly escorted into an HR manager's cabin.

The Indian man sitting behind a desk flashed a big smile at me. He had a worn-out plastic folder in his hand which had some documents including my offer letter and my dumbed down CV.

'Congratulations, you've been hired by a very famous British company,' he began as we shook hands. 'Your offer letter is here,' he said, pretending to read from my job contract. 'Ah, yes, you'll get a salary of Dh18,000, along with family accommodation, annual travel allowance of Dh10,000, and a generous bonus structure.' He paused, giving me a moment to absorb the good news. I nodded in appreciation.

Turning his attention back to the contract, he added, 'Oh, and you'll also get a BlackBerry phone.' His tone grew slightly serious as he continued, 'Now, I understand there's a processing fee that needs to be settled. Do you have that with you today?'

I don't know whether it was the impetuousness of youth, absurdity of the situation, the grin on the recruiter's face, or the forlorn plastic rose protruding from a shabby ceramic flowerpot atop his desk, but I just blew my cool, and also my cover.

Reaching into my pocket I fished out my press ID.

'Look at this,' I said, thrusting the card at him. 'I am a journalist.' I snatched the folder from his hand and extracted my fake CV. 'Now, according to this,' I continued, pointing at the page, 'I am an idiot with bogus degrees, but your client is still willing to offer me a job with these fancy perks. Care to explain?'

The man's smile vanished.

I tapped at the spy pen camera in my breast pocket. 'I have recorded everything,' I said. 'All of you will go to jail.'

Suddenly, the man stood up and grabbed my arms hard.

'I will tell you everything,' he said. 'I have no part in this. I warned Ali this would happen someday, but he didn't listen. Nobody listens to me here. But who told you about us? Shahid, was it?'

I was taken back by his reaction. I had no idea who Shahid was.

'Yes, Shahid and a few others,' I lied.

The man's fear deepened, his voice quivering with dread.

'I knew, I knew. The bastard,' he muttered, beads of sweat forming on his brow. 'I don't want to go to jail. I have small kids,' he pleaded.

'Calm down,' I said, patting his hand. 'Just tell me everything. I will make sure nothing happens to you.'

'No,' he exclaimed as he stood up from the chair and fixed his gaze at me. 'I am not Shahid, I will not rat out my employers.' Then, without warning, he bolted towards the door, his panicked shouts echoing through the corridor.

'Betrayal, betrayal! Where is everyone? We have been betrayed by Shahid. Lock the door! Stop this reporter, he has recorded everything!' he bellowed.

I was not prepared for this.

I sprang out of my chair and stumbled out of their fifth-floor office. Two burly security men, an Indian manager, and an Egyptian man who I guessed was the owner of the agency ran after me. 'Blue blazer, tall man in specs, blue blazer, blue blazer,' the manager shouted. 'Blue blazer, tall man,' the Egyptian repeated after him as he relayed the information to the security men.

There was no time to wait for the sluggish elevator so I dashed down three flights of stairs until I reached the parking level. It wasn't safe to step out of the building yet. I peeped down from my hidden vantage point and saw the Egyptian talking animatedly on the phone while also giving instructions to the security men who were still running helter-skelter down the street.

I waited until it was dark and then climbed down the stairs to my parked car.

The following morning, I rang up the agency's Egyptian owner to seek his response but instead received a barrage of abuses and threats of physical assault.

Over the next three days, I called several recruitment agencies and made enquiries for ridiculous job positions.

At Foreigners Employment Management in Al Majaz, my query for a position of hotel manager-cum-outdoor salesman was met with an affirmative response. Another agency, New Future, confirmed they had an opening for a dentist-cum-accountant. But it was the response of the manager at Waseela Recruiters, near Sharjah City Centre, that took the cake.

'I am a qualified elephant trainer from Ching Pong institute in Thailand,' I told the woman who picked up the phone and identified herself as Asma.

'Oh very good, mashallah,' Asma chirped.

'Thanks, Asma,' I said. 'But since there are no elephants in the UAE my skills have yet to find their purpose. Can you help me get a job as an elephant trainer abroad?'

Asma's response was quick: 'My dear, if you want me to send you to our company's branch office outside the UAE then you have to make a visa payment of Dh300. We do have our company branch in Canada. We have a whole veterinary hospital there and institute … including the zoo … there we have more than 300–400 elephants … and not just elephants but other animals also … we have many trainers but we are looking for more trainers. If you pay us Dh300 we can send you to Canada within fifteen to twenty days and also give you a one-way ticket.'

I recorded Asma's jumbo offer and put the audio file online along with the responses of others in a cover story that shook the country.

My report won me a few awards and led to a massive crackdown against the recruitment agencies mentioned in my report.

Would a sting operation along similar lines also nail Wisdom Jobs? I was nowhere near that degree of optimism but I wasn't entirely without hope either as I registered with them with what could be the worst CV for a chef's position.

Just as I thought, I immediately got a call for a job offer.

Senior career adviser (Middle East) Anurag D. told me that my resume had caught the eyes of several hospitality groups in the country.

Among the four hotels who were keen to utilise my talents, Anurag said, my best bet was Radisson Blu, Abu Dhabi, where I could get up to Dh20,000 per month as salary. That was twice more than what I had asked for.

I vividly recall the excitement in the newsroom when we broke the story on 18 January 2019.

I had expected it to create a stir. It unleashed a full-blown maelstrom. Our phone lines and email inboxes were inundated with messages from every corner of the globe. Hundreds of victims, along with scores of HR managers, who had fallen victim to impersonation, reached out to us. Law enforcement agencies and media outlets started to call us as well. The sheer volume of it left me in a daze.

Amidst this chaos, my editor beckoned me into his office. I entered, thinking he would appreciate my work or discuss the need for follow-ups. 'Ah, there you are. Come, have a seat,' he said. 'I've got an intriguing story for you today.'

As he began to speak, his words took me by surprise. 'You know, it always baffles me how laundry workers manage to identify the clothes of their customers,' he mused. 'They collect garments from so many people, yet they never make a mistake. Not once. Look into it. It will make a good read. Find out how they do it.'

'They use tagging,' I said tersely.

'Ahan, so they used tagging? See, I didn't know that. How many people would know that? Not many, I bet. So, look into it, speak to the laundrymen, get cracking. Assign the photographers.'

'Sure,' I said, 'but you see, right now I am slightly busy, the commissioner of Hyderabad Police just rang me up. They are probing Wisdom Jobs and need my help. Two newspapers want to do a story on us so they are calling us too, as are victims from as far as Singapore, Belgium, Jordan.'

'Yes, of course,' he said, 'it was a decent story, but you have got to move on. Now do something else, like this laundry story. It's very important.'

The events that unfolded over the next few days would make for a Netflix docudrama series.

Hyderabad Police assembled ten teams to get to the bottom of the scam. They raided Wisdom Jobs's office and seized all their computers and documents.

In less than one week Ajay Kolla was arrested and charged for defrauding thousands of unsuspecting jobseekers to the tune of millions of dollars. Thirteen other key members, including the head of operations, team leader of consumer sales and several high-ranking executives, were also taken into custody. Among those arrested were two women. The police released a picture of all of them.

Preliminary investigation showed the company had made $16 million by cheating nearly 70,000 job seekers in India and another 35,000 based abroad. It was a proud moment for all of us when Cyberabad Police Commissioner V.C. Sajjanar announced the arrests at a press conference and praised my investigation.

'Indian newspapers should learn from *Gulf News*,' he declared.

The exposé went on to win a bunch of international awards, including the TRACE Prize for Investigative Reporting in the US. *The New York Times* journalist and bestselling author Dina B. Henriques, who was on the judging panel, tweeted: 'Your work was outstanding, Mazhar. One other judge wrote to me that it "read like a screenplay" that kept her "on the edge of my seat". Great storytelling is so important to making these deep-dive pieces accessible! Bravo!'

The report was also ranked among the best stories of 2019 by the Global Investigative Journalists Network (GIJN) and won the KCK International Merit Award for Excellence in Journalism.

Ajay Kolla was eventually released on bail and resumed his thuggery. He also found time to send me a legal notice threatening to sue me for defamation if we did not remove the story from the website.

'What do we do now?' our legal head asked.

'We do what we do best,' I said.

In November 2019, I exposed Wisdom Jobs all over again.

As part of my investigation, I randomly called twenty UAE-based companies from Wisdom Jobs's Gulf placement listings. None of them had any openings for the advertised positions.

The CEO of a recruitment firm went on record to say they spotted over 500 fake advertisements listed on Wisdom Jobs under their company's name.

Most were fake. Those which weren't had already been filled, in some cases, as long as ten years ago. Among the offers posted on the site was an 'urgent opening for a foods and beverage (F&B) manager at Dubai's Regent Beach Resort in Jumeirah'. The resort had been shut for more than a year. 'Why will we need a F&B manager for a hotel that doesn't exist anymore,' said the marketing manager of Regent Palace Hotel that used to operate the resort.

I wrote all of this in my second story. Wisdom Jobs never bothered me after that but they got many news websites and YouTubers to remove the story about them.

Sydney Lemos: Footballer Turns Forex Fraudster

Inside a gated community in Dubai's South Barsha neighbourhood, not far from the Barsha Police Station, is a five-bedroom villa that sprawls over 15,000 square feet. I don't know who lives in that dirty yellow building now, but in 2017 it was occupied by a thirty-something-year-old Indian man who had cropped hair and owned a forex company in Dubai.

His name was Sydney Lemos and he hailed from the town of Mapusa in Goa, the former Portuguese colony on India's west coast.

Before he was sentenced to 517 years in jail, Sydney lived an insanely lavish life. He wore only the finest suits. His parties were legendary, with tables piled high with exotic delicacies and champagne flowing in a never-ending stream.

Sydney was always on the move, travelling around the world in style. When he was in Dubai, he drove to work in branded luxury sports cars like Ferrari and Maserati. Often, he would show up in a customised gunmetal-grey BMW 3, modelled after a similar car driven by James Bond in many of his movies.

Sydney was a huge fan of the fictional spy character with the code 007. His Arenco Tower office in Dubai Media City was numbered 007, as were the registration plates of a number of cars and motorbikes associated with him. Among his glamorous collection of vehicles was a Range Rover Sport, albeit without the coveted 007 plate, a whimsical purchase inspired by a persuasive salesman who assured Sydney that the unique numerical sequence in the car's chassis would bring him good fortune. At first, fortune did smile on him and he made the most of it. Actually, he made quite a lot of it.

The passionate football lover started a small football club in Dubai called FC Bardez. He owned the club and also played for it. In 2015, one of his companies, FC Prime Markets (FC denoting forex and commodities) became the main sponsor of FC Bardez, a franchise in the Indian Super League.

The move catapulted Sydney to instant fame and recognition. Suddenly, he was rubbing shoulders with the likes of cricketer Sachin Tendulkar and actors Abhishek Bachchan and Ranbir Kapoor, all of whom were part of the cash-rich league.

Sydney hobnobbed with some of football's biggest icons. He partied with Ronaldinho, posed alongside Zico, and got Brazilian superstar Neymar to record a personal video message for his wife Valany Cardozo, sending her a 'big hug and kiss' in her native Portuguese tongue.

Sydney loved Valany and lavished her with expensive gifts and treats. On her birthday, he whisked her to a private island off the coast of Dubai and renewed his vows in an opulent ceremony.

He also pampered his staff with surprise gifts, including foreign jaunts. Sydney's enormous wealth came from his forex trading company, Exential, where an account could be opened with a minimum deposit of $25,000 with the money supposedly invested in foreign currency and traded when markets fluctuated, using a sophisticated computer algorithm.

The promise of 120 per cent was like a siren call to nearly 10,000 investors. They came from all walks of life, entrusting their savings, hopes and dreams to Exential.

For many, it was the chance of a lifetime. At first, investors couldn't believe their luck. Significant profits were paid out each month. Unknown to them, these earnings weren't the fruits of legitimate trading, but rather, funds supplied by fresh investors.

As time passed, the returns continued to pour in, luring even more individuals into the scheme. Young cabin crew, exhausted from their long flights, joined in as word of mouth spread among them. Soon, they too were investing their hard-earned money, inspired by their colleagues' substantial returns.

Professionals from the oil, gas and metal industries also entered the fray, injecting significant sums. A senior Indian executive at Petrofac in Sharjah maintained 625 accounts with Exential, each with $25,000, while a former vice president of an aluminium company held 350.

Sydney had become a master of his own universe, basking in the wealth and power of his fraudulent empire. For over five years, his Ponzi scheme managed to fool over 10,000 investors. But as with any unsustainable scheme, it was only a matter of time before it would all come crashing down.

In 2017, when the music finally stopped playing, panic set in among the investors. The promised returns had been too good to be true, and now many found themselves in financial ruin. Scores of them lodged complaints with the Dubai Economic Department (DED), which eventually shut down Exential's office. Distressed investors, drawn by my track record of exposing deceptive companies, reached out to me. One notable instance involved a company called Sunfeast Infotech that operated from Mai Tower in Al Nahda. Here eager investors were given 'outsourced projects' on a flash drive containing PDF manuscripts that they had to transcribe into text format within twenty-five days. At the end of each twenty-five-day cycle, they pocketed Dh250 for their efforts, with a Dh500 security deposit per project. In theory, they recouped their initial investment within two months; anything thereafter was profit. One enterprising soul even set up a makeshift typing centre under a tarpaulin shade back in India, where fifty typists diligently clacked away at keyboards to churn out these projects. It might have sounded ludicrous, yet around 6,000 UAE residents fell for it. I recall visiting Sunfeast Infotech's office when it all crumbled and its South Indian promoters were jailed.

However, Exential was a far more complicated scheme. As I unravelled the intricacies of their operation, I also delved into the harrowing stories of the victims. An Egyptian pilot, juggling multiple accounts, had contemplated ending his life as his entire salary vanished into the abyss of debt. A Filipino nurse had been reduced to a psychological wreck, and an Indian family became homeless after failing to meet their rent obligations. With every story I exposed, the pressure on Sydney mounted.

One day, a middle-aged British man walked into our office, dressed in an ash-grey suit that matched his wavy hair. He introduced himself as Mark, claiming that he had been sent by Sydney to speak with me. 'I'm here to help with the stories you've been writing,' he said. 'If you need a statement, an update or anything else, just give me a call.' As he spoke, he jotted down a cell phone number on the back of my business card.

Then he added, 'And if any of your friends or relatives invested with Exential and got their money stuck, just let me know. We'll refund their money in less than a day and add a special profit from our side.' He gave me a sly wink. I thought about the Egyptian pilot, the homeless Indian and the Filipina nurse.

'Thank you,' I said. 'I don't have any friends or relatives who could afford to invest $25,000, and I don't want anything from Mr Lemos except his statement.'

'Think about it. This can be mutually beneficial,' Mark said.

I shook my head. 'There's nothing to think about.'

'Well, Mr Sydney specifically requested that I speak to you,' said Mark. 'So if you change your mind, just give me a call.'

I didn't make any calls. Mark did. His approach was more than a conversation; it bordered on intimidation.

Mark claimed that certain members of the royal family were angry with my reporting and demanded a meeting at a hotel lounge that evening.

Initially, I considered it, but my editor Bobby Naqvi suggested I invite them over.

Mark was aghast at the idea. 'That's not how it works. Do you know anything about protocol? Royal family members don't visit newspaper offices. You'll only make it worse for yourself,' he warned.

But I stood my ground. 'Whether they're royals or not, if they want to meet me, they have to come to us.'

Reluctantly, Mark consented. A few days later, he showed up at our office with two men wearing the traditional Emirati dress, complete with headgear.

The younger man spoke in a slow, raspy voice. 'We are from the royal family, and we don't like these rubbish reports about our friend Sydney Lemos,' he said as we took our seats in the meeting room.

It was quite an act, but I remained sceptical about their claims. The men's accent and flashy wristwatches seemed out of place for Emiratis. They looked more like migrant Bangladeshi camel herders than royalty.

Our conversation didn't go anywhere. After about twenty minutes, I politely showed them the door.

By now, hundreds of police complaints had been filed against Sydney. Investigations into Sydney's activities continued to uncover new evidence, so he started another fraudulent scheme under the guise of Pinnacle Asset & Investment Management. This time, he remained behind the scenes, appointing Indian forex educator and author Mario Singh as its executive director.

It didn't take long for me to expose Sydney's deceitful tactics and reveal that Pinnacle was actually his company. The story thwarted Sydney's gameplan.

As the plot thickened, some 250 investors pooled money and hired private detectives from the UK to recover their funds from Exential's parent company FCI Markets Ltd, based in the British Virgin Islands, and its sister concerns Tadawul MidEast and Ellipsys.

Experts from Carlton Huxley flew to Dubai from the UK to chalk out a strategy but instead landed in trouble themselves as they had no permission to investigate the case.

In December 2016, Sydney was arrested. I remember receiving a text message from him when I broke the story. 'Don't spread rumours. I am not in jail.'

A short while after his initial release on bail, Sydney found himself arrested for the second time within a brief span. Subsequently, a Dubai court delivered a verdict that sent shockwaves through the region: Sydney, his wife Valany, and the company's accountant Ryan D'Souza were convicted in the 515 cases filed against them. They were sentenced to one year in jail for each of the 513 cases, and two years for the remaining two. Such a monumental judgment was unprecedented in Dubai and garnered international attention, making headlines across the globe.

I felt sorry for Ryan. He was a football player from Goa and had barely joined Exential. Ryan's brother lives in Dubai. I called him a few times, hoping to meet him, but he refused.

In July 2018, Manohar Parrikar, the then chief minister of Goa, assured the Goa Legislative Assembly to take up Ryan's cause with the Ministry of External Affairs, then headed by Sushma Swaraj. Unfortunately, both Parrikar and Sushma died the following year within a few months of each other.

Valany was sentenced by Dubai courts in absentia as she had already fled to Goa.

Before escaping, she broke into Exential's sealed head-office in Aremco Tower in Media City and stole vital evidence related to the case.

I was stunned by her audacity as I saw CCTV footage of her entering the building with some men and then calmly carting away several boxes in a car.

In the days ahead, I found out that investors' funds amounting to millions of dollars were moved to Australia-based brokerage firm FC Prime Markets owned by Valany.

More surprises awaited me when I uncovered another Dubai-based entity which was part of the elaborate scam. It was S&S Brokerage, a financial intermediary regulated by the Central Bank of the UAE. Its association with Exential deluded investors into believing that their investments were secure. I found out that S&S staff were paid to turn a blind eye because soon after the scam came to light, S&S Brokerage was shut down by regulators. Its manager left for Pakistan and bought a huge property, but a disgruntled investor tracked him down and shot him. He survived. They don't die that easily.

Com Mirza: Serial Swindler

In the mid-2010s, a man burst onto Dubai's social scene like a comet, leaving a blazing trail in his wake. His name was Aziz Com Mirza, and he swiftly became the city's focal point. With a stocky build and a receding hairline, he seemed to be everywhere— at social gatherings, in newspapers, at charitable events, and even on public stages, captivating audiences with his words.

Aziz Com Mirza hailed from Pakistan but held a Canadian passport and had a larger than life persona. He lived in the Burj Khalifa and possessed a fleet of supercars that was the envy of many. He was also a man of many titles, often referring to himself as a serial entrepreneur, mentor, influencer and philanthropist. His numerous charitable initiatives earned him glowing newspaper coverage, one of which aimed to provide meals for 1,50,000 less fortunate individuals during the sacred month of Ramadan.

That carefully crafted image got a further boost when he started attending public speaking events to share his wisdom and talk about his 'Billion Dollar Mastermind' classes. At TEDxMcGill, a TED conference held at McGill University in Montreal, Com charmed the audience with a fifteen-minute talk on his social media business, which he said had the potential to save 1 million human lives in the Third World countries. At other forums, he boasted about successfully launching three dozen companies around the world, making more than a hundred investments in companies like Amazon, and mentoring, training and coaching thousands of entrepreneurs.

Com was so convincing that even internet marketing guru Tai Lopez publicly endorsed his Billion Dollar Mastermind classes. Before long, hundreds signed up for his mentorship courses, while more than 8,00,000 followed him on his verified Instagram account, where he unabashedly flaunted his extravagant lifestyle of private jets, luxury cars and designer clothes.

As his fame spread abroad, Com flew to London in 2016 and, together with elder brother Rafaqat 'Rocky' Mirza, partnered with a community group called Muslim Entrepreneur Network (MEN) that used to operate from a mosque in Barking, a suburban town in East London.

Once onboard, Com announced an investment scheme called the Leverage Programme (LP) that promised financial freedom to MEN members within a year.

'This is a life-changing opportunity. Our systems, which we used for many years and spent millions of dollars on to perfect, will be there to help you,' Com told a packed audience at a promotional event in London. 'This is mentorship taken to the next level. This is us holding your hand and walking you through every step of your successful business. And not just that, this is us standing behind you with our full commitment and resources.'

As the crowd erupted into cheers, Com welcomed his 'far more successful millionaire' brother Rocky onto the stage and introduced the Briton as the brainchild of LP. 'Meet my brother Rocky, he's a mathematical genius, the Steve Jobs of the Muslim world,' Com said amid more applause.

Within days of its launch, 300 people paid anywhere between £1,500 and £25,000 to join the Leverage Programme. Around 1,200 more enrolled a few months later. Among the new recruits was Umme Rayin, a housewife in Sharjah who paid £25,000.

Nobody tried to find how the scheme would make money. The business model had the blessing and backing of Com. For investors, that was enough.

'We were dazzled by Com and trusted him blindly,' MEN co-founder Harun Rashid would tell me later.

Those who enrolled for the LP were encouraged to invest in yet another venture of Com—a real estate–linked Sharia compliant cryptocurrency called Habibi Coin.

Hundreds worldwide invested in Habibi Coin, billed as the Bitcoin of the Middle East. Com had a third scheme called International Success Group (ISG). It was pitched as an educational website where subscribers could learn how to get the best bang for their buck. Hundreds invested in ISG, too.

I began investigating Com in early February 2019 when some disgruntled investors reached out to me from the UK. They had no returns on their investments and suspected foul play. In the beginning I thought their fears were unfounded—that there could be a genuine reason for the delay.

But when they shared Com's investments schemes and I put them under the scanner, it became evidently clear that all of them were bogus.

Conman Com had sold them Ponzi schemes disguised as legitimate investment plans.

Awash with ill-gotten wealth, he was now lolling in wealth without a care in the world.

Roughly £4 million was raised under the LP alone between 2017 and 2019.

Investigations into the money trail showed that £1.8 million was wired to the Dubai bank account of a company owned by

A. Mirza, a third brother of Com, while huge amounts went to pay for personal expenses and fund various ventures owned by the Mirza brothers. Some part of the money was used to pay back old investors—a hallmark of Ponzi schemes.

One such venture under the LP included an app called Empty Trip. The Mirzas said it would revolutionise the taxi industry. Stakeholders were assured that the app was in the final stages of discussion with the UK's Department for International Trade (DIT).

I found out that no one from the DIT had even met Com, let alone had any discussions about Empty Trip.

Another get-rich-quick scheme, ISG had meanwhile morphed into an investment programme called ISG Capital Pool, which guaranteed returns from a real estate project in Dubai. That real estate project didn't exist, nor did Habibi Coin, which was launched as an Initial Coin Offering (ICO). Each Habibi Coin was priced at $0.05, and reportedly created using the ERC20 standard. According to Mirza's own representations online, he raised $39 million in pre-sales of the ICO. Where that money went remained a mystery.

As I put the pieces together, I rang up Com Mirza and asked to see him.

He showed up at our office in a Rolls Royce the following morning. 'Happy birthday, Mazhar bhai,' he greeted me as I met him at the reception and walked him to my favourite meeting room number 7 at *Gulf News*.

'I am one of your most ardent fans in Dubai. I follow you on social media and saw that you have just had your birthday, mashallah. I didn't bring a gift because I wanted to hear from you firsthand what you'd like to—'

'Thank you, Mr Com,' I cut to the chase.

Com listened sagely to me as I lay bare the truth of his dodgy investment schemes one by one.

When I finished, he removed his baseball cap and edged closer to me.

'You know what, Mazhar bhai, all of this is untrue. This is a conspiracy to defame me. I am glad that you are on the case. You need to investigate it thoroughly,' he said.

'Yes,' I replied, 'that's precisely what I have been doing, and it doesn't look good for you.'

Com ran his hand across his balding pate before he replied.

'Yes, there have been problems in Habibi and ISG and I am fixing them but I got nothing to do with the Leverage Programme. That's Rocky's doing. I can't be held accountable for what somebody else did. Plus, I had already quit the Muslim Entrepreneur Network. I am a millionaire businessman, for God's sake. Why would I want to run a Ponzi scheme?'

Com claimed that the money collected under the ISG scheme had gone towards the construction of a real estate project in Dubai. However, he refused to share any details, saying it could sabotage the project and cause 'disastrous damage to the community'. He also claimed that Habibi Coin was a real currency and was nearing acquisition by a big company. Again, he refused to reveal details.

My investigations showed that the company that was supposed to acquire Habibi was a hastily established entity called Makotos run by Com himself.

To give it some semblance of credibility, he had put the name of an Emirati influencer and a US-based entrepreneur of Pakistani origin on its board of advisers. The two were dating each other during that time and had invested over $1,50,000 into Habibi Coin.

Alarmed by the bad publicity surrounding Com and his coin, both washed their hands off the project and filed a police complaint.

We published our exposé on 19 April 2019 under the headline 'Serial Entrepreneur or Serial Scammer'. The story reverberated across the nation and beyond. But it were the stakeholders in Com's money-spinning schemes who were most affected. For days, our phones and email were flooded with calls and messages from investors waking up to the realisation that they had been cheated. The list of his victims kept growing. The amounts were staggering. John Barry ($5,00,000), MK ($1,50,000), Tariq Syed ($1,00,000) and digital entrepreneur Alex Becker ($28,000) from the USA, Ghulam Masktaki ($25,000) from the UAE, Kalib Hussain (£50,000) from the UK and Giannis ($17,000) from Greece ($17,000).

Stung by the damning revelations, Com came out with a five-part Instagram video refuting my report, accusing me of lazy journalism and challenging me to furnish proof within twenty-four hours. 'This report is a textbook example of bad journalism, on purpose to harm others,' he said as he appeared in the video wearing a white T-Shirt and a Louis Vuitton baseball cap. 'Mazhar Farooqui has gone out of his way to write fiction as the truth,' he said, citing the example of former American journalist Janet Leslie Cooke who won a Pulitzer Prize in 1981 for an article written for *The Washington Post*. Cook's story was later discovered to have been fabricated.

Com challenged me to come with evidence to back my story.

I did not respond.

In October 2019, Com was arrested in connection with a fraud investigation on the very investment schemes that I had uncovered. It took us a while to break the story about his arrest as our dedicated crime reporter couldn't get a police confirmation.

Many stories never see the light of the day for want of a police comment. I didn't want Com story to suffer the same fate. So I went to the detention centre at Bur Dubai Police Station and got an officer to confirm that Com was indeed behind bars. The report of his arrest made headlines around the world.

With Com out of action and unable to make any more videos, it was time for his elder brother Rocky to take up the mantle. He did that by coming out with YouTube videos threatening to sue me at the High Court in London for defamation. The videos were interspersed with pictures and statistics and could have been funny if they weren't so absurd.

The following year, Com was convicted for fraud and sentenced to jail.

In October 2023, he was still behind bars. Rocky, meanwhile, sent us a bunch of legal notices from the UK, which were followed by formal notices from Her Majesty's Courts and Tribunal Service. We didn't respond to any of them.

Com's fall from grace was no less spectacular than his rise to fame.

As con artists go, he was up there with the most notorious. He left more than 2,000 persons out of pocket, one of them also with a broken heart. Among the many people who contacted me after the story was a woman to whom I will refer only by her initials, MA. She claimed she was in a long-distance relationship with Com after meeting him on a matrimonial website in 2014. 'He introduced himself as Aariz and said his son and wife were killed in a car accident and he was looking for a life partner,' MA told me. Com was married and had three children at that time. As their relationship blossomed, they shared several emails.

'Pain in my heart I still keep thinking about you for you are the joy of my life,' reads the subject of one such email that Com sent her in November 2014.

MA said their love affair ended prematurely when Com asked her to loan him £25,000 so that he could release a shipment that was stuck with Netherlands Port. MA shared a letter sent to Com by the Netherlands Port Authority asking him to pay the money within ninety-six hours or face strict penalties.

Like his bogus investment schemes, the letter was also fake.

Leonard Charles, a reformed small-time scammer turned laundryman from Pakistan, used to tell me about his interactions with Com over the phone from Al Awir Prison when they were serving time together. 'Com is still delivering lectures, it's just that instead of his fans and followers his audience is his fellow inmates.'

Hayyab Arif Kamboh: Dead Man Walking and Scamming

The Latin American festival el Dia de los Muertos, or the Day of the Dead, is observed on 2 November, when all the souls of the dead are believed to return to the world of the living. Another festival that is more popular and is around the same time is Halloween, during which the souls of the departed are said to return to Earth and become visible to humans.

But for Pakistani businessman Chaudhary Hayyab Arif Kamboh, the worlds of the living and the dead have remained blurred since 19 July 2017. That's the day he 'died' in a road accident in Sharjah only to spring back to life in neighbouring Ajman a couple of years later.

Hayyab, barely in his thirties then, was a member of the Pakistani political party Muttahida Qaumi Movement (MQM).

Muttahida Qaumi Movement Television mourned his death on their Facebook page, describing him as an 'ideological worker'.

The post was accompanied by a photo collage of the deceased. A close-up picture showed Arif lying dead with cotton balls plugged in his nostrils and a white burial shroud wrapped around his body.

Arif's younger brother Mian Zaryab also shared a social media post talking about his struggle to come to grips with the personal loss.

Both posts elicited an outpouring of grief with scores paying glowing tributes to the departed.

But Arif was not dead. My investigation revealed that he was not only alive and kicking, but also busy making a killing scamming overseas companies.

Fourteen months after his purported death, Arif had launched a company in Ajman Freezone and then tricked exporters into shipping him millions of dollars' worth of onions, bananas and coconuts among other foodstuffs. None of them ever got paid.

The list of victims ran over several pages and included exporters from India, Sri Lanka, Indonesia, Malaysia, Thailand, Myanmar and the UAE.

It's not that the exporters didn't do their due diligence. Many even flew to the UAE to verify the antecedents of Arif and his company. Arif laid out the red carpet for them.

He sent his staff with large bouquets of roses to receive the visitors at the airport and then put them up in hotels before meeting them at his office. Secured in the mistaken belief that they were dealing with a legitimate firm, they handed bills of lading to Arif which allowed him to release the shipments from the port.

When the exporters asked for their payment, Arif switched off his phone and vanished. Those who managed to reach out to him were mocked and abused. A trader from Gujarat shared with me a voice note sent to him by Arif via WhatsApp.

'Yes, I scam people … this is my business, I slaughter them like a butcher would slaughter lambs. A bigger crook than me is yet to be born. I pick my victims and prey on greedy dogs like you. This is what I do for a living. You were a fool to fall for me. I don't even remember how many cases I have against me in Pakistan. Why do you think I won't go back there?'

I remember the expression on the face of the managing editor Mohammad Al Mezel when I first told him about the story.

'You mean to tell me this man here is not dead?' he asked as he stared at an enlarged picture of Arif lying dead and then compared it with an image of him sitting behind his office desk in a dark suit.

Before publishing the report, I called Arif to seek his response.

'Mr Arif, are you dead or alive?' I enquired.

He was startled because only his closest confidantes had that cell phone number. However, he kept his cool and responded to all my questions with remarkable nonchalance. Of course, the answers didn't add up.

'I am alive and I will live for a hundred years,' he said.

'So why did MQM post an obituary about you?' I asked.

'I don't know. Maybe there was a mistake. You need to ask them.'

'What about the picture of you lying dead?'

'Oh, that is from my theatre days in Pakistan. I played a dead man in a play.'

With his portly bearing and manly full beard, Arif didn't look anywhere near someone the age of a college-going student in the picture.

'But this appears to be a recent picture,' I said.

'No, it's an old one, I have been like this for many years.'

'So what was the name of the play and when was it staged?'

'I don't remember its name as it's been many years. But it was a good play, a lot of people watched it.'

'Could you share the name of any of your co-actors?'

'No, this is my personal matter.'

'If what you are saying is true, then why did your younger brother also post fake news about your death on his Facebook page?'

'Oh, that was not him. Someone must have hacked his Facebook account and posted it.'

'What about the allegations of exporters?'

'They are lying. I did not pay them because the foodstuff they supplied was of very poor quality. They are spreading lies about me and I will take them to court.'

'You mean all exporters from India to Indonesia have ganged up against you?'

'Yes, all of them.'

'So why don't you confront them? You aren't even taking their calls.'

'I can't take their calls because I lost my old cell phone and couldn't get a replacement SIM card issued as there is an outstanding bill against it.'

'Why don't you clear it?'

'I will when I want to, it's my personal matter.'

We ran the story on the front page, juxtaposing the picture of Arif lying dead with one of him sitting in his office. Nothing remotely of this sort had ever been published in *Gulf News* or any other newspaper in the country.

The story went viral.

It refuses to die (no pun intended) even to this day.

I was told Arif had faked his death to evade people, who had become his sworn enemies after being cheated by him, in Pakistan.

Shortly after the exposé, Ajman Free Zone announced a probe into the matter. Sadly, nothing came out of it. Arif changed his company but not his ways. I never met Arif but remember catching a fleeting glimpse of him through the glass-fronted door of a street-facing restaurant where I was dining with my wife and youngest daughter in April 2022. It was early Ramadan and we had gone to Lucknow Rasoi restaurant in Al Nahda to break our fast with kebab parathas. Halfway into the meal, my wife suddenly gripped my shoulder. 'Look, look, there's your dead man,' she said.

I gazed outside. Arif had put on more weight and his beard looked even fuller. But I could recognise that face even in my sleep.

Nowhera Shaik: Veiled Deception

She was the quintessential Muslim businesswoman—a self-made billionaire who wore a hijab and cared for the community, or so one thought. Islamic scholars in India and Pakistan swore by her. 'In the Interest of All Mankind,' proclaimed her company's tagline.

For thousands of families across South Asia and the Middle East, Nowhera Shaik was a veritable female messiah. But somewhere in October 2018, I found myself caught in her crosshairs when I exposed her. I was abused, threatened, trolled and—when none of this worked—portrayed as a member of an Indian political party, disguised as a journalist.

A big, plump woman, Nowhera Shaik was fondly called 'Apa' (Urdu word for elder sister) but used the 'Dr' prefix, never mind that she had neither earned a research doctorate nor was she a doctor by profession.

In fact, Nowhera was a school dropout. The eldest of five siblings, Nowhera hailed from Tirupati in the Indian state of Andhra Pradesh. Her father, Shaikh Nane Sahib, was a cleric who led prayers at the local mosque while she and her mother, Bilkis, hawked vegetables.

Sometime in the late 1990s, Nowhera came in contact with some illiterate Muslim women from her village and began selling them gold jewellery at a low profit margin, while also preaching to them about Islam. Buoyed by the initial response, she expanded the circle and created a big self-help group of women. Nowhera's gold scheme earned them money while her lectures strengthened their religious beliefs.

As Nowhera's popularity soared, more and more people joined her. In 2012, she launched her proprietary company called Heera Gold.

For the next few years, the company's rise was meteoric. Soon Heera had a finger in everything from gold, forex trading, textile and jewellery, to bottled water, real estate, electronics and e-commerce.

Those who invested in the businesses were promised and given such high returns that financial wizards rubbed their eyes in disbelief.

Heera Gold handed out monthly payouts of Dh3,250 ($884) against an investment of Dh1,00,000 ($27,225) with a minimum lock-in period of one year. Heera Textiles guaranteed annual returns of 65–70 per cent against a minimum deposit of Dh15,000 (lock-in period: two years). At Heera Foodex (lock-in period: two years), the deposit yielded annual profits of up to 80 per cent.

Almost all her investors were Muslims, who were deluded into believing that the schemes were halal and complied with the principles of Islamic law.

Islamic clerics on Heera's payroll strengthened the narrative. I came across a video of one such cleric, Shaikh Arshad Basheer Madani, urging people to invest in Heera.

'We have gold jewellery lying at home, but if we give some of it to Heera company, we will get good profits, which we can use to help our family and also play a productive role in society, like Alima Nowhera Shiekh,' he said. Pamphlets promoting Heera's investment plans were also distributed through mosques in Karnataka and Maharashtra.

The heady mix of halal income and financial freedom worked like magic.

By 2017, some 2,00,000 Muslims from India, Bangladesh, Indonesia, Pakistan, Kuwait, the UAE, Saudi Arabia, Qatar, Bahrain and Oman had invested in various schemes of the conglomerate.

When personal savings were not enough, many borrowed from banks and loan sharks. Assured by a steady flow of halal income, hundreds of housewives in Maharashtra and Andhra Pradesh pawned their jewellery to invest in Heera Group.

Nowhera would splurge investors' money on anything she fancied. In 2017, she forked out an undisclosed amount to secure the title sponsorship of the inaugural edition of the T10 Cricket League held in Dubai.

At the beginning of the month, the investors would get the returns based on their stakes. The higher the investment, the higher the reward.

But when the payment suddenly dried up in mid-2018, investors took to the streets and laid a siege outside Heera's head office in Hyderabad.

Following police complaints, Nowhera, then forty-five, was arrested for cheating, criminal breach of trust and criminal intimidation. The federal probe agency said that Heera Group illegally collected about Dh2.88 billion from investors.

But the enormity of the scam and the devastation it left in its wake didn't dawn on me until a whistleblower, Shahbaz Khan, put me in touch with investors.

I remember speaking to Shabnam Khadri, a middle-aged woman who lived in the Mumbai suburbs of Mira Road. She had invested Rs 1.6 million (Dh80,000) in Heera Group weeks before it shut down. The money belonged to her son Suhel, who was also the family's sole breadwinner. 'It was our life savings and I gave it away without Suhel's knowledge in the hope of getting a steady monthly income,' Shabnam told me.

When her son found out about it, he slipped into depression. He'd keep awake all night worrying about their fate. A few days later he suffered a heart attack and died. Suhel was thirty-eight. Shabnam now survives on alms. She was last spotted begging opposite Mumbai's Umrao Hospital where her son breathed his last.

Closer home the picture was no less bleak.

Shahid, who retired as a school bus driver in Sharjah, told me he put whatever he had saved in thirty years along with his end-of-service benefits into the Heera Group. He didn't even have money to return to India, having worked for over three decades in the UAE.

When news of Nowhera's arrest broke, Shahid rushed to Heera Group's office in Jumeirah Lakes Towers in Dubai. It was locked. Visits to the company's offices in Sharjah and Ras Al Khaimah by panicked investors also drew a blank.

It is estimated that 15,000 people from the Middle East had invested in Heera. A majority of them were from the UAE.

Police investigations revealed that Nowhera had more than 150 bank accounts and multiple offices in India and Gulf countries.

These offices were manned by marketing agents whose primary job was to bring in investments. Like the company's investors, its sales agents were also largely Muslims. Most of them had beards and wore skull caps while women dressed in burqas.

Apparently, Nowhera sensed what was coming. Just before her Ponzi scheme spectacularly collapsed, she tried to dabble in politics.

In 2017, she launched the All India Mahila Empowerment Party (MEP) and went on to contest the 2018 Karnataka Assembly elections with a diamond as the party's election symbol.

Bollywood stars Arbaaz Khan and Sohail Khan campaigned for Nowhera's party which fielded candidates in all 224 constituencies.

Their defeat was a foregone conclusion. Yet, Nowhera tried to influence voters by coming up with a poll falsely claiming that MEP would emerge as the second largest party. The dodgy agency commissioned by her said it used a powerful satellite to conduct the survey. It even shared the details of the satellite with its coordinates. How a satellite could predict election results, Nowhera never answered, and her dumb supporters never asked.

AIMEP could manage only 0.3 per cent of the vote share. All 224 candidates lost their security deposit. Later, seven of them filed a cheating case against Nowhera.

Sami Syed, a Dubai-based entrepreneur and former T10 Cricket League director who joined MEP as general secretary but soon quit, offered a plausible explanation behind the move when I called him to our office for a chat. Sami told me that Nowhera thought she could win some seats and use the resulting political clout to scuttle any probe against her and also counter the regional All India Majlis-e-Ittehadul Muslimeen (AIMIM) party, whose president Asaduddin Owaisi had accused her of fraud.

In the days ahead, I found out that Nowhera used photo manipulation tools to fake awards and gain the trust of investors. She also morphed an image from a 2014 event to show her receiving a book from Sushma Swaraj, India's external affairs minister at that time. Nowhera was present at the release of *The Indian Super 100*, a coffee-table book which contained profiles of one hundred entrepreneurs and professionals from India. In fact, she was featured in the book too. But unlike many others, she did not receive the book from Swaraj.

Immediately after my exposé, Hyderabad Police ordered a probe into the doctored pictures and filed charges against Nowhera, much to the chagrin of her supporters.

Angered by my revelations, they launched a malicious online campaign against me. On a propaganda YouTube news channel, a man accused me of working for Owaisi and urged viewers to report me to local authorities. He called for a boycott of *Gulf News* and said he would not sit idle until he had put me behind bars in Dubai. For weeks I was tagged on hundreds of abusive and absurd posts demanding my arrest.

Among other things I was called a pimp, thief and a member of Owaisi's party disguised as a *Gulf News* journalist.

The truth is that I don't know Owaisi or any of his party members and have never visited Hyderabad where his party is headquartered.

Nowhera Shaik is out on bail and facing investigations by various agencies in India. In March 2023, the Enforcement Directorate attached her properties in a money-laundering case. But she remains unfazed. Last heard she was hawking the Heera Digital Gold app, claiming a surge from $2 to $44 in digital gold value, without revealing the source or unit size of this dramatic increase.

Russell King: Trillion Dollar Conman

One day in February 2017, a short European woman called Paula Frances King walked into the luxurious Palazzo Versace Hotel in Dubai and asked to see the manager. She wore a smart blue blazer over a white tunic shirt and carried the inaugural issue of the *Financial Times Arabia* magazine.

At the meeting, she told the manager that her publishing house in Bahrain had just launched the Middle East edition of the internationally renowned *Financial Times (FT)* newspaper and wanted to host a gala at the hotel to celebrate the momentous occasion.

The manager flipped through the slick publication which carried *FT*'s unmistakable salmon-pink logo. The magazine had a cover story on Mohammed bin Salman who had been appointed as the crown prince of Saudi Arabia weeks earlier. Inside, there were other well-researched articles. There was an interview with the CEO of McLaren, an insightful piece on Tesla and a feature on cricket's bid for the Olympics. Every few pages there were advertisements by leading hospitality and retail brands of the region.

As the manager nodded appreciatively, Paula handed him a digital publication report of the magazine. It showed a detailed summary of how the publication was faring online. There were statistics on the number of visitors to the website along with figures of country-wise readers.

Seeing that she had sufficiently impressed the manager, Paula offered him a barter deal.

The hotel would foot the bill of a gala to mark the launch of *FT Arabia*. It would also pay for an awards night for one of their other publications, *Food and Travel Arabia*. In return, Palazzo Versace would get free coverage and advertisements in *FT Arabia* as well as the 'Best destination hotel' and 'Best chic restaurant' awards. It looked like a good deal.

The manager readily agreed. A few days later they signed a contract.

The event cost Palazzo Versace nearly $90,000. For them, it was a small price to pay for a chance to be featured in a *FT* publication.

'We had opened barely a year back and wanted publicity,' the hotel's marketing manager would tell me later.

He had a fair point. But there was a problem and a big one at that. *Financial Times* had nothing to do with *FT Arabia*. In fact, they hadn't even heard of it.

The magazine presented to the hotel manager as *FT*'s sister publication was the first and last issue of a fraudulent magazine, of which only a dozen odd copies were ever printed. They served just one purpose—as bait, to rake in millions of dollars in advertising revenue and barter deals.

Palazzo Versace was not the only one who fell for the con job.

Scores of other UAE-based organisations got similarly trapped and signed contracts in lieu of editorial coverage and advertisements. They included a coffee brand ($35,000), confectionery manufacturer ($16,500), beach resort ($4,350), real estate giant ($45,000), trading firm ($25,000) and a freight company that paid upwards of $50,000.

None of them had an inkling that they had been duped until I broke the story and unmasked the real mastermind of the scam.

His name was Russell King and he was no ordinary criminal.

He was a convicted globe-trotting fraudster who tricked dictators in the heart of the world's most repressive regime, stole the world's oldest football club, duped a royal family and pulled off a massive insurance fraud.

King was on the run for over ten years and faced twenty-five counts of fraud and larceny in his home country when he appeared on my radar.

Originally from Jersey, the big, burly, bespectacled man, who looked like a Bond movie villain, was sentenced to two years in prison in 1991 for insurance fraud after trying to get £6,00,000 in theft claims for his Aston Martin that never left his garage. After a string of other frauds, he pulled off a scam so big it earned him the sobriquet 'The Trillion Dollar Conman' from the BBC, who subsequently featured him in their documentary series *Panorama*.

In 2009, King founded a company called Swiss Commodity Holding, which claimed it had assets worth $2 trillion besides the rights to all the gold, iron ore and coal in North Korea.

The fraudster then engineered the takeover of British investment bank First London. By falsely claiming he was managing billions of dollars for the Bahraini royal family, he got the bank to turn over 49 per cent of its share to him.

The sweet-talker's next step was to gain control of Notts County Football Club, the world's oldest football club, where he lured former England coach Eriksson to be the director of football with promises of shares worth £10 million.

With Eriksson on board and the backing of First Bank of London, Notts County Football Club agreed to be sold to King.

The scammer then took Eriksson to North Korea where he signed a deal with the communist leadership, which gave one of his front companies the rights to mine all the country's minerals in return for £1 billion from Bahrain.

When the money didn't come, King took a plane out of England. He moved to Bahrain and it is from there that he planned and executed the audacious *FT Arabia* scam.

I marvelled at his ingenuity. At a time when established newspapers with vast resources were struggling to get advertisements, he had managed to get millions of dollars of adverts for a magazine that didn't exist. And he did all of this without ever stepping foot in Dubai.

I found out that King had hired two of the best sales personnel in the industry. One of them was a former staff member of *Gulf News*. Both had been sucked into his web of deceit.

The woman who showed up at the Palazzo Versace with the fake magazine and false name was none other than King's partner in crime and wife Francesca Jackson.

My revelations caused ripples in the UAE, particularly among the city's elite who had attended the gala and boasted about it to their friends. The story also sent shockwaves at *FT*'s headquarters in London. They issued a statement denying association with *FT Arabia* and also launched an investigation.

When our story came out in February 2018, King was all set to host another awards night in collaboration with Palazzo Versace. Following the exposé, the hotel slammed the door in his face while the Global Restaurant Investment Forum (GRIF) that had tied up with the bogus publication immediately snapped ties with them.

Saved the blushes and their dollars, Palazzo Versace expressed their thanks by hosting me and my wife in their signature suite. Ironically, it was the same room where they had hosted Francesca Jackson days earlier.

A few months later, King was extradited from Bahrain to Jersey and charged with multiple counts of fraud that took place while he was living in Jersey in 2008. These included allegedly selling a financial company in a fraudulent manner, as well as falsification of accounts. King is said to have misappropriated something to the order of £16 million. In April 2019, he was sentenced to six years' imprisonment for stealing £6,70,000 from the financial company and told to pay back £3,20,000 or face additional time in jail.

In February 2022, the BBC featured me in a five-part programme on Russell King for their *Sport's Strangest Crimes* series. From Nottingham to North Korea, it traced how the conman took the oldest club in the football league to the brink of oblivion with promises beyond their wildest dreams. For me, King was the ultimate con artist who had the foresight of a chess grandmaster. I admired his wits and quirks in equal measure. He rarely put his name on back accounts, shareholdings or directorship. Instead he used monikers. Sometimes he signed off as Barry Appleby or John Taylors, at others Lord Voldemort, after the character in the Harry Potter books, also known as 'He-Who-Must-Not-Be-Named'.

Nowraid Awan Malik: Flight of Fancy

Remember *Catch Me If You Can*? The Hollywood blockbuster depicted the exploits of conman extraordinaire Frank Abagnale who posed as a pilot to bum free Pan Am flights. But while Abagnale's story may have been the stuff of Hollywood legend, the reality of modern-day fraud is no less intriguing.

In February 2021, I unmasked Nigerian scammer Lawal Isiaka Babatunde who masqueraded as an Emirates pilot for six years, peddling forged tickets, visas and fake aviation jobs across South Africa, Ghana, Nigeria and Zimbabwe. Babatunde was a master of deception, dressing up in crisp white shirts with epaulettes on his shoulders and a golden aviation badge pinned above his shirt's left pocket. And should there be any doubt about his profession, the thirty-six-year-old also wore a lanyard neck strap with the Emirates airlines name emblazoned in its distinctive font and colour across the length of the cord.

But even Babatunde was no match for Noureed Awan Malik, a young man with a goatee and big girth, who owned the MMA Group in Dubai and ran an international airline that just did not exist.

Noureed Awan Malik was from Abbottabad, the city notorious as Osama Bin Laden's hideout, in the Khyber Pakhtunkhwa province of Northern Pakistan.

He also shared the Al Qaeda chief's penchant for assault rifles. There's a chilling YouTube video of Awan smilingly firing thirty rounds from an M4 carbine in the air in his hometown as an elderly man looks on. Bin Laden might have heard the staccato burst of gunfire if he were alive as Malik's September 2011 video is from around the same place where Bin Laden was killed four months earlier by the US Marines in a predawn operation.

From afar, Awan appeared to be one of the biggest stories of entrepreneurial success in the UAE. Aside from a private airline, the MMA Group also claimed to own a bank, forex platform, heavy machinery equipment company, advertising firm, online radio and social networking platform.

Awan was unabashed about his meteoric rise and thirst for fame and wealth.

His website called him the 'youngest successful businessman of Asia with an aim to conquer the world'. For a long time, he looked to be on course to do that, living it up in style on Palm Jumeirah, jet-setting around the world, hobnobbing with the UAE's elite and handing out trophies at international cricket matches in Sharjah and Dubai.

In the midst of all this, Awan found time to marry and divorce two women from the glamour industry in quick succession. His relationships with British singer-model Annie Khalid and Pakistani actor Sataesh Khan were tumultuous, to say the least. Despite their short-lived marriages to Awan, both women shared harrowing tales of domestic abuse. They claimed that Awan regularly subjected them to physical violence, including kicking them in the stomach and slapping them as if it were routine.

A badly traumatised Sataesh once sought protection, saying her ex-husband had threatened to kill her if she exposed his wrongdoings.

Awan's seemingly limitless wealth always intrigued me, but my suspicions of its source were confirmed in early 2012 when I received a tip-off that he was involved in dubious business practices.

I wanted to go after him with all guns blazing. But what if he did that too? The video of him peppering the air with bullets was fresh in my mind.

Moreover, there was no evidence against Awan, who was riding a tidal wave of success those days. The man who gave the tip-off had disappeared and efforts to trace him had drawn a blank. Meanwhile, MMA Airline had been registered in Ras Al Khaimah, with the first commercial flights expected to take off for Karachi and Lahore in May 2012.

Awan claimed that his company had invested $50 million in the airline.

'We have acquired two Airbus A320s to start flights. Two Boeing 777-300s are expected to join the fleet when we plan to add more destinations, such as Mumbai,' Awan gloated in a statement that was promptly reported by local and international media.

The flights might have taken off if they were not flights of fancy.

We found out, from the General Civil Aviation Authority (GCAA), that MMA Airline just didn't exist and had no approval to operate anywhere in the country.

A visit to the airline's website would, however, delude one into believing that it was a full-fledged international carrier operating out of Ras Al Khaimah. Not only did it have a daily operational schedule but also a platform that appeared to accept online bookings to various destinations. MMA Airline also boasted a team of 'dedicated professionals, including pilots, navigators, ATC controllers, flight engineers and airline marketing gurus, ensuring excellence in everything'.

There were even 'benefits and privileges of Skywards membership' under the MMA Sky Perks Program, and the 'best halal food including Asian, Chinese and Thai cuisines'. Frills included video games, free wi-fi and noise-cancelling headphones for 'true music nerds'.

Upon closer inspection, we discovered that the pictures of the Boeing 777 fleet on MMA Airline's website were actually taken from United Airlines planes, while the managing director's message was plagiarised from the website of Biman Bangladesh, the national airline of Bangladesh.

Awan's other business ventures were equally deceptive. For instance, MMA Bank was nothing more than a trading company, while MMA Forex, the group's heavily promoted forex trading arm with over 1,00,000 clients and millions of dollars in monthly transactions, was an elaborate Ponzi scheme that left over 8,000 people from the UAE, India and Pakistan out of pocket. Exact figures were hard to come by but according to an estimate, the victims had collectively lost over $10 million to the fraudulent scheme.

I met scores of devastated victims outside Mai Tower in Al Nahda, Dubai, where MMA's office was located on the eleventh floor. Most had put their life savings into the company after being promised 36 per cent annual returns. Those who didn't have money mortgaged personal assets.

Their earnings dried up, many had been forced to quit their jobs and go underground after being hounded by banks and loan sharks.

I remember encountering a middle-aged Indian woman one afternoon as I made my way to Mai Tower. She sat behind the wheel of a white Nissan Pathfinder parked outside the building. As I strolled past her, she opened the passenger side front door and called out to me. 'Excuse me, are you the journalist who has been writing about MMA?' she asked nervously. I hesitated for a moment, but then crawled into the car.

As I settled into the passenger seat, I could feel the weight of her desperation, her trembling hands on the steering wheel, and the anguish in her voice as she pleaded with me for help.

'Please do something,' she said, her eyes welling with tears. 'I have pawned all my jewellery and also that of my mother-in-law. Help me, I beg of you.'

'How much was it for?'

'The pawn shop gave me Dh1,50,000 but it was worth a lot more as it included family heirlooms.'

'Does your husband know?'

She shook her head. 'I don't know how long I could hide it from him. He will divorce me if he finds out. My mother-in-law will throw me out.'

I don't know what happened to her. Her fate couldn't have been worse than that of chartered accountant Shahid Zulfiqar who couldn't get a liver transplant for his five-year-old son Shamoil as all his life's savings were stuck in MMA when he needed them the most.

Zulfiqar couldn't save Shamoil. He was his only child.

Zulfiqar had invested $1,00,000 in MMA Forex before Dubai Police shut it down on suspicion of fraud and took Awan into custody.

Awan was later convicted and sentenced to three years in jail but like the Phoenix, MMA Forex rose again.

Five years after being shut down for fraud, it reopened in 2017 and began seeking investments all over again. If this was not worrying enough, it started operations from the same building.

I had a feeling of déjà vu as I visited Mai Tower. This time I was not alone. I was accompanied by a woman in her early thirties. Her name was Sara Waqar. A mother of two, Sara was a forex trader from Pakistan and had surprised me with her grit and intelligence when I first met her while investigating the $300 million Exential forex scam in Dubai.

At that time, Sara worked for S&S Brokerage House, a financial intermediary licensed by the Central Bank of the UAE.

Her revelations helped me get to the bottom of the Exential racket. Before long, we struck up a friendship. Sara joined as an intern at *XPRESS, Gulf News'* bold weekly tabloid that I headed those days. It proved to be a fruitful endeavour as we teamed up to uncover numerous fraudulent activities. Working as a pair, we quickly established ourselves as the scourge of scammers. In February 2017, we embarked on our first joint operation, going undercover to expose a forex racket. I reached out to Sara when I found out that representatives of the dodgy FXUnited were hosting a public event at an Al Barsha hotel to lure unsuspecting investors.

We met them a week before the event posing as a couple looking to invest. A Filipina team member of FXActionTeam International introduced us to Allan, a self-styled Malaysian forex guru of Indian origin. Allan claimed he was part of FXUnited and had been camping in Dubai to prepare the ground for their two-day public sessions where the UAE residents would learn more about forex and have a 'recession-proof means of improving their family's financial wellness'.

Sara and I exchanged amused glances as Allan blabbered on.

'Nearly $6 trillion is traded in the forex market daily and I can show you how to scalp some bits off it in a matter of minutes,' Allan began as he connected the hotel's television set to what he said was a live trading platform.

'I will start with a $500 investment,' he said, clicking some commands on his computer. A few minutes later, his investment had swelled to $2,000.

'This is nothing. I have made up to $5,60,000 in a single day,' he said as he boasted about his extravagant lifestyle.

'I don't have to work for anyone. I have 3,800 traders under me. I make money every time they trade. I am my own boss. Now my mission is to share the secret with others,' he said.

'So what do we need to do to partake of this enormous wealth?' I asked naively.

'You need to open an account with us by paying $500,' he replied, claiming that the return on investments (ROI) would be generated through foreign exchange, specifically Capital Gain Auto Trading (CGAT). 'You'd also get referral commissions to recruit new affiliates, via a binary plan.'

We pretended to be impressed as Allan explained how we could revel in incredible profits for the rest of our lives.

After the meeting with Allan, Sara and I couldn't wait to get our hands on some delicious dal gosht at the nearby Daily Restaurant. As we dug into our plates, we discussed how we were going to run the story and bring this scam to light.

We joked about how we could have easily been swept up in the scheme if we weren't seasoned investigative journalists. 'I almost wanted to give him my $500 just to see if this CGAT thing was real!' I said, before we both burst out laughing.

But we quickly sobered up and got to work, determined to expose the truth behind FXUnited's so-called 'legitimate foreign currency scam'. And that's exactly what we did, with our hard-hitting headline: 'New Scam: Stay away from Forex Convention in Al Barsha This Weekend'.

The story went on to detail how FXUnited was peddling a multi-level marketing (MLM) scam as a legitimate foreign currency scheme.

The event was called off and FXUnited staff took to their heels. 'What you did was not right,' Allan messaged me from the airport.

We put on our best acting skills and visited the MMA Forex office, posing as a couple eager to invest, just like we did when we met Allan at the Al Barsha hotel.

I thought we looked the part.

As we were ushered into a conference room, promotional videos ran on a TV screen about the group's 'diversified' portfolio that included a private airline operating from Ras Al Khaimah airport and the MMA Bank.

Of course, we knew that MMA was not a bank. In fact, it was a general trading company called Mabaank. Malik chose this name specifically so that he could split it into two separate words, 'MMA' and 'Bank', to mislead investors. In small letters, almost negligible to the eye were the letters GT, which was an acronym for general trading.

Mabaank GT had already been listed under 'firms you should avoid doing business with' while MMA Forex was on the watchlist of the Investor Alerts of the International Organization of Securities Commissions. But this didn't stop an MMA manager from demonstrating how we could make windfall profits by trading in foreign currencies.

'You can start with just $300,' said the man as he ran us through a demo account on his laptop and explained how we could register with MMA Forex and start trading in currencies and commodities.

We played along.

I wonder how he would have reacted if he knew that the woman sitting before him was a certified forex trader and her partner was the journalist who had busted them five years earlier.

But we had to seek MMA's response so we called them a few days later and revealed our real identities.

MMA Group was caught off guard. Their manager said they had no links to MMA Forex but the argument didn't cut ice because we had secretly recorded their staff encouraging us to invest in forex.

'But you still have promotional videos of the airline,' I said.

'Yes,' the manager replied. 'We don't have an airline but we plan to have one in the future. Just like when you have kids and you start preparing for their future, we are also looking at the future.'

Sara and I had great fun putting together our experience in a story which appeared in May 2017 under the headline 'Forex Firm Shut Down for Fraud Reopens in Same Building'.

Awan was livid. He shot off a letter to investors and also released a video saying that journalists were out to tarnish his image as he refused to pay them.

'I will not let that happen. I will take them to court,' he threatened.

We never got sued. Awan was instead banned from travelling and his passport was withheld by the court. However, he continued the charade of a high-flying businessman by visiting Dubai Airport and flaunting fake check-ins.

Gill Wallace: Queen of Con

Unmasking criminals is an exhilarating experience. The adrenaline rush that comes with it is the lifeblood of investigative journalists. It's what keeps us going. It's what made me go after Gill Wallace aka Ambassador Hope, a middle-aged British blonde who had relocated to Abu Dhabi with stunning credentials. Gill's LinkedIn profile and Facebook page described her as an advisor to Obama and the UAE government on economic and environmental sustainability. She also claimed to have been nominated for the Nobel Peace Prize.

Her mission: launch a grand project called CULA Liquidity Programme to help 2,00,000 UAE residents with a cash injection of $1.47 billion.

Gill told everyone that the project was backed by the United Nations, G20 countries and the UAE government. But that's not what the anonymous caller who tipped me about her said on the phone. 'Gill is a convicted globetrotting fraudster. Everything you see about her is fake. Her CULA programme is nothing but rip-off scheme targeting the UAE,' he warned.

By now Gill had posted a video of herself citing an official decree instructing 'all UAE government employees to collaborate and cooperate'.

I had to get to the bottom of the story, and if what the caller said was true, stop the woman in her tracks. But how could I do that without alerting her? The caller's words rang in my ears: 'You have to tread carefully, my friend. Gill is no ordinary con artist. She is the best out there. She will eat you alive.'

I thought of meeting her as a potential investor but quickly ruled out the idea. Even in my Massimo Dutti blazer, I didn't look anywhere close to someone who could be part of a $1.5m project.

'What if you try to get a job with her?' a colleague suggested. 'You will get first-hand insights into what she does or at least meet her.'

The idea was shot down too. It was highly unlikely that she would hire me. If she indeed did, there was no way *Gulf News* would spare me to work for her in the hope of getting a story that may just not be there.

Finally, my wife solved my dilemma.

'Why don't you see her as who you are?' she said.

'You mean as a journalist? But that would be a dead giveaway,' I protested.

'On the contrary, it would be the perfect foil. You don't need to tell her that you are investigating her. Tell her instead that you came across her wonderful humanitarian initiatives and want to interview her for the newspaper's lifestyle section.'

She was right.

The plan worked perfectly. Lest Gill looked me up online, I got our newly hired Armenian reporter, Razmig Bedrian, to call her and seek time for an interview.

She readily agreed. We were asked to meet her at Abu Dhabi's Etihad Tower 3 the next day.

I remember it was a blistering hot Ramadan day in 2014 when we drove down to the UAE capital city. I was fasting but Razmig and our photographer Virendra Saklani weren't. There wasn't much they could do as food outlets in the country remained closed during Ramadan those days.

Gill made us wait as she needed to go to a salon. 'I want to look good for the camera. You will put me on the cover, right?' she said over the phone. We spent our time window shopping at Marina Mall.

Nearly three hours after the scheduled time, Gill showed up accompanied by a pint-sized clean-shaven Egyptian man wearing a dark grey suit and lugging two heavy leather bags. Gill introduced him as her manager Yasir as they led us to a plush twenty-seventh-floor conference room overlooking the Abu Dhabi coastline.

As Gill sat regally behind a large oval table, Yasir unzipped the bags and pulled out several sheets of paper.

Gill didn't waste any time on sociability.

'We've been very busy,' she said, pointing to the large stack.

'And this is just the beginning. Under CULA, we shall help 2,00,000 residents put the crisis behind them. And we will do that by injecting Dh5.4 billion at the street level.'

Razmig and I exchanged a subtle glance, uncertainty clouding our expressions as Gill continued confidently, 'I've got Dh69 million ($18.79 million) in the UAE Central Bank awaiting clearance. It will be released within two weeks and used to help 200 applicants in the first phase. In phase two, we will reach out to even more people.'

She didn't bat an eyelid as she rattled the benefits of CULA, which she said was the Arabic word for liquidity. Over the next hour we were told how the US, Poland and Cyprus among other nations were all waiting to see the outcome of the programme in the UAE so that they could replicate it in their own countries. 'Help the poor, and get the UAE's economy on track, that's what CULA will do,' she said.

Gill said she was assisting people who were in jail or hospital or had overstayed in the country. We were told CULA was also reaching out to students facing dropouts because of financial constraints.

'As a third party we'll cover all pending school fees. I am already coordinating with the Abu Dhabi Education Council,' she claimed.

Midway through the meeting, Yasir also chipped in. 'We help all this poor very much.'

Gill said she was glad to have him on board. 'Yasir is so devoted he has left his family and quit his job to focus on CULA,' she said.

Sitting before the confident woman it was hard to believe that she had been jailed abroad twice and was wanted in multiple countries.

Her confidence remained unwavering throughout the conversation as she ran us through her fanciful schemes, dropping names of international celebs and political heavyweights and using obscure financial jargon to bubble wrap her sham show.

'I want to inject cash at the street level to end gridlock, get cash flowing and pay down debt so that businesses can pivot their ambitions towards unrestrained growth. The paramount objective, my friends, is to achieve quantitative easing while adroitly refiguring the economic landscape through horizontal collaboration, ultimately heralding an era of self-employment and micro entrepreneurship.'

I feigned that our recording device had paused, and asked her to repeat, and she complied, word for word.

At one point she fished out a letter from the bag. 'See this,' she said handing us the document, 'UK prime minister David Cameron believes in our cause and has personally appointed me as a diplomat to take forward my initiatives. That's his signature and stamp here.'

Gill told us she was leading an international network of stakeholders committed to improving the 'quality of life' of one billion people who live on $1 a day or less.

And yes, she had also invented a solar cooker that could prepare a meal for ten in under an hour.

All of this was hogwash.

We found out that the woman's real name was Gill Edwards. She was a fugitive who had fled Britain for the US in 2001 following an arrest warrant. Gill was convicted for fraud in 1994 and also served a jail term. In the US, she was accused of trying to rip off victims of 9/11, and in Uganda, she had been arrested for failing to pay a hotel bill.

However, none of this had deterred her from reinventing herself as a champion of the poor and seeking investments in seemingly innovative concepts and projects such as detox centres for NYC responders of 9/11, IPO forex for funding the green economy, and now CULA.

A 2010 video posted on the sidelines of a sustainability conference in Sharjah showed the 'Queen of Green', as she called herself then, boasting a $1 billion investment in the UAE. 'We are going to green the Sharjah Chamber of Commerce and the Sharjah Ladies Club,' she is seen saying in the video.

It wasn't true, of course. Both Sharjah Chamber of Commerce and Sharjah Ladies Club denied the claim. There were also videos of phony interviews with Oprah Winfrey and Larry King, where Gill can be seen rambling about her harebrained schemes but the presenters and Gill are never in the same frame. I found the man who stitched the videos together. He lived in Dubai. Gill had promised to pay him but didn't.

We spotted a picture on Gill's Facebook and X (formerly known as Twitter) accounts showing her standing next to footballer David Beckham. The caption read: 'Discussing Africa with Beckham in Dubai. Met with David Beckcham to discuss how football can teach orphans in Africa how to be team players.'

I found out that the man in the picture was not Beckham but his UK-based lookalike Jamie Gleeson. He even wrote back to us when I contacted him for a comment.

But Gill was calm when I confronted her. 'Oh, it was not Beckham?' she asked, mildly surprised. 'I thought it was him. We still discussed football and Africa. They are important, not the individual. Do you know what's happening in Sub-Saharan Africa?'

She also denied any wrongdoing and instead blamed the Ku Klux Klan for tarnishing her image when we called her later.

'All of this is a lie. I've never served time in jail … it's a smear campaign run by racists in San Diego. The Ku Klux Klan is behind it. They've been after me since 2002 when I took on the Africa project,' she said, adding this priceless gem: 'Human capital is the driver of robust TFP [total factor productivity]-driven growth as the coefficient correlation of the CULA initiative has a far better aggregate than what is pursued by traditional economies in pursuant of UN policies which may not be financially rewarding from the investment point of view.'

A few days earlier, an Abu Dhabi real estate company had nearly fallen for the mumbo jumbo after Gill tried to talk its owners into transferring a Dh50 million building in her name.

Georges de Castro, the firm's French manager, told me that Gill was so convincing that they almost got duped.

Later, we also reached out to Martin Seward-Case, a Dubai-based chartered surveyor who was approached by Gill to build 2,200 orphanages in Africa at costs running into millions of pounds. Initially tempted to go ahead, Martin backtracked when he found out about Gill's criminal past.

She was horrified when we put her picture on the front page under the screaming headline 'Queen of Con Exposed' and followed up with another stinking article.

She shot off a series of tweets accusing me of trying to sabotage her charity initiatives. One of the tweets carried my picture with a caption that read: 'Mazhar is an economic terrorist who has been reported to Interpol, DHS, ECIPS, UN and intell comm.'

Who would have thought an HR manager at a publication would come across these mad ramblings while doing a background check upon me and, believing them to be true, turn down my job application.

In one of her tweets, she claimed that President Obama had accepted her invitation to visit the UAE, sparking a storm on the microblogging site.

She was the butt of jokes on X. Hundreds trolled her. 'Breaking News. @AmbassadorHHope signs a cooperation deal with Godzilla. Godzilla will plough land in Africa to make way for agriculture development,' said one user.

Gill responded by mounting a fierce attack targeting me and my family.

I asked our legal department if we could sue her for slander but they said they wouldn't want to get involved as it was a personal matter between me and her. I was livid. How could it be a personal matter? My story was published in the newspaper, not my blog, I argued. But the Indian man heading our legal team refused to budge. But that changed quickly when Gill attacked the newspaper. And she did it in her own inimitable style: she issued a fake press release claiming that the UAE's Telecommunications Regulations Authority had sued *Gulf News* and me for $5.4 billion for an act of economic terrorism plus slander and libel. That got the legal team moving. A meeting was hurriedly called. After a long discussion, our British editor-at-large, Francis Matthew, was tasked to write to the National Media Council drawing their attention to Gill's press release demanding action against her.

Roughly two years after this incident, on 4 July 2016 to be precise, Matthew, sixty, was arrested for killing his wife Jane with a hammer at their Dubai home. By a quirk of fate, I was also arrested on the same day. But more on that later.

Gill and his Egyptian partner, who turned out to be her husband, were arrested. But Gill was sprinted out of the UAE by the UK Foreign Office while her accomplice and hubby Yasir remained in jail to face fraud charges.

The setbacks had no effect on Gill. Two years later, she resurfaced as a guest speaker at Rotary Club's 5 meet in Warwickshire, UK, claiming she had received a Nobel Prize nomination for her project to slash school fees in Abu Dhabi.

Fortunately, someone among the audience googled her, came across our reports and asked the club president to stop her speech. I haven't heard from Gill since then and often wonder what she's up to now.

Shoaib Shaikh: Figurehead of Global Fake Degree Empire

In May 2015, *The New York Times* journalist Declan Walsh did an exposé that shook the world but left me feeling happy, sad and vindicated, all at the same time

Walsh's damning report revealed how a secretive Pakistani software company with the motto of 'winning and caring' earned millions of dollars from selling fake qualifications globally.

The degrees had no true accreditation. The university campus existed only on the internet. The professors were paid actors.

The company behind this massive scam was called Axact and it was run by Shoaib Shaikh, a young man who portrayed himself as a self-made tycoon with a passion for charity and plans to educate 10 million children in Pakistan.

Shaikh operated Axact from the port city of Karachi and had over 2,000 people on its rolls.

Most of them were telephone sales agents working in shifts round the clock. Their main job was to pose as professors and counsellors of fictitious Western universities and manipulate those seeking a real education into signing up for expensive courses.

To boost profits, the agents would often follow up with ruses that included impersonating top American and UAE government officials to persuade customers to cough up money for authentication charges.

Declan Walsh took three months to put together the story after being tipped off by a whistleblower. I don't want to take away anything from him. It was a great story. It led to Shoaib Shaikh's arrest and got everyone from the FBI and Interpol excited.

It's just that I had uncovered the racket nearly a year earlier. And I had done it in less than two weeks without anyone's aid.

My report, published in *Gulf News* on 4 June 2014, details how hundreds of vice presidents and CEOs in the UAE had climbed the corporate ladder on the basis of academic credentials from universities that didn't exist. All these online degree mills were run by Axact.

Sadly, my editor didn't allow me to mention Axact's name in our story. 'What's the point of uncovering a racket if we don't tell readers who's behind it,' I argued. It was a wasted effort.

'No name means no names,' he growled at me from behind his thick-rimmed spectacles. 'If you insist, I will kill the story. I don't want any debate on this.'

I stormed out of his room in disgust. As soon as our story went online, I shot out emails to senior journalists in India categorically mentioning Axact's name and their fake universities uncovered by me. I hoped it would raise the antennae because my investigation suggested that Axact was backed by the notorious D Syndicate run from Pakistan by India's most wanted gangster and international terrorist Dawood Ibrahim.

Here's a verbatim reproduction of the email I sent on 6 June 2014, nearly eleven months before Walsh's report in *The New York Times*:

The D company has found a new way to make money— selling degrees; and trust me it's more lucrative than trafficking and smuggling put together.

Shockingly, several Indians are unwittingly filling up their coffers.

Visit any of the following links:

www.edgebrookuniversity.com

http://www.experiencebasedgraduates.com/

www.affordabledegrees.com

www.midtownuniversity.com

They are all non-existent colleges offering college degrees based on life experiences. Prices range from $500 to $4000. Open any of them and go to the chat option and ask for a college degree.

We did a story today.

http://gulfnews.com/news/gulf/uae/education/online-fake-degrees-xpress-investigation-part-2-1.1342936

It has now emerged that all of these bogus universities—there are hundreds of them worldwide—are backed by the Pakistan-based company AXACT.

They have set up call centres where Brit-US educated Pakistan students masquerade as US professors in heavily accented English.

This is their main business … The annual turnover according to an insider is $500 million—The sad part is anywhere between 2,000–4,000 unsuspecting Indian job aspirants/students enrol for their bogus courses every day. (India is their biggest market in Asia), thus unknowingly funding the D empire.

I thought the journalists would jump at the story, but they ignored the lead.

I was tempted to embarrass them by resending my email with the link to the article of *The New York Times*. I didn't do that. Not because I am a gentleman but because it would have been akin to the pot calling the kettle black.

Indian media weren't the only ones who had a scoop and sat over it. We did that too.

Before reaching out to Walsh, Axact whistleblower and former employee Yasir Jamshed had visited the office of *Gulf News* thrice with incriminating evidence against the company.

Jamshed came looking for me but I was vacationing in India those days. Each time he came to the office, he was turned away by a junior Arab reporter who was sent to the reception to meet him.

'She would listen to me intently and then ask, so what's the story?' Jamshed told me later as we sat at Tim Hortons in Sharjah's Al Majaz Waterfront from midnight to dawn.

'I got so frustrated by your newspaper's response that I rang up the desk of *The New York Times* who heard me out. A few days later they flew Walsh into Dubai to meet me. The rest as they say … '

'Yes, I know,' I said lamely.

Jamshed recalled the reaction at Axact's office when my report came out in May 2014. 'It rattled us because you named some of our most lucrative online mills. But why didn't you mention our company? Did you not know it?'

I didn't have the heart to tell him the truth.

Even without Axact's name, our story had created shockwaves in the region.

As part of my investigation, I conducted a simple experiment. I went to LinkedIn and typed in its search box the names of the bogus universities + UAE + CEO + manager.

I found a deluge of profiles flaunting qualifications from these universities.

From vice presidents and CEOs to top managers, they were all there.

Many were unsuspecting victims. In fact, they didn't know that their costly degrees weren't even worth the paper they were printed on.

The realisation left them shattered. Many immediately pulled off their profiles from LinkedIn after our story came out. Others remained in denial.

'My degree is genuine and attested by all relevant agencies,' said an Indian manager in Dubai who had listed an MBA degree from Rochville in his LinkedIn credentials.

'What's your problem?' he demanded.

'The problem,' I said politely, 'is that your fellow alumni is a dog.'

The year he got his degree, Rochville had also awarded an MBA to a canine. This happened when a Singapore-based journalist enrolled his pup, Chester, for the university's online MBA programme.

The degree came in a parcel couriered from a Dubai address. Chester has since become the mascot of a website that helps people understand the importance of distance learning accreditation and warns them about degree mills and life experience colleges.

To get to the bottom of the scam, I registered with several online degree mills that offered 'affordable, accredited and instant' US college degrees for as little as Dh1,800.

All of them followed the same predatory trajectory.

Within seconds of registering, a live chat window would pop up on the computer screen. Soon I was connected to a 'counsellor' or a 'professor'. They would ask for my phone number and then call me instantaneously, pestering me to pay the $199 enrolment fee. For good measure, I was sent a degree sample along with a payment link.

I captured screenshots of live chats and audio recordings of many such interactions.

A chat with a man who introduced himself as Professor James Marshall of Edgebrook University in California went like this:

'Can I get an MBA degree quickly?' I enquired.

'You have experience?' he asked in heavily accented English.

'Yes, around six years.'

'Wonderful, we are offering degrees on the basis of a candidate's experience. We will convert your work experience into credit hours and, on behalf of that experience, our university will award you the master's degree. You don't need classes. You'll get the degree in four weeks, sir. It will cost you $500. Attestation will cost extra.'

At www.experiencebasedgraduate.com, counsellor Djvon Connor claimed the degrees were recognised internationally and at www.gcconlinedegrees.com, the caller rattled out the names of several UAE firms where the alumni of their partner universities were supposedly employed.

The sales pitch was always high pressure, often aggressive.

In two days, Midtown University called me twenty-seven times and Edgebrook, twenty-four.

'Why waste this opportunity? Give me your credit card details, I will make the payment on your behalf,' suggested Professor Peter Hill from Midtown University.

All these university websites carried glowing endorsements, video testimonials and authentication certificates from the United States Department of State, bearing the signature of the then secretary of state John Kerry.

Between 2009 and 2015, over 2,50,000 people in 197 countries, paid up to Dh1,00,000 for professional online courses at Axact-run bogus universities such as Midtown, Rochville, Brooklyn Park, Gibson, Grant Town, Ashley, Nixon, Campbell, Belford and Paramount California.

'Hands down, this is probably the largest operation we've ever seen,' said Allen Ezell, a former FBI agent and author of a book on diploma mills. 'It's a breathtaking scam.'

The majority of Axact's clients were from the Middle East.

'At our 24/7 Karachi headquarters, we handled roughly 5,000 calls daily. Of them 60 per cent came from the UAE and Saudi Arabia,' Jamshed told me.

As one of the 110 quality assurance auditors, his job was to listen to the interactions between customers and sales agents.

Jamshed gave me credit card transaction details and payment receipts of several high-profile clients based in Abu Dhabi, Dubai and Al Ain who had paid ridiculous amounts to obtain degrees from institutions that existed only in stock photos and on computer servers.

Jamshed told me how Axact made money from three key areas—priority learning assessment (PLA), research and sponsored programmes (RSP), sale of degrees and legalisation/attestation through embassies/ministry of foreign affairs/ministry of higher education.

Legalisation charges started from $5,000 and went up to $60,000. In September 2014, when Jamshed quit, Axact made $8,00,000 from PLA and $4,00,000 from RSP where PhD aspirants seeking help for writing theses were directed to other websites operated by Axact. Sales of degrees accounted for $1.7 million.

Hundreds of school dropouts from the US bought our degrees to land army jobs in Iraq and other cities in the Middle East.

Dr R. Srivastava, who worked at a reputed hospital in Dubai, was in disbelief when I told her that her PhD in quality management from Midtown University amounted to nothing.

She had spent Dh40,000 on the 'course' between 2011 and 2014.

An IT manager at a software firm, who forked out Dh18,000 for an online computer networking degree from Edgebrook University, was equally gutted.

He had been saving for the course for years and threw a party to celebrate his graduation.

Jamshed said he felt sickened when he saw Axact duping the same people that they sold the fake degrees to.

He decided to quit when he overheard a young salesperson trick an Emirati nurse in Al Ain into believing she was calling from the UAE embassy in the US and forced her to sell all her jewellery overnight to pay $5,000 dollars for each of her eighteen degrees.

'It was around 6.30 p.m. when I picked up this call that had been going on for quite a while. What I heard was beyond shocking. Here was this twenty-five-year-old girl pretending to be a highly placed US-based UAE diplomat who could land this woman in trouble if she didn't pay up.

'The conversation went on for at least another hour as the woman haggled for the best price for her jewellery.'

Fearing action, the woman sold all her jewellery to raise almost $70,000 of which $30,000 was remitted to Axact that very night.

Later that week, the salesperson, who was struggling to meet her monthly target, was given a $1,000 bonus for closing this job.

A few days later, Jamshed resigned and fled to the UAE with records of nearly two dozen customers who paid around $6,00,000 collectively. He gave all of it to me. Among other things, it has evidence showing that the Emirati nurse wired $69,100 to Axact-owned bogus Cambell University over two days after getting spoofed calls.

Armed with this invaluable information and testimonies of victims, I reported how Axact call centre agents in Pakistan were impersonating government officials to extort 'legalisation fees' from fake degree and diploma holders in the country.

Speaking in an Emirati accent, the telesale agents would call clients and demand thousands of dollars from degree holders towards the 'legalisation fees' of their certificates.

And since they used spoofing techniques that allow them to mimic any phone number—complete with area code—the recipients were deceived into believing that the calls were legitimate.

A South African expat in Dubai who forked out thousands of dollars for an academic certificate said he was shocked when a man claiming to be a Dubai Police officer called him and asked him to remit $5,000 to the university towards degree 'legalisation fee' or face action.

When he rang up the number that showed up on his cell phone it was answered by someone at Dubai Police Headquarters.

Another expat who bought a degree from one such university said he got a similar call from a man who claimed he was from the Ministry of Human Resources. When I called the phone numbers they turned out to be the board line numbers of two actual government entities. Jamshed told me the company used caller ID–spoofing that enabled them to display a number different from the one from which the call was placed.

Stunned by our revelations, Pakistan's chief justice took suo motu notice of the matter and directed the country's Federal Investigation Agency (FIA) to submit a report on the issue. 'Our heads hang in shame due to the Axact scandal,' he said.

Pakistan had already sought help from the Interpol and the FBI to probe the matter. Soon, the scope of investigation shifted to the UAE where forging academic qualifications is punishable by ten years in jail. Among those who bought degrees in the UAE were airline employees and medical workers.

A Dubai-based Lebanese who shelled out Dh85,000 for Gibson University's MBA programme said he never suspected a thing. 'Who would've thought that the soft-spoken professor Terry Howard I interacted with for months was not a university faculty based in the USA's Virgin Islands but someone sitting in a call centre in Pakistan? I am ruined,' he told me.

A simple Google Reverse Image search revealed that pictures of the purported teaching staff of these universities were either stolen from other websites or taken from Shutterstock.

Shoaib Ahmad Shaikh was arrested by Pakistan authorities in May 2015. However, in September 2016, he was granted bail by a District and Sessions Judge who later admitted before an inquiry panel to have taken a bribe of Rs 50,00,000 (Dh1,67,000) to pass the bail order.

After his release, Facebook newsfeeds in the UAE were again inundated with advertisements offering 'accredited online degrees' in various streams.

Posing as a candidate, I again registered with one of Axact's online degree mills offering 'affordable MBA degrees' from a university in California. Within minutes, a US telephone number flashed on my cell phone. The caller identified himself as the university's counsellor, Professor John Smith.

Here's how our conversation went:

Professor John Smith: I understand you're looking for a master's degree in business administration.

Me: That's right.

Professor Smith: Great, do you have any work experience?

Me: About seven years as a sales executive in Dubai.

Professor Smith: That's very good. We'll convert your work experience into credit hours and, on behalf of that experience, our university will award you the master's degree. Does it sound good?

Me: Yes, but I am not sure if I can clear the examinations as I doubt if I will get any time to study.

Professor Smith: Don't worry about that … our online courses are specifically designed to help working professionals like you.

Me: Thank you, Professor Smith, but I still have concerns. Can I ask some questions?

Professor Smith: Yeah, sure.

Me: So how long have you been living in California?

Professor Smith: Since birth, why?

Me: Could you tell me what time is it in California now? (It was 2.40 a.m. in California, 2.40 p.m. in the UAE and 3.40 p.m. in Pakistan at the time.)

Professor Smith: Ugh … the time, here is … Well ….

Me: Never mind, can you tell me who is the governor of California?

Professor Smith: The governor, err … You see Donald Trump is our president.

Me: Yes, but who is your governor?

Professor Smith: Aah … actually [long silence] … so I was talking about this MBA degree …

Me: Can you name any five counties in California?

Professor Smith: Well … they are … [sound of feverish typing].

Me: Are you seeking Google's help?

Professor Smith: Ugh … [sighs].

Me: *Abey Pakistan mein ho na? Theek thaak angrezi bolte ho kuch halal ki rozi kamao.* (You are in Pakistan, right? You speak decent English, make an honest living.)

Professor Smith: Aaah … I'm sorry, I don't understand what you said.

Me: Of course you do.

Professor Smith: *Baatein mat chodo. Bhaag yahan sey bhosdi waley* [swear words in Urdu that Google cannot effectively translate].

Degree mills continually devise new strategies to deceive people, even going so far as to use images of well-known figures to appear legitimate.

In 2015, their audacity reached new heights. The shady University of Atlanta managed to secure a booth at the Gulf Education Training Exhibition (GETEX), the premier annual education fair held at the Dubai World Trade Centre. Surprisingly, their booth was the largest, proving that ill-gotten wealth can take you far.

Unsuspecting college students, looking to make a quick buck, were hired to promote this fictitious institution. They cheerfully distributed brochures and enrolled students in their bogus courses.

Digging deeper, I discovered that the University of Atlanta, formerly known as Barrington University, had been successfully sued for fraud.

When I confronted their representatives who were on the brink of running newspaper advertisements, they resorted to an email threat, involving the US embassy. Panic ensued among our management. I was asked to provide evidence to support my claims. I promptly shared all the proof, including the fact that the University of Atlanta and Axact shared the same address and that their supposed physical campus was merely a rented postbox.

I also revealed the name and phone number of a Dubai woman who somehow acquired an MBA degree from the university without ever taking an exam.

The most damning evidence was the bank account statements of the fake university, displaying all their transactions and overseas account balances. I posed a question that answered itself: 'If the university is genuine, how do I have access to these minute details?' The answer was clear—everything had been handed to me on a USB drive by an Axact whistleblower.

In the face of this overwhelming evidence, the University of Atlanta hastily packed its bags and disappeared. They never returned to Dubai.

Madhav Patel, Baghubhai Patel: The Thugs of Hindustan

A throaty laughter followed by an announcement that his mailbox was full greeted anyone who called Sharjah metal trader Madhav Patel on his cell phone in the early 1990s. But for the scores of banks that lost over £1 billion in credit exposure following the suave Indian businessman's sudden disappearance, it was not funny. One billion pounds is a lot of money. Back then, it was a hell of a lot more. So much money doesn't just vanish into thin air. Yet it did along with the man who stole it.

In the UAE alone, twenty-six banks lost close to $500 million. Even Donald Trump didn't have that kind of money those days.

Mashreq, Emirates Bank, Habib Bank, Al Baraka Islamic Bank, Gulf Bank International, First Gulf Bank, Arab Banking Corporation and Bahrain-based Arab Banking Corporation were all major creditors of Solo Industries and other businesses run by Madhav. Around fifteen blue chip global banks, including Citibank, ABN Amro and Barclays, were also hit along with many financial institutions in India. Such was the scale of their losses that a multinational bank in Dubai had to delay its 1999 balance sheet. Some banks lost as much as two years of profits.

Another bank got hurt so badly it quit the Middle East forever. Several bankers lost their jobs.

By the time I began investigating the case in 2006, the trail had gone cold. But one head-scratching oddity about Madhav intrigued me. His wife Nita happened to be the daughter of Dhirubhai Ambani's elder brother Ramnikbhai Ambani.

This in effect meant that the world's most wanted fugitive was married into the world's then sixth richest family.

In fact, Madhav's real father-in-law was a director at Reliance—at the time just another big Indian company and no match for industrial giants like the Tatas and Birlas that had been thriving since pre-Independence despite colonial efforts to push them down.

Old-timers described Madhav as a charming Gujarati businessman who had meticulously crafted an impeccable reputation in UAE business circles. He was brought up in Iran where his father Baghubhai Patel ran a scrap business.

After the fall of the Shah in 1979, Baghubhai returned to India and established the Hamco Group while Madhav set up Solo Industries in Sharjah. Madhav also established a smelting unit. Bankers visiting the facility were told the smelting plant dealt with top-notch blue chip companies. It was later found that the only time the smelting unit worked was when a bank manager visited the premises.

The father-and-son duo also launched a string of companies in Switzerland, the UK, Belgium, Germany, France, the Netherlands, Hong Kong, and the US. All of them served a singular purpose: carry out transactions with each other to project a flourishing trade in aluminium, lead and other metals. The shipping agents used by them were either pliant family members or friends.

Madhav led a lavish lifestyle, travelling between India, the UAE and the UK as his business empire grew.

His credibility increased when his brand got registered on the London Metals Exchange and Solo Industries got an ISO 9002 accreditation. Not one to lose a high net worth client, banks across three continents fell over each other to offer him credit facilities and loans.

Then one day, in 1999, Madhav disappeared—or rather 'fled' the UAE, as per a statement issued by the country's banking regulatory authority.

Around the same time, his father Baghubhai Patel also did a runner, defrauding several banks in India out of Rs 1,200 crores ($168 million) through his Hamco group which was listed on the Bombay Stock Exchange. Hamco was the first private sector company to be granted mining leases in Orissa (now Odisha), never mind that it never did any mining.

As baffled investigators put the pieces together, they made a startling discovery. The Patel empire existed only on paper. All this while they were raising fake letters of credit (LCs) against goods that were never shipped. In many instances, LCs were raised against high-value metals that were nothing but scrap. Unknown to banks, their own funds were being recycled to create the chimaera of a prosperous business. Years later, many other Gujarati conglomerates would use the same modus operandi to make billions.

The scam couldn't be detected as the Patels held the strings of both the importers as well as the exporters through a complex web of firms in India and the Middle East to as far as the UK, France, Switzerland and the Netherlands Antilles.

New credit was routinely used to clear debts to give the impression that the company was doing dynamic trade.

Hamco would import goods against which suppliers were sent LCs. In reality, the cargos were fictitious. On the rare occasions when any goods were dispatched, they were of a fraction of the value stated on import documents. The beneficiaries of these LCs were Madhav and a Swiss company called Frobevia SA run by the son of Baghubhai's oldest friend.

Subsequent investigations revealed that most bills of lading were issued through three Dubai-based shipping firms owned by Baghubhai Patel's son-in-law Ashok Verma, who, along with wife Alpana, was a director at Hamco. Verma was arrested by Dubai Police while the UK's Serious Fraud Office (SFO) nabbed Milton Kounnou, the London-based import agent for Solo. He pleaded guilty and was jailed for two years. But Madhav evaded the net.

Investigators found that out of his last 3,000 transactions barely twenty were genuine. There were 200 instances where documents listed high-value alloys like silver or titanium on the shipping document, while the actual shipment was for lead ingots.

The evidence against Madhav was overwhelming. But he continued to feign innocence. As the heat got to him, Madhav's brother-in-law, Vimal Ambani, after whom the Reliance's Vimal brand was named, flew down to the UAE to placate the creditors. He tried to play down the scam by telling banks that the 'cash-flow problem' was temporary and would be resolved soon even as Madhav issued a statement from London promising to return to the UAE.

But UAE banks doubted if he had any intention of coming back. They knew he could not be brought back to face trial as the UAE was not a signatory to the Hague Convention and hence did not have an extradition treaty with the UK.

Left with no option, many banks sent their managers to London for a face-to-face chat with the runaway thug. They held several rounds of meetings with Madhav. Nothing came out of them. As the banks exchanged information about their dealings with Madav, what came out instead was the realisation that scores of banks had been caught in the crosshairs of one of the biggest scams in the history of maritime finance.

Many banks brought legal proceedings against Madhav while the UAE's regulatory authority sent circulars asking local financial institutions to conduct background checks on expat business owners with big exposure levels. It was too little too late.

The mega fraud took a macabre twist in July 1999 when Solo's financial controller and Madhav's most trusted aide Paul Thottan was found dead at his home in Kochi, Kerala. The cause of his death was poisoning and it was classified as a case of suicide. No postmortem was carried out, nor was there any probe into his mysterious death. Many believe he was murdered, while others reckon he faked his death and fled abroad.

Thottan, then forty-seven, had left the UAE in April 1999 shortly after Madhav.

The finance controller had signed loan and credit documentation papers on behalf of Madhav who was now missing. For the next eight years, his whereabouts remained unknown. He disappeared like a ghost, eluding a worldwide manhunt by the police forces of half a dozen countries, Interpol and private investigators representing the affected banks.

Also hot on Madhav's heels was underworld don Abu Salem. If a statement made by gangster Rajender Kumar Anankat before Gujarat Police could be believed Salem had his sights on Madhav and had asked him about his whereabouts shortly before the scammer fled the UAE.

In September 2002, Salem was arrested along with Monica Bedi in Portugal. Three years later, Salem was extradited to India and sentenced to life imprisonment.

It is speculated that he went to Portugal as he was told that Madhav was living there in hiding.

In 2007, there was news about Madhav's arrest in India. His absconding dad Baghubhai was also caught. I remember reporting the story for *Gulf News* and speaking to a former country manager of ABN Amro Bank. Madhav was one of their oldest and most important clients.

The UAE banks affected by the scam were thrilled when they heard about Madhav's arrest. They wrote to Dubai Police requesting Madhav's extradition. Their hopes faded when both father and son got bail and the court trial against them in India hit an impasse. Fifteen years later, they still haven't been brought to book. Today, the Patels enjoy a luxurious life in India. And because media houses in India are either owned by the Ambanis or are dependent on the conglomerate for advertising revenue, the world's greatest bank robbery never drew any media attention. Following the UPA government's ouster, the case was put on the backburner and remains there.

So what happened to the money? A large part of it is believed to have been laundered through a trust account in the tax haven of Guernsey in the Channel Islands. What remained went to fund multiple businesses.

The Lords of Trading Scams

If I could interview anyone I wanted, who could it be? Narendra Modi? Elon Musk? Cristiano Ronaldo? All likely answers, but the correct answer is a middle-aged Indian family man named Deepak Raheja who lives in obscurity in Dubai.

Bearded, bespectacled, balding and mostly dressed in grey safari suits, Deepak looks nothing like a criminal, much less the uncrowned lord of scammers who has pulled off so many mega financial frauds that I have lost count. But that's not exactly why he fascinates me to the point of obsession. There are deeper reasons. First, he invented a new form of scam. Second, he spawned a whole generation of fraudsters. Third, he remains unstoppable despite his advancing age, being arrested and forced to eat shit. Yes, you read that right.

Deepak may have invented the scam but I gave it a name. For want of a better term I will call it GADs, which is a lame acronym for Goods Against Duds. It's a pity that people don't know about GADs or its scale. I do, so I will stick out my neck and say it's the single biggest threat facing the UAE. Already, GAD scams have destroyed thousands of lives and wiped out billions of dollars from local markets.

By a conservative estimate, there have been 700 GAD scams between 2016 and 2023. That's a hundred companies being launched annually to cheat businesses and then vanishing without a trace. Each runaway company leaves behind anywhere between fifty and a hundred victims. Do the maths.

That's 5,000–10,000 victims every year, if you are still calculating.

In many business neighbourhoods, nearly one out of every four traders I spoke to has been a victim of the scam with many losing up to $2 million individually.

It took me almost two years to get to the bottom of the racket. The painstaking investigation involved sifting through hundreds of documents, speaking with dozens of confidential informants besides innumerable tails and stakeouts, often in the dead of the night from my tinted Kia Mohave.

'Are you sure you are working on a story? Because I don't see any,' Eram said after I came home past midnight for the fifth straight day.

My investigation revealed a deeply disturbing picture. It showed that GAD scams are largely the handiwork of just four gangs.

They are led by long-time UAE residents like Deepak Raheja who stay in the shadows, perfecting the game, building smuggling and distribution networks through China, India, Pakistan, Iraq and East Asia, without leaving so much as a fingerprint.

Even those working with them don't know the scale of the operations. It's a parallel industry that's more lucrative than drug trafficking, and the gangs run it like well-oiled machinery. Secure in the belief that the law will never catch up with them, their criminal activities have assumed frighteningly grotesque proportions.

Even as I am writing this, I have the names and addresses of ten trading companies propped by these gangs. Their names are Spicy Dine, Bait Al Barakah Electric Sanitary Trading, Goutam Star Trading, Al Rukh Al Mas Building Material, Zahrat Al Marjan Foodstuff, Kapaz Trading, CGR General Trading, Masterstroke Technical Services, Arvolan General Trading and Unique Prestige General Trading.

By the time you read this, each of these firms would have disappeared with millions of dollars' worth of stolen goods.

Try living with the knowledge of crimes that are about to happen and the frustration of not being able to prevent them. It's not that I didn't try. I sat down with senior policemen multiple times to make them understand the gravity of the situation. I even shared my findings in a PowerPoint presentation. Cheques worth Dh15 billion bounced in the first quarter of 2018 alone. It didn't take rocket science to figure out where most of them were from.

My revelations left the officials stunned. They appreciated my efforts but that was about it. No tangible effort was ever made to do anything about GAD scams. Sometimes I wonder if they thought of me as a desperate lunatic.

They should have known better. In September 2018, when I was editing the weekly *XPRESS*, I published the initials of eight companies that were about to run away.

As I had predicted, each of these firms disappeared within two months.

I know who was behind those companies just as I know who is behind the ones preparing to run away in the next few days.

Not only do I know the names of these masterminds, I also have an exhaustive record of their entire criminal history along with personal details of all their key accomplices—in some cases, down to what cars they drive, where they dine and who they date. I have their pictures too.

The corollary question is: why don't I name and shame these scammers? It's not that easy.

Remember, these are no ordinary criminals but seasoned serial swindlers who have mastered the art of deceit to perfection.

They operate from behind curtains and rarely leave a shred of evidence that can be held against them. They know every loophole in the law and exploit them to the hilt. For starters, they never put their names on any company document.

The owners and signatories of firms they help set up are mostly handpicked dummies. In one case, it was a mason, in another, a driver and in a third, a cafeteria worker. The cafeteria worker told me he was paid Dh5,000 to play along.

These front men are flown out of the country before the scam comes to light, as are salespersons and other staffers who are brought on visit visas from India and Pakistan and given fake business cards.

Sure enough, instead of someone to prosecute, what's left with the police after each scam are stacks of dud cheques.

Well, not always. Deepak has been caught in the act on CCTV at least once. There are a bunch of people who can testify against him. He has also been briefly jailed. After his release he called me and offered to meet. Unfortunately, that didn't happen. He didn't call back. Calls made to him went unanswered. Messages didn't elicit the response I was looking for. 'I told you before that I am out of this world,' he said in a text message in May 2022 when I asked him out for coffee.

Originally from Hyderabad, Deepak first came on my radar in February 2016 when he duped fifty UAE businesses out of Dh35 million through the phoney SR Global Trading, which operated from a building on Bank Street in Bur Dubai. Those days he lived near the Gold Souk in Deira with his Russian wife and drove a 7 Series silver BMW.

Deepak's foray into crime, however, started twelve years earlier when he opened a garment store called Christy Fashion that shut down overnight after buying textiles against post-dated cheques. The following year, Deepak carried out a similar scam in Abu Dhabi through Afroon Trading.

He then moved to Singapore and carried out a string of GAD scams there between 2006 and 2010.

In 2011, he shifted to China where he stole goods worth Dh5.5 million in Yiwu City in Zhejiang province while acting as purchase officer for Euro Global Trading International Limited. But this time Lady Luck ditched him. As he was about to flee, the Chinese got a whiff of his plan. They abducted Deepak and his accomplice Shyam Sunder Agarwal and locked them in a warehouse. Here they were stripped naked, beaten mercilessly and force-fed their own poop and urine.

The news of their abduction and torture made headlines in India after Deepak's brother wrote to the Indian government seeking their release.

Following the intervention of the Indian embassy in Beijing, Deepak and Agarwal were finally freed after seventeen days. The Indian embassy went on to issue an advisory warning to their countrymen not to do business in Yiwu. Alas, they didn't know.

One would have thought Deepak would mend his ways after the China debacle.

Instead, he turned into an even more hardened criminal. In 2015, Deepak returned to his favourite hunting ground, the UAE, and picked up from where he left, improving his strike rate each year.

DKC Electronics set up by him near Al Mulla Plaza and Omar Al Kalsi in Abu Hail stole goods worth Dh25 million in 2015. These were followed by SR Global in 2016, Rock Bottom Trading in 2017 and Triumph Fortune in 2018.

All these fraudulent firms were backed by Deepak.

To this day, he continues to operate with impunity but his hegemony has waned.

By the time Deepak returned from China, the competition in the UAE had grown exponentially with two other gangs vying for a piece of the pie.

Deepak's strongest competitor is S. Badshah (SB), a short clean-shaven Bangladeshi man who lives with his two wives in Ajman and splurges most of his ill-gotten wealth on a bar dancer near Al Qiyadah Metro Station in Dubai. How do I know this? Because I followed him to the bar on several occasions.

Formerly a tea boy, Badshah is behind Crystal City Building Material (2012), SunLink Marine (2013), Steelite Electrical and Mechanical Engineering (2014), Alpha Impex GT (2015), Explore Fareast Marine (2016), Bright Way Technical Services (2017) and Black Star Electronics (2018), among many other UAE-based companies that have disappeared after defrauding traders.

Their collective haul runs into millions of dollars.

Badshah's most trusted aide is EPJ from Pakistan who lives with his wife and thirteen-year-old daughter in Umm Ramool, Dubai, and runs a facilities management firm.

Badshah's gang has around forty members with specific duties assigned to each one of them. Murtaza from Pakistan handles the website. Humayun prepares fake audit reports. Bilal, Abhishek and two pretty young girls Zoya and Neha act as purchase managers. Filipina Anna plays receptionist. It's a long list.

The third gang is led by Moidinabba who once ran a stationery shop in Ajman. The dad-of-three from Hyderabad was behind Royal General Trading, Brazza General Trading, Lifeline Surgical Trading, Salim Electrical Devices, Seven Emirates Spices and Pulse Trading, among many other runaway firms. He was arrested by Ajman Police in August 2023. Along with cash, the police also seized fake cheques from his apartment.

The gangs behind GAD steal anything they can get their hands on but their top favourites are building material, electronics, printers, food stuff, home appliances, industrial equipment, hotel stays and international flight tickets.

So meticulous is their planning and its execution that the victims rarely suspect anything. Many are snared at trade shows. I remember meeting S.A. Akhtar of Sharjah-based Jabal Al Toor Building Material who lost granite and marble worth nearly Dh1 million. Akhtar said he had no misgivings about the immaculately dressed men who walked up to him at the international building and construction show, The Big 5, at the Dubai World Trade Centre where he was showcasing his company's products. 'They made trade enquiries and we exchanged business cards. A few weeks later they turned up at our yard in Sharjah industrial area and placed orders for high-grade Italian marble tiles,' Akhtar recalled.

There have also been instances of the conmen stealing 2,000 goats and buffaloes. I wonder where they were kept. Other crazy stuff that was stolen include hundreds of Ferrari World Tickets, 10,000 fire extinguishers and 60,000 gallons of diesel, and 100 cartons of Panadol. Seriously?

In October 2014, I found myself outside Ronnington Steel Services in Al Quoz where a familiar scene awaited me: a runaway company and dozens of victims clutching dud cheques. On a table inside the abandoned office lay a copy of Vikas Swarup's bestselling novel *Six Suspects*.

I suppressed a smile. It was ironic that Ronnington's owner Mazhar Khan was reading a murder mystery while his namesake journalist was looking for clues in a mystery theft.

Besides electronics and building material, Mazhar Khan had also stolen 660 tonnes of industrial chemicals worth Dh1.2 million.

That's a lot of chemicals. It's not something you could sell off easily. But 660 tonnes of chemicals is still nothing compared to the 6,000 tonnes of rice worth Dh15.3 million stolen in 2019.

It was enough to feed the UAE's entire population for five days.

The audacious theft left investigators baffled as the rice came in 250 rice shipping containers that measured 20X8 feet each. Put end to end, they could have occupied a football field.

It was hard to believe they could vanish. But vanish they did—not just the containers but also the owner and the entire staff of Dubai's Al Rawnaq Al Thahbhi General.

The twenty-odd Indian exporters who dispatched the rice handed a telegraphic transfer (TT) receipt for each shipment as 'proof' that their payments were being electronically remitted to their banks.

The money never arrived. Instead, one by one, twenty-three TTs totalling $4.18 million got cancelled after cheques issued against them bounced because of insufficient funds.

Vinod Goel of NM Food Impex company in Haryana, who shipped twenty-two containers of Basmati rice, lost over $3,15,000 as did Kamla Mills' Vipin who sent seventeen containers.

Other rice exporters similarly duped included KG Industries ($1.02 million), Harman Rice ($5,53,640), Amritsar Riceland ($4,51,250), Aarna Foodstuff ($2,89,925), AS Impex ($2,87,985) and Heera Rice Mills ($1,31,435).

Spice and coconut wholesalers were also hit. Karnataka's Joseph International lost $1,09,200 and Manna Organic $1,25,835, while Tamil Nadu's SJN Coir Export lost $2,10,000.

It's not that the exporters didn't do any due diligence.

They visited Al Rawnaq Al Thahbhi's Dubai office, checked its trade licence, met its general manager and, more importantly, released the shipments only after they had received TT receipts from UAE Exchange confirming the acceptance of the remittance request and the initiation of the transaction.

Vinod Goel told me that the firm's owner Tariq Sheikh

presented himself as a multimillionaire when they came to Dubai to firm up the deal.

'He invited me to his sprawling six-bedroom villa in Living Legends in Al Barari for dinner and sent a chauffeur-driven SUV to pick me up from the hotel. I was impressed. At his house, I met his wife, son and mother for whom I carried gifts. In fact, his mother lovingly put her hand on my head to bless me,' recalls Vinod Goel.

I found out that Tariq never owned the villa but had rented it for Dh20,000 monthly just weeks earlier. For all you know, his wife, mum and son were also rented.

My story remained the talk of the town when I broke it in July 2019.

The scam destroyed exporters overnight. Some of them had to sell off their homes and factories to recover their losses.

The exporters alleged that the UAE Exchange staff deliberately held their cheques for days, allowing scammers enough time to receive the containers and sell off the rice before the cheques could be banked.

Had the UAE Exchange followed standard procedure and submitted the cheques on time, they would have bounced. As a result, their corresponding TTs would have also been cancelled.

Alarmed by the revelations, the Indian consulate in Dubai asked local authorities and Central Bank to probe the matter and also investigate if any UAE Exchange staff were involved. Vipul, who was then the consul general of India in Dubai, also appealed to the Reserve Bank of India (RBI) to 'explore the possibility of action against the UAE Exchange in India for its questionable conduct'.

The UAE Exchange, however, denied any wrongdoing saying that the issuance of a receipt (TT) neither confirms nor guarantees that the amount would be credited to the beneficiary account or received by the beneficiary.

Regardless of their stance, the public prosecutor ordered Jebel Ali Police to investigate accusations of fraud against six men and two companies, Al Rawnaq Al Thahbhi and the UAE Exchange.

In December 2020, a key suspect of the scam was sentenced to six months in prison and was also ordered to pay $1.20 million to one of his victims.

He didn't belong to any of the three–four gangs but was instead linked to one of the many splinter groups that had spread their tentacles across the country.

At the height of the COVID-19 pandemic in May 2020, one such gang stole beef, cheese, dates and face masks worth nearly $2 million. Before he could be caught, Yogesh Ashok Yariava, the owner of the fraudulent Royal Luck Foodstuff, escaped to India on a Vande Bharat Mission flight meant for the elderly, pregnant women and children.

The scam came barely a month after an audacious fruit loot in which 810 tonnes of bananas, grapes and coconut were similarly stolen by the fraudulent OPC Foodstuff Trading operating from Deira.

The exporters were paid 25–30 per cent upfront via telex transfers. The balance was to be paid within one to three weeks of delivery. That never happened. Instead, OPC Foodstuff suddenly downed for a month and its entire staff disappeared.

A few months earlier, another bogus firm Triumph Fortune scooted off with saffron, frozen chicken and dry fruits worth Dh25 million.

One company lost cashew nuts worth Dh1.8 million. Another firm that supplied five containers of rice pegged its losses at Dh4,00,000 while a third reported losing stationery worth Dh6,25,000.

In October 2022, the scammers used the same method to steal tonnes of avocados, coconut and strawberries from dozens of overseas and local companies. The fraudulent Max Star Trading even posted a job listing for fifty packaging helpers to pack, weigh and load the stolen goods into containers.

Now I have become an expert at GAD scams. Like doctors who can tell things about your health just by looking at you, I can also tell if the GAD scam is the handiwork of Deepak, Badshah, Moidinabba, Tariq Sheikh, or any of the new gangs.

Each gang has its own distinct style. Lost electronics and building material? It could be Deepak. Food items? Sardar Imdad or SB. Go to the fruit and vegetable market in Al Aweer and ask for Jameel. Hundreds of air tickets and hotel bookings made against dud cheques? That would be SB. See if you could find him or any of his relatives on the list of guests and passengers.

Most GAD scams follow predictable lines but there have been some creative ones too. A few years back, around twenty people turned up at the ballroom of a five-star hotel in Dubai dressed to the nines. They had been invited to a gala dinner as part of an event meant to 'inspire creativity and honour relationships'.

Unknown to the guests, the organisers had fled the country days earlier, not just deserting the attendees but also leaving several firms counting losses running into millions of dollars.

Over forty rooms and six suites were booked, and paid for, at the hotel for the gala along with hundreds of flights originating from the USA, Azerbaijan, Thailand, India and Pakistan by the fraudulent Spear International LLC.

The Egyptian sales director of the travel firm that lost Dh7,50,000 to the scam said Spear staff made them believe that the tickets and hotel bookings were for an awards night.

'All their cheques have bounced,' he said as we sat in a meeting room at *Gulf News*. 'Maybe you could take your family and friends to stay in the hotel as it's all paid for. The suites are nice, your kids will like them.'

Over the past fifteen years, I have uncovered so many GAD scams that I can write about them with my eyes closed. In fact, I have a ready-made template to report them. All I often do is change the names and amounts.

But in 2017 I decided to go public with the initials of the top three masterminds. I ran a four-page cover story titled 'Masterminds of Trading Scams Exposed'.

Our designer Ador Bustmante came up with stunning visuals for the story, which became an instant hit.

For weeks, it remained on top of the charts, both in terms of page views and time spent.

After the story, a delegation of twenty-five business owners came to the *Gulf News* office to thank us.

All of them had fallen victim to GAD scams at some point in their lives.

I felt flattered when they handed a memorandum to our editor-in-chief appreciating our effort and demanding swift and detrimental action against the criminals.

But any hope of authorities acting on the exposé turned out to be wishful thinking. They continue to treat the blatant organised crime naively as cases of bounced cheques.

As a result, GAD scams have become endemic like cancer with no early remedy in sight.

They have also changed the rule of business in the UAE. Fear-stricken traders are reluctant to strike deals with new firms. Many have also withdrawn credit facilities to existing clients.

The stolen goods are either shipped out of the UAE or resold locally by people known as 'cutters' in gang parlance. I know one of them. He is known as Johnny and hangs around the Sharaf DG Metro Station. Local markets crumble each time stolen goods enter them.

Who would buy Indian basmati rice from the local supermarket for Dh15 per kilogram when it's readily available for Dh5 per kilogram elsewhere.

The same applies to all other stolen items.

Victims follow a predictable pattern after each scam.

They form WhatsApp groups, hold meetings, visit their consulate, tag local authorities on social media, visit lawyers and police stations in the same order.

There is a lot of chatter on these WhatsApp groups in the first few days. By the second week, the number of messages dwindles from a hundred a day to ten. By the third week, the groups are as quiet as mice as the victims resign themselves to fate.

I have exited around fifty such groups that I was added to after the scam.

Now I am part of just one GAD scam–related group that comprises roughly a hundred victims across various companies. I can't stop the scams but I can certainly stop at least some traders from falling for them. On this WhatsApp group, I do just that by identifying dodgy companies and flagging them. Often I am tipped off by disgruntled gang members themselves.

In April 2022, a woman employed with Spicy Dine sent me a bunch of frantic messages on WhatsApp.

'A lot of people will be in trouble … my God a lot of people will cry.'

I immediately alerted a senior police officer.

A few days later, he got one of his deputies to call me. I remember it was towards the end of Ramadan.

'How do you know this crime is going to happen?'

'I am a journalist and I got this lead and—'

The cop interrupted me. 'How do you know someone is not making it up?'

'I don't think so,' I replied. 'The information is credible and this company will indeed shut shop and run away. Millions will be lost.'

'What if they don't?'

'What if they do?' I shot back.

'Look,' I said politely, 'I can come down to the police station now or anytime you want and explain. You've got to stop this.'

'We don't have time for your stories,' he said and hung up.

A few weeks later Spicy Dine shut shop, leaving a trail of devastated victims.

One of them was Yamini Iyer, an Indian woman I got acquainted with when she lost Dh50,000 in another GAD scam in 2017. Spicy Dine cost her Dh67,000.

I sent a message to the senior cop. I kept it crisp and simple. 'Good morning, sir. The company, SpicyDine, about which I alerted you in April has shut shop and run away after cheating Dubai traders out of more than $12 million.'

The officer responded saying they couldn't have opened a case on mere suspicion.

'Ask people who lost their money to complain,' he said in the message.

I conveyed the message to Yamini. I don't know if she visited the police station but many did.

The outcome was a foregone conclusion.

In August 2023, Vietnam Television visited my apartment in Dubai to conduct an interview with me about the recurring scams after a significant incident involving five containers of spices and cashews, valued at over half a million dollars, were shipped to Dubai. Shockingly, these containers were claimed by unidentified individuals at Jebel Ali Dubai Port, without remitting payment to the Vietnamese companies.

Shortly thereafter, the Vietnamese embassy contacted me, urgently requesting a meeting with the ambassador and the head of trade. We convened at Raw Coffee in Al Quoz. During our meeting, the ambassador confided that he was under tremendous pressure, given that even the Vietnamese prime minister himself was closely monitoring this perplexing case. The masterminds of the scam collectively wreaked havoc on thousands of lives. However, it was a trio of resilient women who took them to task. An Emirati woman in Al Ain imprisoned Deepak for a month. A British woman unravelled Badshah's web of deceit, and a woman from Kerala led to Moidinabba's arrest.

Amit Bhardwaj: World's Biggest Crypto Fraudster

In life and death, they were kindred spirits—two hucksters from opposite sides of the globe, united by their involvement in the world of cryptocurrency and their inexplicable end.

Amit Bhardwaj and Gerald Cotten were once celebrated figures in the realm of digital finance. They were revered as pioneers of a new era, visionaries who were reshaping global finance with their cryptocurrency schemes. But their veneer of respectability was a smokescreen as they were nothing more than con artists who defrauded countless individuals out of billions of dollars.

The striking parallels between these two men, despite their diverse backgrounds and geographical locations, are remarkable. Both were at the helm of cryptocurrency ventures—Gain Bitcoin and QuadrigaCX—that ultimately crumbled under the weight of fraud allegations. Both met their untimely demise in India in Fortis hospitals under mysterious circumstances. What's most perplexing is that both left behind encrypted cryptocurrency wallets, the passwords of which remain unknown, leaving behind a substantial digital asset trove that may never be recovered.

Speculations abound to this day that Amit and Gerald may have faked their own deaths to evade legal accountability. The details surrounding their funerals remain shrouded in secrecy, lending credence to the theory that they may still be alive.

I am not a conspiracy theorist, but what I do know is that the stories of Amit and Gerald serve as stark reminders of the risks in the digital finance universe. Here people can fake their own death or vanish without a trace, as shown by Dr Ruja Plamenova Ignatova, the Bulgarian woman behind the $4.2 billion OneCoin scam and an FBI most wanted fugitive.

Ruja had significant business interests in the UAE, including a company in Ras Al Khaimah Free Zone. I started investigating her in 2018, but when my leads took me down a path my newspaper deemed unsuitable, I shifted my focus to Amit Bhardwaj.

He was in jail in Pune, India for orchestrating one of the biggest crypto frauds in history.

Initially it was thought that the scam was worth $1 billion, but fresh investigations suggest it was ten times larger.

Amit's arrest was also dramatic. He was first caught at Dubai Airport in March 2018 but faked a heart attack to escape to Bangkok. Eventually, he and his younger brother Vivek were arrested with the help of Thai authorities and brought to India to face trial.

Amit and Vivek along with five others—popularly known as 'seven stars'—floated several companies to market the concept of crypto currencies. They posed as innovators and the only ones in India mining Bitcoins, successfully duping nearly half a million people worldwide. Among them were Varun and Gagan who lived in Dubai. I met them over dinner at a restaurant in Karama where I gained insights into Amit's operating methods. Amit, who completed his education in New Delhi, pursued a bachelor of technology (B.Tech.) degree in Maharashtra. He later secured a software developer's position at Infosys in Pune. However, it was the emerging world of cryptocurrency that truly fascinated him.

He co-founded HighKart, India's first e-commerce platform that accepted Bitcoin as payment, long before the concept had caught on. In 2016, he founded Amaze Mining & Blockchain Research Ltd, which claimed to be the world's largest individual Bitcoin miner. Amit further established his place in the Bitcoin world with GB Miners, a Bitcoin mining pool he touted as the fastest growing in the world.

His fixation with cryptocurrency didn't stop there. He wrote an e-book titled *Cryptocurrency for Beginners*, which gained him widespread acclaim. Bollywood stars including Shilpa Shetty, Neha Dhupia, Huma Qureshi, Bipasha Basu and Nargis Fakhri, took to X to sing its praises. Shilpa Shetty, in particular, thanked Amit for enlightening her on Bitcoin investing and claimed she would add the book to her reading list. However, it's unclear if she ever read it. Amit also went on a property-buying spree in Dubai, acquiring several high-end properties in the city's posh enclaves, including Shilpa's Burj Khalifa apartment, which she had received as a gift from her husband Raj Kundra.

Amit's fascination with Bollywood celebrities extended beyond praise for his e-book. He sought to add glamour to the GBC Ultra Miners Summit, a gathering of top GainBitcoin investors in Dubai in November 2017. To achieve this, he flew in actors like Sunny Leone, Prachi Desai, Aarti Chabria, Sonal Chauhan and Karishma Tanna to the Grand Hyatt Hotel. The summit was a front for Amit's multi-level marketing (MLM) scheme promising a highly inflated monthly return of 10 per cent on Bitcoin investments in just eighteen months. Despite the implausible returns, over 1,00,000 investors, including Varun and Gagan, were lured in by the allure of quick riches.

To sweeten the deal, Amit dazzled investors with lavish launch and rewards programme parties in Thailand and Dubai, all documented for future hard sell. He even picked people like

Ashish Dabbas, a UAE-based dentist, to be the face of the company and populate YouTube with videos of him engaging with potential investors. GainBitcoin's marketing blitz included seminars where promoters took the stage like motivational speakers to convince people to buy into their supposed gold mine. They preyed on people's desperation for financial security, especially during times of economic uncertainty.

The fraud came to light in mid-2017 when Amit failed to fulfil his promise of 10 per cent returns in Bitcoin. Undeterred, he devised a cunning scheme to force payouts in an in-house crypto token called MCAP, with the audacious prediction that its price would grow twenty-fold. The promise turned out to be nothing more than empty words, as disgruntled investors discovered that MCAP—or 'Mcrap', as many of them call it—was worth a measly $0.61, compared to the $5.78 it was once listed at.

As the heat intensified in India, Amit fled to Dubai but his investors were not willing to let him off the hook so easily. Many of them tried to barge into the GBC Ultra Miners Summit in Dubai, but were stopped by bouncers. Amit left the event in haste, claiming he needed to rest as he had had a renal transplant.

However, some investors tracked him down to his eightieth-floor apartment at Elite Residence in Dubai Marina. They cornered him but Amit evaded their questions and refused to take responsibility.

A police officer, who had flown from Punjab, claimed he lost $2 million to the scheme.

'I gave the money within two-three days of demonetisation. It wasn't safe to keep cash at home,' he told me with a casual shrug over tea in his Bur Dubai hotel room during a subsequent visit. How he had that kind of money is anyone's guess.

Indian police tracked down 60,000 user IDs and email addresses in the GainBitcoin fraud case. Amit Bhardwaj and his eight associates were charged with fraud. Since Amit's death on 15 January 2022, two days before his thirty-ninth birthday, India's enforcement director has been urging the Supreme Court to instruct Amit's brother Ajay to give access to, and the username and password for, his late brother's crypto wallet. They argue that the issue of the 'legality of cryptocurrency' is irrelevant, as it is clearly a Ponzi scheme. Ajay's lawyer has claimed that his client is unaware of the username and password of his late brother's crypto wallet.

It is estimated that Amit may have collected anywhere between 3,85,000 and 6,00,000 Bitcoins, amounting to around $11.5 billion at the peak of Bitcoin prices in November 2021.

Till now, the Pune Cyber Police team has uncovered a string of companies that Amit registered across the globe, including in Singapore, Hong Kong, the British Virgin Islands, Estonia, Dubai and the US, where Amit, his brothers Vivek and Ajay, and their father Mahendra Kumar held directorship. Amit was also found to have multiple bank accounts in Dubai.

Amit's GainBitcoin fraud case will go down in history as one of the biggest crypto scams, challenging even Ruja's audacious exploits.

In March 2023, a German film crew flew me to Mumbai for a documentary about the crypto queen, Ruja. Originally, they planned for me to visit Berlin, but due to visa constraints, Mumbai became our chosen location.

We conducted the interview at the Taj Hotel in Bandra, and I was filmed walking along Carter Road and the beach, dressed in a suit and tie. It was an amusing contrast, as investigative journalists usually blend into the crowd, but I now stood out in the city's landscape. In June 2024, the docuseries called *The Queen of Crypto: Kill Bitcoin*, also known as *Kill Bitcoin*, was released in Europe.

Serial Sex Predator

For ten months a sex predator posed as the CEO of a bogus chartered airline, lured young women to hotel rooms in Dubai on the pretext of job interviews and then drugged and sexually assaulted them.

It took me three weeks of painstaking investigation and meticulous collaboration with Dubai Police to put an end to his reign of terror.

Job scams are cruel. What this scumbag was doing was truly abominable. Only a sexual deviant with psychopathic traits would spin a treacherous web like this man had. That is what he was.

This was at the height of the COVID-19 pandemic in May 2020.

At a time when the aviation industry was downsizing, he created a fancy website of a non-existent chartered airline. Job adverts were then posted on social media and classified sites seeking applications from aspiring female flight attendants.

Candidates were asked to share their pictures, videos and vital statistics. The dream job came with up to Dh25,000 in monthly salary besides perks such as insurance and free accommodation in Dubai Marina.

From the many applicants who responded, the man would pick his target.

In the beginning, I didn't quite believe that something so brazen and vile would be happening in Dubai. So much so that when I first met an assault victim, I almost doubted her story. I genuinely thought that High Fly Jets was a bona fide company and Ryan was indeed its CEO.

Yes, he could have called the woman for an interview and then ended up having consensual sex with her. And now the woman was trying to frame him because she didn't get the job. But as I dug deeper and found more unrelated women who had gone through the same traumatic experience, I realised the gravity of the threat the man posed every day that he was out on the street.

I urged the victims to report him to the police but they flatly refused. I contacted the hotels where the incidents took place. They also declined to help.

As part of an elaborate plan, the job applicants would get an email from a purported HR manager asking them to meet the airline's CEO in a hotel for the final interview.

The women were made to believe that the CEO was a very busy man and they should consider themselves lucky that he was meeting them in person.

Once the women reached the hotel, the man would tell them that the hotel meeting rooms and business centres were closed because of COVID-19 safety regulations. For the same reasons, the interview couldn't be conducted in the lobby either.

'It was a plausible explanation,' recalled expatriate Russian Karine Petrova as we sat in a coffee shop in Mall of the Emirates, days after the assault.

She was an attractive young woman with a slender body, green eyes and chestnut brown hair that fell to her shoulders.

Like many before her, Karine reached the hotel for the interview at the scheduled time.

Little did she know then that her much-awaited meeting with a 'Ryan Fernandez', the visiting CEO of High Fly Jets, was to become an ordeal that would end in subterfuge, drugging and a sexual assault.

The interview had been arranged by Linda Gomez, a recruitment manager for an American private jet charter company.

A WhatsApp message sent from California days earlier had seemed encouraging. It said: 'Ever heard of this … "right place at the right time". There is something good coming for you … good things happen to good people … don't forget to treat me to dinner at Burj Al Arab when you get that job.'

Karine and Linda had never met, but Karine told me that Linda had been friendly throughout the recruitment process.

'He's [Ryan] the right hand of the CEO. He decides who to hire and what to pay them. Two women have met him since he landed. They got hired at salaries of Dh18,000 each. Maybe you won't get 18,000. Maybe you'll get 15. But hey, it's still freaking good,' she was told by Linda via text message.

At 7.15 p.m., Karine stepped into the hotel on Al Mina Road. She was met by a bearded Indian man in his mid-thirties who introduced himself in an American accent as Ryan Fernandes, the CEO of High Fly Jets.

'He didn't look anything like the boss of an airline, much less an American, but who was I to judge a rich and successful man by his appearance?' Karine told me.

'I followed him to the hotel room, hoping to finish the interview and return home before the 10 p.m. coronavirus movement restrictions.'

Once inside, the man asked Karine to sit on a sofa chair while he propped himself up on the double bed. He started with common questions as he lit a cigarette and read her CV on his laptop.

Ryan told her that their company was headquartered in the US but operated air charter services in forty-three countries, including the UAE, and that their clients were mostly VIPs like top CEOs, senior government officials and foreign dignitaries.

Karine was impressed.

He then asked why Karine wanted the job and listened intently as she rattled off her well-rehearsed answers.

After some time, he got up from his bed, came around and handed Karine his laptop with its screen open. It showed a web page with a hundred questions. Karine was told the company had an opening for a team leader and she could be hired if she satisfactorily answered all questions.

'I thought I had been randomly blessed. The questions looked easy. I took the laptop and began typing the answers,' said Karine.

She was halfway done when Ryan asked if he should order some food for her.

'I thought it was nice of him. I was in a hurry so I politely declined. He smiled and poured a glass of water from a disposable bottle next to his bed and offered it to me, saying I should at least have some water. I was thirsty and gulped it in two quick swigs.'

According to Karine, it was at this point that the interview took a turn for the sinister. The water contained a date-rape drug. The colourless, odourless and taste-free drug can have a paralysing effect on victims. It works quickly, causing drowsiness and inducing hypnotic effects, often within minutes.

Karine told me how the words on the computer's screen began to swim and blur before her eyes.

'I felt I would faint. I tried to stand up, but my legs buckled under me. As my vision started to fade away, I saw Ryan's face inches away. There was a furtive gleam in his eyes and an evil sneer around his lips as he forcibly kissed and groped me. I wanted to resist but couldn't move my limbs. I felt woozy. Barely awake, I watched helplessly as he dropped his pants and ordered me to perform lewd sexual acts. I begged him to leave me alone, but he held me firmly as I drifted into unconsciousness.'

Between September 2019 and May 2020, more than a dozen women in the UAE were similarly drugged and sexually assaulted after being called to different Dubai hotels.

Yana Litvin, twenty-seven, of Ukraine, Malike Hadad, twenty-nine, of Lebanon, Dylla Santos, twenty-six, of Italy. It was a long list.

I spoke to eight victims, each of whom was threatened with dire consequences if they reported the matter to the police.

Karine, who had stayed past nightly COVID-19 restrictions, was warned she could be arrested and fined. Yana and Malike were told they could be charged with prostitution 'because they came to the hotel room willingly'. Dylla was threatened with sextortion. She told me the man had clicked her nude photographs and threatened to post them online.

'I got scared. I am not sure if he took any snaps because I have only a faint recollection of that evening. I went into a trance-like state almost immediately after drinking the water,' recalled the former usherer who visited the man at a hotel in Jumeirah.

She spent two weeks under psychiatric care after being plagued by nightmares that woke her up in the middle of the night and left her sweating and gasping for breath.

Dylla said she saw a young European blonde sitting beside Ryan on his bed when she entered his hotel room.

'He introduced her as his assistant and began the conversation by giving me an overview of his airline as I perched on a chair in the far corner. He claimed he had a master's degree from Harvard University and had worked himself up in the aviation industry with sheer determination. He said I don't have to be intimidated by his position as they had a friendly work culture and their staff was like one big family. He then offered me a glass of water and suggested we play the game "Simon Says" to "calm my nerves" before the interview.'

Simon Says is a popular ice-breaker game involving three or more players where one player takes the role of 'Simon' and issues instructions to the other players, which should be followed only when prefaced with the phrase 'Simon says'.

'I felt amused, but I thought this is how they do it. At his cue, a blonde (present in the room) started the game by asking me to pat my head and stick out my tongue. To my utter surprise, I found myself stupidly following the instructions. She said "Simon says, Jump" and I jumped. It was as if I had been hypnotised. Slowly, my mind went blank. I didn't even realise when the blonde had left and I was alone with the man who was completely undressed now,' said Dylla.

Yana, who worked in the hospitality industry, described how the man touched her breast several times and forced her to perform sexual acts while she was under sedation in his room at a hotel on Shaikh Zayed Road.

'Linda had messaged me saying Mr Ryan would be flying into Dubai for just one night and this was my best chance,' said Yana. 'I was asked to carry along my Emirates ID and A4 size papers for a written test. He was courteous and polite when I showed up past midnight. He even apologised for the late-night interview. He claimed he had a flight the following morning. I believed him. He then lit a cigarette and handed me a paper containing a hundred job interview questions.

'As I got busy with the answers, he passed me a glass of water. I drank half of it. Soon I started to feel dizzy and disoriented. I was conscious of my surroundings, but had no control over my body when the man removed his clothes and held me close to his bare chest.

'He was murmuring, "Don't worry, it will be alright." Everything appeared to be happening in slow motion. I was terrified. I thought, what if he had a knife tucked under his pillow?'

The more harrowing accounts I heard, the angrier I got.

A sex predator was on the prowl, and yet there was nothing I could do to stop him. I couldn't even discuss the story with my editors face-to-face as we worked from home those days.

I missed the comforting familiarity of editorial meetings. Online editorial meetings can never be a substitute for physical interactions. The daily newsroom conference is where the real magic takes place. That's where ideas harden and you get to the nuts and bolts of a story. You can't replicate that on a computer screen. But I had no choice. So I called a Zoom meeting and shared my findings with senior editors on a hastily made PowerPoint presentation.

The editors heard attentively.

At the end of my presentation, Abdul Hamid said, 'Go ahead, make sure you involve the authorities.'

I had got the green signal but didn't know how to approach the story or, more importantly, get the man busted. I didn't have a shred of evidence and no one to testify against him. The purported chartered airline didn't exist. The fancy job advertisements and the detailed enrolment forms were also fake. Probably there was no real Linda Gomez either. I could have run a story alerting potential victims about the racket but it would have also alerted the man.

Mercifully, I met a senior police officer who heard me out and offered to help, provided, of course, that the victims lodge a formal complaint. He assured me that the women had nothing to fear. 'If they feel uncomfortable visiting a police station, we will get our officers to meet them in civilian clothes anywhere they like,' he said. 'Now it's your job to convince them.'

I saw a glimmer of hope, but persuading the victims to report the predator was like trying to blow out an electric light bulb.

'I don't trust anyone,' said Dylla as we sat around a table at a cafe. Her Pakistani boyfriend nodded knowingly. 'I don't trust you either,' he said. 'You say you are from a newspaper, but how do we know your identity card is not fake.' 'Your ID,' he said, 'can I see it again?'

Calls and messages to many other women went unanswered but I didn't give up.

After several days of persistent persuasion, I succeeded in convincing Karine and Yana to meet the officers in my presence. We met Karine at a coffee shop at the Mall of Emirates and Yana at Starbucks on Sheikh Zayed Road.

I acted as interpreter as the women described the sordid details of their experience. It was embarrassing translating terms like 'jerk off' and 'wank'.

A few days later, the women were directed to make a formal call to the government's 24/7 Al Ameen Service Hotline, which allows people to report crimes anonymously.

They were then asked to visit the Al Barsha Police Station, which was tasked to investigate the case. Yana was called first. I picked the Ukrainian from her house at 8 p.m. and drove her to the police station where her statement was recorded. She finished around midnight. The cops gave us cookies and coffee. In 2017, I was at Al Barsha Police Station in handcuffs. Now I was there as a special guest.

Based on the information provided by us, the police mounted a massive investigation. They trawled through hours of CCTV footage from the hotels where the sexual assaults took place. I was worried the perpetrator would have left the country but the cops worked tirelessly to track him down, using all the resources at their disposal.

In August, the authorities finally had their man. He was a Canadian of Indian origin.

For me, the news of his arrest was more than just a victory for justice. It was a personal triumph too. I had played my part in exposing his sickening actions, helping the police to catch the perpetrator. The satisfaction I felt was indescribable, knowing that my investigation had contributed to putting a stop to his crimes and no other innocent woman would have to suffer the horrors that his victims had experienced.

'What did he say when he was caught?' I asked an officer who was part of the team that nabbed him.

'Nothing,' said the officer. 'He was speechless.'

Karine and Yana have since relocated to their countries. Once in a while, I hear from them.

As part of my story I had asked a psychologist why the predator created such an elaborate ruse and risked arrest to quench his sexual desires when he could have simply paid a sex worker. He told me it's a misconception that sexual crimes are committed for sexual desire. In fact, sexual gratification is only one of the factors behind why an assailant will choose to attack.

For him sex is a control operation and seeking conquest the overriding aspect, he explained.

It made sense, but not entirely. Around the same time a sex predator was arrested in neighbouring Oman. Eerily, he had used the same modus operandi to target fifty-six women. The country's Royal Oman Police said the Muscat-based suspect posed as the head of recruitment at an airline and lured female aviation enthusiasts with fake social networking accounts.

Women who responded to the job openings were asked to share suggestive personal photographs, which were then used to blackmail them.

Could there be a link between the two cases? Were the predators in some kind of evil race? I will never know.

The victims' identities in this story have been altered for their protection.

PART 3

INTRIGUING SCOOPS AND EXPOSÉS

Bribes are a common currency in the world of investigative journalism, and I've certainly been offered my fair share: Dh1 million in cash twice, iPhones thrice and a slightly used Land Cruiser once. Additionally, 'donations' to my NGO back home, an 'all-expenses-paid family holiday' and a 'relaxing' yacht party followed by a stay on a private island have all been presented to tempt me to bury various investigative stories.

Once, a thug approached me, offering to do 'something very good for me' in exchange for not publishing a story, which had been held back for an entirely different reason. The fool mistakenly assumed I had accepted the offer and wanted to know how he could repay the favour.

Life as an investigative journalist in the UAE is exhilarating, as there's never a shortage of stories. Every few days, I receive leads, for which I am grateful. However, I also have to contend with individuals who believe they are obligated to provide tip-offs, or who think they can tap into my insights whenever they please. I'm fed up with random calls from people asking me inane questions or seeking my opinion on topics I have no clue about, such as when the Russia–Ukraine War will end or if Bitcoin will rise or fall.

Some time ago, I had written an article about counterfeit perfume, which often contains toxic chemicals, and in some cases, even urine. The morning after its publication, I was awakened at 6.00 a.m. by an Arab caller demanding to know if the urine in the counterfeit perfume was camel's or human's. I had never considered it.

Then there are individuals who present absurd and vague leads and become upset if I don't drop everything to pursue them. At *Gulf News*, we had one such individual in the marketing department—an affable South Indian man in his late fifties—whose leads consistently fell through. One day, he pulled me aside and whispered conspiratorially, 'I have a scoop for you.' Wary after his past fruitless leads, I asked, 'Okay, what is it?'

'I was on the Metro last night and I saw a group of foreigners, speaking in hushed tones.'

'Nationality?' I probed.

'Couldn't say for sure, but definitely not locals.'

'Topic of discussion?'

'I couldn't catch it. You are the investigative journalist here—go dig.'

The next day, he eagerly awaited updates, only to slump in disappointment at my lack of progress, as if he'd entrusted me with the next Watergate scandal. Nonetheless, many seemingly trivial leads have blossomed into captivating stories.

'Did you hear about the hi-tech public toilet in Sharjah that flings opens automatically after twenty minutes regardless of whether you are done with your business or not?' my daughter Unaiza once asked me. It made for a fascinating read. There's also the story of a blind judge from the US Supreme Court who stayed at the Atlantis resort in Dubai for a month and delivered verdicts in the US while running thirty-five kilometres along the Boardwalk daily.

Some stories seem unbelievable, but that's what makes them stories. Journalists understand this, but individuals from other departments, who often attend editorial meetings, sometimes do not. I met an Indian manager whose life was turned upside down after accidentally tossing a bag of cash into a garbage bin. The bag contained over Dh1,00,000 that belonged to his company. His carelessness cost him his job and triggered a series of unfortunate events, leaving him penniless and homeless. Yet, an IT manager in our editorial meetings refused to believe the story. When he challenged me, I simply asked, 'What are the odds of a man mistakenly throwing a bag of cash into a bin?' He replied, 'One in ten thousand.' 'Exactly,' I said. 'That's precisely why this is a story.'

In Part 3, you will find a mix of intriguing scoops and stories, including a chilling exposé on cyber slaves who are forced to work for a burgeoning Chinese cybercrime syndicate. Back in the day, the UAE residents had to contend with Pakistani scammers calling individuals and telling them they had won an Etisalat raffle and asking for their credit card details. Now, however, Chinese scammers have upped the cybercrime game several levels. Be afraid, be very, very afraid.

Investigating Cyber Slaves in the UAE

Like many groundbreaking investigations, this global exposé began with a simple lead. In late February 2024, Farhaan Wasti, a friend from Dubai, contacted me about a situation involving a mother of two from my hometown.

Rose Jehan, a physiotherapist, had travelled to Dubai from Lucknow in search of employment. When job opportunities proved elusive, she accepted a digital marketing position offering a salary of Dh3,000, along with accommodation and meals.

For many South Asians facing unemployment in their home countries, it seemed like a lifeline. Little did Rose know, however, that this seemingly promising offer would soon reveal its dark side. Before long, she found herself ensnared in a cybercrime syndicate run by Chinese scammers engaging in forced labour and human trafficking.

In a desperate voice message to Farhaan, Rose described how she was held captive and forced to defraud people with promises of additional income, only to drain their bank accounts. Her passport had been confiscated and her phone remained under the custody of her employers from 7.30 a.m. to 8.30 p.m., during which period she impersonated a representative from a purported Mumbai-based company called Coin DCX Company. When I tried to reach her after work hours, she became frightened and hastily ended the call.

It took many days of gently persuading her through text messages before she finally opened up. 'Please help me,' she pleaded. 'I'm holed up in a cramped seventh-floor apartment with six other girls from India, Pakistan and Bangladesh. Our workspace is on the ninth floor. We're trapped with Nigerian security guards monitoring every exit. It's like a jail.'

'Do you ever get to step out for food or something?' I inquired.

'No, the meals are served in the call centre,' she replied. 'Breakfast is just bread with tea. Sometimes, if the company's had a good run with their scams, they toss in some butter. Lunch is at noon, dinner at five. It's usually watery daal, kabooz, noodles, hummus, and salad.'

From Rose's detailed account, I could imagine the scene of her workplace: a crowded room filled with nearly a hundred men and women, each hunched over a computer, generating lists of Indian cell phone numbers to call throughout the day. Their mission? To entice unsuspecting individuals with deceptive part-time online income opportunities. Rose described her gruelling schedule, working thirteen-hour shifts for thirty days straight.

'Every day, each of us makes anywhere between 700–800 calls, all of which are recorded, with many randomly monitored by our Pakistani handlers,' she explained. 'The moment I finish one call, another appears on the dialler. Yesterday, I took Rs 5,00,000 from a retiree's account. His life savings, gone in an instant. It weighs heavily on my conscience, leaving me unable to sleep.'

I had read about how Chinese syndicates recruit individuals in locations such as Bangkok, promising job opportunities, only to traffic them to countries like Myanmar and Cambodia. The UN reports around 2,20,000 people in Southeast Asia trapped in these scams. Surely, this can't be happening in the UAE, I told myself. I assumed it was a rare case or some idiot trying to establish operations here without understanding the consequences.

I believed I could intervene by contacting the Indian consulate and Ajman Police to rescue Rose and the other girls and shut down the operations within a day or two.

However, the more I delved into the racket, the clearer it became how ignorant I was. The realisation hit me hard when I discovered that the UAE had become the global epicentre of cyber scams. These schemes enslaved not merely a few dozens or hundreds, but thousands of computer-literate and educated young people across high-security compounds in Ajman, Ras Al Khaimah and Dubai.

Before the COVID-19 pandemic, cyber syndicates predominantly operated from China, Cambodia and Myanmar. However, a crackdown prompted them to seek new havens. In 2023, Chinese authorities pressed charges against 2,80,000 individuals involved in cybercrimes, marking a 35.5 per cent increase from the previous year. Additionally, China targeted cybercrime syndicates in the border areas of military-ruled Myanmar, resulting in the extradition of 31,000 suspects. Faced with mounting pressure, the cybercriminals sought sanctuary in other countries, with the UAE emerging as a favoured destination.

The cyber slaves told me they face harsh financial targets and quotas. Failure leads to fines, termination and sometimes torture, including electric shocks, isolation, physical punishment, waterboarding, starvation and sexual exploitation.

A Vietnamese man who escaped from a compound shared chilling videos. They depicted men being stripped naked, waterboarded and subjected to tasering.

I learnt of a heartbreaking incident involving a Bangladeshi man who suffered a fatal heart attack at a scamming compound in Ajman. Eyewitnesses recounted how they pleaded for an ambulance, only to be callously refused.

When I spoke to Rose the following evening, she was worried about her colleague Laxmi. A young Indian girl from Punjab, Laxmi had been denied medical aid despite running a fever. 'I begged them to let her see a doctor,' Rose said. 'But they silenced me, insisting that nobody leaves this place.'

Over the course of three days, I identified four scamming compounds in Ajman, along with one each in Ras Al Khaimah and Dubai. In some instances, these gangs had control over entire buildings, effectively imprisoning thousands of cyber slaves within their confines. One particularly fortified compound, located behind Ajman's Al Ain Hotel, stood as a daunting fortress, guarded by vigilant Nigerian security personnel, and monitored by CCTV cameras. It was within these imposing walls that Rose and countless others were held captive, leaving me with no recourse but to observe from a distance in my tinted glass car.

On Dubai-Al Ain Road, the Chinese scammers had taken over a cluster of buildings. Parked outside was a truck van with an antenna protruding from its back. When I showed its picture to a telecom expert, he explained that it was a cell tower designed to bolster communication networks. Given the large number of people using mobile devices simultaneously, such a measure was necessary for ensuring a strong signal.

I had heard rumours of a major operation running from Ajman's Grand Mall, but what I saw exceeded my expectations. Up to eight scamming compounds operated openly there. I observed hundreds of young men and women flowing into and out of the building. Unlike the compound behind Al Ain Hotel, the workers here had more freedom. I caught up with some of them during their smoking break. For many it appeared to be their first job. 'Why do you do this?' I inquired of a young Pakistani man in his mid-twenties as he lit a cigarette and took swigs from a packaged box of labaan. 'Give me a job with the same perks, and I'll quit today,' he chuckled. Another young man told me that he used to feel guilty, but not anymore. 'It's just a job to me now. If I don't do it, someone else will. There are plenty of people who would take my place gladly.'

As I conversed with the workers wearing company lanyards around their necks, a troubling comparison dawned on me: were they fundamentally different from burglars? While burglars invade homes, these individuals breach banks. I couldn't shake off the concern for their future. Their initial employment thrust them into a world where criminality seemed routine. How would this influence their paths? Would they hold onto any semblance of morality? Before my eyes, I witnessed the potential cultivation of thousands of future criminals. Who's to say how many might eventually establish their own scamming enterprises?

I was desperate to meet Rose, but she needed an out pass to leave, and there was only one way she could obtain it: by meeting her daily target of twelve clients. Every evening, I would drive down to Ajman and linger near her building, locally known as the Chinese Tower, hoping she would achieve her target, even though it meant more lives being ruined. Then, finally, on 11 March 2024, the first day of Ramadan, I received the green signal around mid-afternoon. Rose informed me that she could leave at 10.00 p.m. That evening, after Taraweeh prayers, I took my wife Eram and headed to Ajman. She insisted on joining me, having heard my accounts of the dangers from previous visits. I didn't object; I welcomed her company for the long drive and having someone to hold the phone camera.

Usually, for such assignments, I would use my Kia Mohave or Mercedes E300, both equipped with tinted windows. However, that day, the SUV was parked elsewhere, and the Mercedes had a flat tire, so I reluctantly took my official Mazda 6 Saloon, which had clear windows.

I parked a little further down the building where Rose worked, to avoid the CCTV cameras and patrolling guards. At 10.15, Rose arrived, quickly taking her place in the back seat as we drove away. There was little time to spare so we didn't venture far. Instead, we found a rundown mandi restaurant nearby, offering separate dining areas for families with floor seating. It was an ideal spot. Handing the camera to Eram, we ordered some food while Rose recounted her tale, describing every detail.

Rose said her Pakistani handler, Ahmad, referred to them as 'opening batsmen'. 'We're the ones who make the first call, initiate conversation, and assign people simple tasks like posting Google reviews and liking YouTube videos,' she explained. 'The handlers and Chinese gang monitor our calls as we stick to a script.'

Initially, victims are promised small sums ranging from Rs 200 to Rs 500. But as their trust is gained and involvement deepens, they are ushered into a larger Telegram group with hundreds of participants. Here, they are coaxed into paying subscription fees for tasks that promise greater financial rewards. The fraudsters employ deceptive tactics, using fabricated screenshots of individuals purportedly earning significant sums to lure in new victims. 'We collectively defraud hundreds of people daily, and when our illicit gains surpass Dh1,00,000, pre-recorded applause and cheers echo through the room.'

She outlined the hierarchy within the scam centre. At the bottom were telesales agents like herself. Above them were receptionists, responsible for grooming the callers. Then came the teachers, and at the top were the 'killers'. The latter two categories could rake in thousands of dollars daily in incentives, given their expertise in hacking.

I reached out to four Indian victims, including Rupal, an assistant professor from Udaipur whose numbers Rose had shared. Each confessed to losing anywhere between Rs 50,000–10,00,000.

Bewildered by my unexpected call, they bombarded me with questions: Who are you? How did you get my number? Can I trust you as a journalist, or are you another scammer? Amidst the barrage of inquiries and expletives, I patiently explained my role as an investigative journalist. Slowly, their scepticism gave way to relief as they realised I was there to uncover the truth behind their losses. With a sense of catharsis, they eagerly recounted their experiences, hoping that their stories would lead to justice, or at least some form of resolution.

Sadly, not everyone made it out alive to share their story. Rose told me about a couple in Hyderabad who, after losing their life savings, took their own lives. They posted a video on their Telegram before ending it all.

'Could the video have been faked?' I asked.

'I'm not sure; I didn't see it myself. But those who did were deeply disturbed and believed it was real. Just the other day, a victim posted a video of himself cutting his wrist. These kinds of incidents happen all too often. Some people vent their frustration at us, while others resort to extreme measures.'

We said our goodbyes with heavy hearts as we dropped Rose back. 'Can't you stay?' I asked as she stepped out of the car. 'I'll retrieve your passport and settle the company debts.'

She offered a weak smile. 'What about the other women inside? If I don't return, they'll become suspicious and move their operations elsewhere.'

It made sense.

Outside Grand Mall, I met an Indian man who sheepishly revealed his specialisation in pig butchering or romance scams—an insidious operation employing social media, dating apps, WhatsApp and text messages to ensnare victims. Starting with seemingly innocuous conversations that feigned errors, the scammers gradually earned the trust of their targets, ultimately persuading them to invest in cryptocurrency trading under false pretences.

Victims were directed to download apps or visit websites secretly controlled by the scammers, leading to devastating financial losses. My mind drifted to my stories in *Khaleej Times* recounting the stories of individuals hit by these scams. A father of five in Ajman lost $47,000 while seeking a second wife on Tinder, while an IT director in Dubai was drained of $1,47,000. Similarly, an Indian businessman in Abu Dhabi lost $2,00,000, and an Emirati mother in Sharjah over $2,75,000. Pig-butchering scammers have likely stolen more than $75 billion from victims worldwide, a figure surpassing previous estimates, as per a recent study.

I pondered how many of these scams occurred in the UAE and whether any were perpetrated by the wiry-framed man with frizzled hair whom I had met.

I also marvel at a striking paradox: while taking chunks of Indian land along its border, China is also nibbling away at Indian bank accounts worth millions of dollars daily, using its own people to do so. So much for calls to boycott Chinese products.

I have alerted the UAE authorities and the Indian consulate in Dubai, but now, I'm in a tense waiting game, aware that dismantling such a deeply rooted network won't be easy. It's a heavy burden knowing that with each passing hour, thousands are falling victim to financial deception. My heart aches for the cyber slaves, hoping for their freedom. And as for Rose, I hold onto the hope of one day meeting her as a free woman. Without her courage, there would be no crackdown, no story to tell.

Based on the investigations, on 26 June 2024, UAE special forces conducted an all-night operation, dismantling cyber syndicates across multiple locations in the country. The operation led to the arrest and rescue of thousands of cybercriminals and cyber slaves, many of whom have since been deported.

Inside Dubai's Hidden Liquor Empires

In the fading light of that August evening in 2010, my formal attire seemed conspicuously out of place against the rugged backdrop of Jebel Ali's industrial district. Beads of sweat glistened on my forehead as I discreetly wove my way through the maze-like network of narrow streets that concealed the clandestine alcohol trade.

An astonishing scene unfolded before my eyes.

A multitude of people stood in line at covert liquor hotspots near a supermarket, hidden behind worn-out buses parked on sandy patches, and sprawled across the expansive ground affectionately known as 'the big ground' among the labourers. It was Indian electrician Mushtaq, a resident of a nearby labour camp, who had tipped me off about this place.

Mushtaq, our informant, provided crucial guidance. 'The first queue is for beer, the second for whisky,' he explained. 'Come on a weekend, that's when queues stretch into the streets.'

As we hurried past, he jutted his chin to point to a man standing on oil drums. 'He's a spotter,' Mushtaq whispered. He must have been very good at his job because as soon as our eyes met, his face etched with a deepening sense of concern. 'Let's go,' Mushtaq urged, tugging at my sleeves, 'It's not safe here.'

During the mid-2000s, Jebel Ali, with its massive expatriate workforce, had become a fertile breeding ground for bootleggers and criminal activity. The alarming statistics underscored the severity of the issue, with 374 reported crimes in one year placing the neighbourhood among the most crime-ridden areas in Dubai.

But the real peril lay in the ruthless gangs running this illicit trade. A savage sword battle had left thirty injured, and two men suffered the horrifying fate of being gang-raped and buried alive in the desert. In neighbouring Sharjah, the situation was equally grim, with two men, one from India and one from Pakistan, meeting their end in a brutal turf battle.

Amid this grim scenario, I, together with Bobby Naqvi, the *XPRESS* editor at the time, chief reporter Jay Hilotin and our photographer Ahmad Ramzan, ventured to the location at sundown on a weekend, this time adopting a more inconspicuous appearance in tattered T-shirts and track pants. Our rendezvous point was the Parco Supermarket, the labourers' hub and our contact's chosen meeting place.

'Much better,' Mushtaq nodded approvingly.

As the booze bazaar sprang to life, it was quite a sight. Massive orderly queues, each containing more than 250 people, had formed. We decided to join one of them. To mask the camera's noise whenever our photographer Ahmad Ramzan took a picture, we employed a subtle yet necessary tactic—fake coughs and sneezes.

As we inched forward in the queue, we couldn't help but notice the thriving secondary businesses around the liquor trade. Omelettes, boiled eggs, salted peanuts, and even gambling tables flourished alongside, creating a unique microcosm within this hidden world.

Finally, our turn arrived, and we purchased a bottle of French brandy and three cans of Filipino beer. The transaction felt extraordinary, considering that the individuals who handed us the bottles appeared to be not much older than those who had been convicted of bootlegging and now faced the death penalty in Sharjah.

Stacks of garbage bags and crates of whisky lay to replenish the stock.

As night descended upon Dubai, we ventured to the 'big ground', where hundreds revelled under the open sky. Spotters kept a vigilant watch, and photography remained a challenge.

In the distance, the radiant lights of Dubai's cityscape contrasted starkly with the hidden revelry taking place in the dark.

Our journey had taken us deep into the heart of the liquor syndicate orchestrated by a web of Iranian, Baloch and Indian men. The staggering estimates of millions of dollars of illegal liquor entering the UAE each year underscored the scale of this clandestine operation.

A few years later, I found myself uncovering another illicit liquor trade hub, this time in a car park in Naif. The place offered not only a variety of alcohol but also ice cubes, soda, boiled eggs and even drugs. A young man approached us, offering an array of drugs, including hash, African weed and speed.

'What have you got now?' I asked.

'Whisky,' he responded, producing a bottle from a sling bag.

Here too the supply seemed endless, with beer cans continuously emerging from big white plastic sacks loosely hanging from a nearby tree.

Liquor bottles remained concealed beneath stacks of mattresses in pickup trucks, and some were stashed in sling backpacks hidden underneath parked vehicles. I even spotted one car replenishing the stock. Crates full of alcohol were unloaded from its trunk and discreetly relocated to secluded spots. Well-built African men, armed with cell phones, stationed themselves on the four corners of the car park to keep watch over the tightly knit streets.

We purchased an Indian whisky for Dh20 and a can of Filipino beer for Dh7. The complementary offerings, such as chicken kebabs, salted peanuts and boiled eggs, sold as briskly as the alcohol itself.

Drinking in public is strictly illegal in the UAE, with a zero-tolerance policy in place. The consequences for engaging in bootlegging, which often leads to violent turf wars, are even more severe.

In the wake of both stories, Dubai Police launched crackdowns, leading to the apprehension of numerous individuals involved in the illicit trade.

A few years later, we attempted to uncover a similar operation in neighbouring Sharjah, where alcohol has remained banned since 1979, making it the only dry Emirate in the UAE. The epicentre of this illegal trade was a laundry shop in Rolla, where a nearby building concealed crates of alcohol of all types. It was astonishingly easy to obtain these prohibited items. However, the story had to be abandoned due to its sensitive nature. Another story that was not permitted involved a sting operation aimed at exposing the bump-and-blackmail scam in Sharjah. While cheap alcohol is legally available in Ajman, expats transporting it to Dubai had to pass through Sharjah, creating a lucrative opportunity for criminals. They would intentionally collide with your car, creating a fake minor accident, and then demand significant sums of money while threatening to involve the police due to the alcohol transportation.

This scam has persisted for over two decades without interruption. I proposed catching these criminals in the act by visiting a liquor shop and returning with empty coke bottles to give the impression to the criminals monitoring us that I was carrying liquor. Behind me in the car, we would have our camera team and undercover police officials. The plan was to drive away from the liquor shop and then wait for someone to collide with our car. An officer at the Sharjah Police agreed to be part of this exposé; however, my office deemed it too risky and disallowed the operation.

Uncovering Blood Gold in Zimbabwe

In October 2019, I found myself in the badlands of Zimbabwe as part of a cross-border investigation to uncover the country's multi-billion-dollar illegal gold trade.

There were two other journalists with me—a male reporter from Zimbabwe and a radical feminist female freelancer from India.

We were part of a collaborative project funded by an independent nonprofit organisation called Journalismfund. The local journalist, whom I will address by his initials SM, was the team leader.

SM had pitched the story to Journalismfund and then reached out to me to ask if I was interested. I readily agreed. Artisan gold mining is a major concern worldwide, particularly in Zimbabwe where an estimated half a million of its poverty-stricken population pans for gold in dangerous shafts amid bloody turf wars.

All that glittered was not gold here.

The decriminalisation of artisanal gold mining was supposed to fuel the economy. Instead, it had plunged the country into turmoil and given rise to brutal cartels.

Machete-wielding gangs ran amok the mines. In the space of just three months, they had killed hundreds in a single town.

Yet the killings represented only a fraction of the toll around the gold mines that dotted the country's ten provinces.

I landed at the Robert Gabriel Mugabe International Airport in Harare, hoping to do an insightful report on the subject but my enthusiasm quickly petered out when immigration officials refused to let me into the country because of my profession. 'You are a journalist. So, what brings you to Zimbabwe?' a big woman with sunflower yellow eyes asked, flipping through my passport at the immigration counter.

'Sightseeing,' I lied.

'Really, and where's your family?'

'I travel alone mostly, but yes, if I like this place I will bring them next time.'

She didn't appear convinced. With that lame answer nobody would. 'And where are you staying? Do you have a hotel booking?'

Our bookings had been made by SM.

'Yes, I said, showing her the confirmation receipt on my phone.

The woman looked at it incredulously.

'You sure you want to stay at this place?'

'Yes, why?' I asked.

'Nothing. Best of luck,' she said, stamping my passport.

I realised what she meant when we checked into the dreadful run-down resort in the back of beyond.

I didn't expect to find a hotel of Dubai standards in Harare but I didn't expect something so pathetic either.

SM sensed my discomfort.

'I chose this resort deliberately so that we could remain under the radar,' he explained. 'This is a dangerous place. We got to work discreetly.'

It didn't make sense but there was nothing I could do at that time. It was near midnight. I had a long flight so I unwillingly checked into my room and hit the sack.

An hour later I woke up with a start.

It was as dark as a grave. I didn't remember turning off the bedside lamp. I flipped its switch a couple of times. It didn't work. I tried the other lights. Nothing. I picked the house phone. It was dead. I reached for my cell phone. It was out of battery. I went to the washroom. It had no water. I stumbled out of my room. It was even darker outside. Mosquitoes nearly the size of locusts buzzed excitedly around me. I was not vaccinated for yellow fever so I beat a hasty retreat. In any case, the reception was nearly half a kilometre away and I didn't know in which direction.

It was just the beginning of an unforgettable ordeal. In the days ahead I would run out of money as well as a journalist's most important virtue—patience.

When the electricity and water supplies couldn't be restored until the following evening, I put my foot down. I wasn't going to stay there.

But SM and the woman journalist didn't want to leave.

'Stop throwing your Dubai tantrums,' Ms Radical Feminist chided me.

We had developed an instant dislike for each other from the day I landed.

I was aghast. I was not asking for a pool or spa, only the basics: food, water and electricity. And because there was no power, the hotel's lone restaurant was also shut. 'Can we have some tea at least?' I asked a man who doubled as waiter, receptionist, manager and everything in between.

'Sure, sir,' he replied politely, 'but it may take some time.'

'How long?' I asked exasperatedly.

'Two hours maybe, but I will try to hurry up. Do you want anything else, sir?'

We were the only guests in that ghost resort.

I'd had enough. With my phone's battery on its last legs, I booked three rooms at the Cresta Jameson, a four-star hotel in the heart of Harare, using my credit card.

But there was a problem. The grant money that was supposed to cover our expenses had still not arrived in the bank. This meant

I had to not just pay for everyone's accommodation, but also foot all food and travel bills.

By day two, I had maxed out my credit card because SM loved steaks. I had just a few hundred American dollars left. I exchanged $150 for Zimbabwean Rands and used some of the money to pay a local man who drove us to gold mines located along the banks of Mazowe Dam, around sixty kilometres from downtown Harare.

Common sense told me it was stupid to go there, but SM assured us that we would be safe so I relented. He was a local journalist who had spent all his life in Zimbabwe. Who was I to question his judgement? Ms Radical Feminist also didn't have any qualms.

'You can stay back if you are afraid,' she teased me when I suggested we do a recce first.

We reached the mining area a little after 2 p.m.

The miners regarded us suspiciously as we parked the car and walked down an embankment where scores of men panned for gold in shallow open pits.

Ms Radical Feminist and I stuck out like sore thumbs. We had hardly gone a few steps when two huge black men came menacingly towards us, their naked upper bodies glistening with sweat under the blazing sun. One of them carried a machete. It was a weapon of choice for miners.

'What are you doin' here?' he sneered, rolling back his lips and showing his toothless gums.

I pretended not to understand English and looked the other way.

'I am talking to you,' he yelled as he drew level with me and held the machete to my neck. I smelled the cheap tobacco on his breath. My heart was pounding like a blacksmith's hammer but I remained calm and smiled absently at my tormentor. 'Pretend that we don't understand the language,' I said to Ms Radical Feminist in chaste Hindi.

At the same time, I pulled out a packet of Esse super slims from a sling bag and made a hand gesture for a lighter. The man hesitated, lowering his machete and studying my face with a puzzled expression before fishing out a matchbox from his pocket. As I graciously accepted the matchbox and lit my cigarette, I extended the pack of Esse towards him. Greedily, he plucked out six sticks and examined them with reverence, seemingly unfamiliar with the concept of super slims, let alone those with menthol crush balls.

I gently pressed my cigarette filter until it popped. He was impressed.

'Take his phone and watch also,' shouted a miner standing knee deep in a nearby pit.

'Shoes too,' egged another one.

'And don't let him go until we find out what he's doin' here,' commanded a third man.

I turned in the direction of the rasping voice. It came from an elderly man with a wiry frame and tuft of white hair. Ringleader, I deduced.

He was engaged in an animated conversation with SM.

'Please let us go, we just lost our way,' SM pleaded.

'Who is the woman and the tall guy with you?' he asked

'My guests and they can't speak English,' SM replied.

The old man scoffed at the answer.

'So how do you communicate with them? Do you use sign language?'

SM looked around sheepishly.

The old man spat on the ground.

'You think I am dumb,' he snarled. 'Take your guests away from my sight and never come back again. Now get lost.'

As we got into the car, I checked my phone's gallery. In the welter of all this, I had tapped the shutter button a few times as I held the phone behind my back, hoping its camera would capture the miners in action. The results surprised me. The snaps came out perfect.

By day three, I was down to my last few dollars and the grant had not yet arrived. SM and Ms Radical Feminist had no money left either. 'This is all I have,' I said, holding up a $50 bill at the breakfast table. 'We need to use it carefully.'

Imagine my horror when I had to hand it to a cabbie the very next day because SM kept him waiting while we spent four hours interviewing some people in the jewellery industry and aimlessly loitering around a local market.

I lost my temper. 'Have you gone completely nuts?' I shouted at SM.

The following day we were supposed to interview a minister at his house but had no money to get there.

'We will walk. It's just three kilometres,' SM announced.

I was not going to turn up at a minister's house huffing and panting and sweating like the miners.

I did not sign up for this. I flatly refused. 'Aren't we a team? If SM and I can walk, why can't you?' Ms Radical Feminist protested. I had already had several spats with her over her misandrist rhetoric about male supremacy. Just two days earlier she had labelled me a male chauvinist. My crime: heeding the warning of the hotel security, I had asked her to stay back while SM and I went out to get food from a late night diner in a crime-infested neighbourhood.

'What makes you think a criminal will target a woman and not a man? Because women are vulnerable? Is that what you think this is all about? Male supremacy? You think you are better than us?' she argued.

I'd had enough of her. 'Yes, we are a unit.' I said testily, but like a film unit, the star shows up only when the camera is ready and the director calls for action. The lead actor doesn't arrange the props. That's the job of spot boys although they are part of the same unit.'

This really got her. 'You think you are Shah Rukh Khan and we are spot boys?' she asked.

'I didn't want to say this in as many words but yes, I have come here to work, not stand in queues outside banks and walk on foot for miles because of someone's stupidity.'

I refused to accompany them. For the next two days, while Ms Radical Feminist and SM put on their best suits and trekked several kilometres to the bank to claim the grant, I lounged in bed and binge-watched the *Rush Hour* series on TV. The bank had imposed an onerous bureaucratic process before releasing the funds, and I wanted no part in it.

One afternoon, the house phone rang as I lay angry and hungry in my room. It was the food and beverage manager. He had called to enquire if we could grade the culinary skills of some hotel management students who had prepared a five-course meal as part of their final exams. We couldn't have asked for anything more.

Mercifully, the grant money finally arrived and we began our investigation. Gold is Zimbabwe's chief export product, accounting for $1.2 billion in annual forex receipts. Half of it (roughly 33 tonnes) came from thousands of illegal gold miners who panned for the precious yellow metal along hazardous riverbeds strewn with dangerous pits.

By law, the miners were required to sell the gold to the Reserve Bank–owned Fidelity Printers and Refineries (FPR), the sole official gold buyer, refiner and exporter. The miners were happy dealing with Fidelity, which offered them an incentive of $44,000 per kilogram ($1,368.55/ounce), a premium of nearly 7 per cent on the daily gold trading price at the London Bullion Market Association.

But all that changed in June 2019 when Zimbabwe banned local trading in foreign currencies.

The move turned out to be catastrophic for artisanal miners when Fidelity began paying them 55 per cent in US dollars and the remaining in worthless RTGS dollars.

Instead of selling gold to Fidelity, the miners began channelling it to informal markets, leading to smuggling.

Our investigations showed that most of the gold was smuggled to China, India and the Middle East through middlemen and syndicates operating out of Harare, Mashava, Bindura, Mazowe and Mutare.

The surreptitious milking of Zimbabwe's biggest natural resource was wrecking the country's economy while having a devastating impact on the environment.

I published my findings independently in *Gulf News* while my teammates published theirs in *The Mail* and *The Guardian*.

In September 2020, environment groups in Zimbabwe presented our reports in the Cabinet, which subsequently banned riverbed and alluvial mining and directed holders of mining titles to obtain environmental clearance.

I hope to revisit Zimbabwe someday and explore its landscape, wildlife and culture. I wonder if things have improved at the place where we stayed. I remember asking their receptionist-cum-manager if he could arrange some water so that I could bathe. Half an hour later, he returned with a bucket that was two-thirds empty. 'How am I supposed to take a bath with this little water,' I asked, staring at the bucket.

The manager/receptionist seemed unfazed by my concern and responded with a confident smile. He pulled out a towel, soaked it in the water and made a vigorous gesture of scrubbing it around his underarms. 'Sponge bath, sir,' he said with a grin as he continued his demonstration, scrubbing his arms and legs with the damp towel. It was like watching a pro athlete warm up before a game.

Despite the absurdity of the situation, I couldn't help but applaud when he finished. 'Bravo!' I said clapping.

The manager/receptionist, grinning from ear to ear, basked in the unexpected applause. His confident demeanour remained intact, as if he had just received a standing ovation at a grand theatre performance.

I often chuckle at the memory and think no matter the state of that rundown resort, one thing's for sure—that receptionist's unforgettable charm and resourcefulness will forever be etched in my mind.

The Great Kashmir Bluff

As our private jet soared over the snow-capped peaks of the Himalayas, I found myself entranced by the stunning view of Kashmir. The landscape was something out of a dream, with its rugged, majestic mountains and lush valleys stretching out as far as the eye could see. But as we approached our destination, a sense of unease began to creep up on me.

It was March 2022, and I was part of a delegation from the UAE that had purportedly come to the strife-torn region to explore investment opportunities. If you remember reading about the much-publicised visit, you might assume it was a business trip. It was anything but.

Most members of our thirty-something strong group were nothing more than pawns in a game of chess. For over two years, I have carried this tale of deceit within me. I can no longer keep it to myself even if it means losing friends and facing potential consequences.

So let me start from the beginning.

In August 2019, the Indian government led by Indian Prime Minister Narendra Modi took the controversial and, some might argue, ill-advised action of revoking Article 370 of the Constitution, which had granted special autonomous status to the state of Jammu and Kashmir for seventy years.

The move was met with widespread protest from Kashmiris, who saw it as a violation of their rights and an attack on their identity. In response, the government imposed an intense military lockdown on the region, deploying thousands of troops and imposing a curfew. Communication lines were cut off, and anyone expressing dissent was arrested, leading to months of unimaginable hardship for the people of Kashmir.

In an attempt to restore its image and attract foreign investment, the government began a propaganda campaign to portray a façade of normalcy. One element of this effort was to highlight supposed interest from businesses in the UAE.

Organising the trip to Kashmir was a simple task for the Indian government. They found a willing collaborator in Bal Krishen, an Indian billionaire based in Dubai to whom I was introduced by my lawyer friend Farhat Khan.

Bala, as he is fondly known, had risen from humble beginnings as a dishwasher to become the CEO of Century Financial, a prominent global financial services provider.

Originally from Doda, a small district in Jammu and Kashmir, Bala's personal ties to the region made him an attractive partner for the government. Frankly, he didn't have much of a choice.

Despite his immense success, Bala had long been under scrutiny from Indian investigative agencies, leaving him vulnerable to manipulation.

Prior to the abrogation of Article 370, Indian intelligence officials had conducted searches at Safa Valley, a project of Bala's construction company in Jammu, and had fined him $60,000 for tax evasion. In September 2019, the Anti-Corruption Bureau probed him for illegal constructions and encroachment upon state land. And in March 2020, the Enforcement Directorate raided his offices and seized fixed deposits and sovereign gold bonds worth

$3.3 million for violating the Foreign Exchange Management Act (FEMA).

I can't say for sure whether these crackdowns played a role, but during Expo 2020 Dubai, Bala made a surprising announcement: a $100 million investment in Jammu and Kashmir. He signed an MoU to build three hotels in the union territory. I remember covering the event for *Khaleej Times* in January 2022. The get-together was presided over by Manoj Sinha, the lieutenant governor of Jammu and Kashmir, and Ranjan Thakur, the principal secretary of the industries and commerce department. Amid thunderous claps, the document was signed in the presence of Aman Puri, the consul general of India in Dubai.

Bala gathered several Emirati friends at the Oberoi Business Bay hotel to keep the Indian government in good spirits. But if he thought he had earned their approval, he was mistaken. Shortly after the $100 million announcement, the government exerted pressure, insisting that he organise a trip of Emirati businessmen to visit Kashmir.

Bala initially tried to wriggle out of the situation, but in the end, he couldn't evade the demand. He chartered a private jet and took a thirty-six-member delegation, of which I was a part, to the region. The group comprised roughly a dozen Emiratis, and several Indian expats, including Ashok Kotecha of BAPS Swaminarayan Temple in Abu Dhabi. Among the passengers there was a businessman from Saudi Arabia and another from Hong Kong. For most people on the trip, it had nothing to do with investments; it was just a fancy all-expenses paid vacation to a place called the 'paradise on earth'.

We flew from DWC World Central Airport at 9.30 a.m. on 20 March and arrived in Srinagar around 5 p.m. It took us over five hours to reach our destination as we did not have permission to fly over Pakistan. It was my first time aboard a chartered plane, and I absolutely loved it. No one even asked us to fasten our seat belts as we frolicked about the cabin, indulging in the choicest food served by the friendly cabin crew, who hailed from Russia.

As the plane taxied down the runway, the Emirati delegates eagerly pulled out their cell phones, hoping to get a signal and check their messages. Their faces fell when I explained that only SIM cards purchased within Kashmir work due to security reasons.

'What, no network? How can anyone do business here when you can't even use your phone?' lamented an Emirati man.

Senior Indian government officials were present at the airport to greet us upon our arrival. We were quickly bundled into waiting cars and started our journey through a heavily guarded convoy of seventeen black SUVs, escorted by armed bodyguards, armoured police, military vehicles, ambulances and mine sweepers. Leading the way was a bomb jammer. It was an unnerving spectacle. As we drove, the Emirati sitting next to me in the back attempted to roll down the window and enjoy the fresh mountain air. He fiddled with the buttons on the door, but nothing happened. 'Excuse me, how do I roll down the window?' he asked. The driver, watching the scene from the rear-view mirror, sensed the confusion and replied, 'I have BP, sir.' The Emirati looked puzzled. 'Wallah, but you're so young and fit. Do you smoke?'

The driver chuckled. 'No, sir, it is not what you think. I meant that the windows won't roll down as the car is BP as in bulletproof. We are prime targets.'

We drove in silence for the rest of the journey.

As we passed through checkpoints barricaded by sandbags, bunkers and razor wires every few kilometres, my heart ached for the residents who faced this daily ordeal just to go about their lives. Kashmir is undeniably beautiful, but it holds an unexplainable sadness in the atmosphere, a sorrow beyond words.

Our stay in Kashmir was arranged by Bala at Lalit Palace Hotel, an impressive palace-like structure that offered all the amenities one could wish for. To ensure we stay connected, we were also provided with local SIM cards. Later that evening, we were hosted for a dinner by Ranjan Thakur, whom I had briefly met in Dubai during the signing of the $100 million MoU.

The following day, we set out on a two-hour drive to Pahalgam. I had seen the town only in movies. It is far more picturesque.

Driving on the Jammu–Srinagar Highway, we briefly slowed down at Pulwama where forty CRPF personnel were killed in a suicide bombing on Valentine's Day in 2019.

As we arrived in Pahalgam, we were greeted by a frenzy of media personnel. They thrust their microphones in front of the Emirati delegates and snapped photos and videos of them donning traditional clothing against stunning backdrops. For the Indian government, images from our carefully curated tour were like gold, serving as a powerful tool to showcase the region's supposed normalcy and stability.

In the evening, we were invited to a dinner hosted by Lt Governor Manoj Sinha at Raj Bhawan, his official residence. The meal featured a wide array of traditional dishes including the famed wazwan, but to be frank, I didn't like it much.

On the third day of our trip, we were chauffeured to a business event at the Sher-e-Kashmir International Convention Centre, where a banner hung proudly, welcoming the Gulf delegation for the Gulf Investment Summit. Lt Governor Manoj Sinha himself joined us and urged the delegates to consider investing in the region. Bala delivered a rousing speech while Ranjan Thakur conducted a PowerPoint presentation showcasing the potential for business growth in Jammu and Kashmir. Thakur even presented slides demonstrating how Kashmir had a lower crime rate than other Indian states. It was rather amusing, considering we were sitting in one of the most heavily guarded places in the world, to see Thakur presenting slides demonstrating Kashmir's lower crime rate compared to other Indian states. An Emirati man sitting next to me sniggered in my ear and asked, 'Has he always been like this or is today a special day?'

Over tea that evening, I asked the delegates if they would consider investing in Kashmir. One of them looked at me like I had suggested jumping off from Jebel Jais. 'Invest in what? Bullet-proof car business?' he exclaimed. Another shook his head, 'Do I look stupid to you?' The third delegate replied, 'I am just a simple salaried employee. I don't know why the media thinks I'm some kind of hotshot businessman.' His apprehension was warranted. Arab men strolling in kandoura through Kashmir were as rare a sight as spotting a snow leopard in the Sahara. The Indian media pursued them relentlessly, thrusting microphones into their bewildered faces wherever they went. Whatever words spilled from their mouths became instant headlines.

A huge shock awaited us when we saw the following day's newspaper. There, splashed across the front page, were pictures of Manoj Sinha posing with the delegates, proudly declaring that investments worth over Rs 70,000 crores ($8.4 billion) were expected to flow into the region in the next six months.

Not a single member of the delegation had pledged a single dirham towards investment in Kashmir.

The initial amusement among the delegates soon turned to consternation as Indian media began to report that their visit coincided with Pakistan's hosting of an Organisation of Islamic Cooperation (OIC) meeting. The OIC, a formidable organisation comprising fifty-seven Islamic nations, including the UAE, had been a vocal critic of India's actions in Kashmir. The insinuation that the delegates had timed their visit to Kashmir during the OIC meeting was viewed as an implicit endorsement of India's stance on the disputed region. This revelation left the delegates furious, with some anxiously fearing that their governments might reprimand them for inadvertently causing a diplomatically embarrassing incident.

For many of the delegates, it felt as if they had been caught in a political game. The bitter realisation that they had been used for someone else's gain was a hard pill to swallow, and its bitter aftertaste lingered with them long after they had left Kashmir.

I Am ISO-certified. Huh?

There are many award-winning journalists out there. But ever heard of a journalist with an ISO 9001 certificate?

In February 2017, my colleague Abhishek Sen Gupta and I got that distinguished honour when we became the first and perhaps the last journalists in the world to bag the globally recognised stamp of quality.

Usually, the ISO 9001 certificate is awarded to select companies only after a detailed audit and compliance survey. The process takes weeks if not months. But we got the ISO certificate in three days and that too for 'our' company that had been long shut for fraud.

So how did this happen? Before you read further, bear in mind that the line between legitimate investigation and entrapment is fuzzy. Journalists who disguise identities or use hidden cameras are frowned upon.

I am not too much of a fan of sting operations either. But there are times when subterfuge and deception are the only way to get a public interest story. How else could I have smoked out the evil geniuses behind Wisdom Jobs, Axact and some of the other fraudsters? So when I got a tip that ISO certificates were up for sale, I immediately decided to dig into my time-tested repertoire.

We decided to sting the Bureau of Assessment Services (BAS), one of Dubai's most reputed agencies authorised to issue ISO certificates.

The plan was to approach the agency posing as the owners of a company desperately looking for an ISO certificate and see if they took the bait.

But there were two problems. First, we needed some credentials to prove that we owned a company. Second, we needed $3,000 to purchase the certificate. The latter problem was more vexing as our newspaper initially refused to give the money.

'ISO certificates for sale, here in Dubai?' Abdul Hamid asked incredulously when I pitched the story to him after work hours.

'Yes, sir, and we need money to show it can be bought.'

At that time Dubai was getting ready to host Expo 2020 and many companies were trying to acquire an ISO certificate as it gave them an unrivalled edge over competitors while bidding for lucrative tenders.

I explained how the Expo had suddenly fuelled the demand for ISO certificates.

Abdul Hamid remained unconvinced.

'But how will you do it? You don't own a company.'

'Leave that to me,' I said. 'We just want you to sanction the money.'

'And you will get this certificate in three days.'

'Yes, sir, we hope to.'

He shook his head. 'We are running into losses and you want me to give you $3,000 for a story you aren't even sure of. How will I justify that?'

'Consider this as an investment. This story will be the talk of the town,' I reasoned.

After three days of haggling, he reluctantly agreed to part with $1,500.

'Ask for a discount,' he said as I left his room.

Abhishek was hanging around outside.

'Did he agree?'

'Yes, but for $1,500,' I replied. 'He said we should ask for a discount.'

'That's great,' Abhishek beamed. His enthusiasm is infectious. 'This means he's given his nod to do the story. We will make for the shortfall from our pockets but let's ask for a discount first. Who knows, they might agree.'

The next step was to find a company and pose as its owners.

Luckily we had trade licence copies of dozens of runaway firms from the GAD scams.

We picked up a defunct company called Van Der Hurst which had downed shutters and disappeared after defrauding scores of traders.

Once we had the documents ready, we rang up BAS.

We told them that we had tendered for a contract and needed the ISO certificate urgently to strengthen our bid. And since we were still a fledgling company we could give them only $1,500.

BAS fell for the ruse.

The following day, we visited their office and handed them the supporting documents and $1,500 in cold cash.

The arrow had left the bow. Now all we could do was wait. A thousand thoughts crossed our mind in those three days. What if BAS found out about us and alerted the authorities?

Using the personal information of another person to make unauthorised transactions amounted to identity theft—a grave criminal offence that can be considered a misdemeanour or felony under the UAE laws. Punishment for the crime can result in a federal sentence of three years in federal prison, community service, probation and a harsh monetary fine.

I avoided walking past Abdul Hamid's cabin, fearing he might spot me and seek an update.

Three days later we got the call we had been waiting for. 'We have good news, sir,' a BAS manager chirped. 'Your certificate is ready, you could come anytime to collect it,' he said.

I took a deep breath and flashed a victory sign at Abhishek. He jumped from his seat and hugged me tightly, almost knocking the phone from my hand.

'Can we come now?' I asked the BAS manager.

'Sure, sir,' the man replied. 'We will be waiting for you.'

Soon Abhishek and I were scampering up the stairs of a modest building in Karama where BAS's office was located.

We made no efforts to conceal our glee as BAS staff posed with us for pictures while handing over the certificate.

'Congratulations, sir, now you are ISO-certified,' the manager said, shaking my hand warmly. 'You can have it framed for your office and impress your clients.'

'Yes, this certificate will go a long way,' I said.

I remember the wonderful feeling of elation and relief that swept over us when we left their office with a scoop in hand.

In a real sense, getting a certificate like ISO on the sly is like earning a prestigious MBA degree without ever going to a business school.

As we walked out with the ISO certificate, that's exactly what we felt. We were now eligible to bid for tenders. Imagine if Van Der Hurst were for real.

Abhishek suggested we celebrate the occasion with a hearty meal. It was around lunchtime so we headed to Kulcha King next door and binged on soft leavened Indian flatbreads filled with assorted veggies and cheese.

The next day, Abhishek got BAS to send us an audit report. The thirteen-page document detailed how BAS officers visited our facility to assess our operations and found it to be fully compliant with ISO standards on various parameters.

Of course, none of this happened—and it couldn't have, even if the auditors had wanted, because Van Der Hurst didn't exist.

The audit report was a one-size-fits-all template that certificate mills like BAS had been blatantly giving out to clients for years. In the process, no accreditation guidelines were adhered to; you pay them, they print you a certificate. What they lacked in morals, they simply made up for with the toner.

There are nearly forty government-accredited certification bodies in the UAE. We found out that nearly one-third of them will issue a certificate to just about anyone who wants it.

We randomly called two agencies.

'ISO certificate? No problem. We will give it. It will take three days and cost Dh5,000. So when can we meet?' said a Filipina sales executive of a company we found out about after a simple online search for 'ISO in UAE'.

Another agency promised a discount as they had an 'attractive promotion'.

Curiously, some of these accredited bodies were not even based in the UAE. They don't necessarily have to be. Their agents fly into the country on visit visas every few months to peddle ISO certificates in industrial areas like Al Quoz and Jebel Ali.

'We start from the moment we set foot here,' said the staff of one such agency from New Delhi.

On 16 February 2017, we splashed the story on the front page with a picture of us holding the ISO certificate. 'We are a bogus company yet we got an ISO certificate,' screamed the headline.

We had acquired the certificate by devious means but it was just as bona fide as those obtained by top government institutions and corporate groups using genuine methods for up to ten times the amount.

Every year, roughly Dh20 million worth of dodgy ISO certificates are issued in the Middle East with no audits or checks.

Most entities have acquired them knowingly but then there are many who have taken them unwittingly as they are not aware of what ISO certification entails.

Our story shook the certification industry. It also caused a huge uproar in government circles.

Within days, Dubai Municipality's Dubai Accreditation Centre (DAC) withdrew the accreditation of BAS and launched a probe into the company

BAS was also ordered to immediately withdraw all certificates issued by them, including the one given to us.

I had great fun receiving a phone call from their receptionist. 'Is that Van De Hurst?' a woman asked sheepishly.

'No, this is the newspaper that busted you.'

She ignored me but I thought I heard a stifled sigh.

'I am from BAS, and we need to retract the certificate issued to you.'

'Oh really?' I responded. 'But why would you do that, dear? Didn't we meet all the requirements? Your audit report says we fared pretty well on all the parameters. Did we not?'

'Yes, sir, but there are some technical problems,' she explained

'Like fraud, you mean?' I quipped.

'No, sir, there are other issues, so we are also refunding the money. We will send someone to your office to collect the certificate and hand back the money.'

Our mission was accomplished. We didn't need the certificate. I bet Abdul Hamid would have been very happy to get back the $1,500. But an inner voice told me to politely decline the offer.

'Ma'am, we can't return the certificate. In any case it was not issued to us. You granted it to Van Der Hurst. So call them,' I said before hanging up. I didn't want to embarrass her further.

She was just doing what she was told.

It's not immediately clear how many certificates were issued by BAS in the UAE but some estimates suggested that their number was over 1,500. All of them were now worthless.

In September 2018, our story went on to bag the *Rajasthan Patrika*'s KC Kulish International Award for Excellence in Journalism. I flew to New Delhi with Eram to receive a certificate and medal from General Bipin Rawat, then India's chief of the army staff, at a ceremony at the Taj Hotel. The award is displayed in my trophy cabinet along with our prized ISO 9001: 2015 certificate.

Dubai's Bajrangi Bhaijaan

In July 2015, an Indian fiction drama starring Salman Khan took the box office by storm.

Bajrangi Bhaijaan told the story of a Hindu man who takes a mute Pakistani Muslim girl, separated in India from her parents, back to her homeland.

In December 2016, I also attracted Bollywood attention when one of my stories reunited an Indian mother, Zainab Fawad, with her four-year-old twins against all odds.

Mustafa and Muzzamil had been stuck in Pakistan for over two-and-a half years following a catastrophic turn of events. There was no telling if Zainab could ever meet her boys given the thorny relationship between India and Pakistan and Zainab's own pathetic situation.

In addition to being separated from her children, she was also homeless and broke.

Out of desperation she once tried to kill herself.

The movie was to be directed by Ribhu Dasgupta who made some forgettable movies like *Te3n* and *The Girl on the Train*. Arslan Goni, Sam Fernandes and Rajat Shrivastav were to produce it.

Goni, who's currently dating Hrithik Roshan's ex-wife Suzanne Khan, flew down to Dubai with script writer Roopa Desai after he came across my report.

We had several rounds of meetings with Goni who then got Zainab to sign a contract.

In exchange she got a few thousand dollars.

Sadly, the project never took off. It would have been really good if it did because it had all the elements of a pulse-quickening drama: love, betrayal, heartbreak, separation and reunion, played across three countries.

It was rumoured that Vidya Balan or Kareena Kapoor would play Zainab.

I wonder who would have played me. Eram thought Irrfan Khan was best suited for the role but my daughters felt someone suave and handsome was needed to portray me.

I remember how I met Zainab. It was a crisp morning in Dubai on 3 November 2016. I had just switched on my office desktop when a message popped up on Facebook messenger.

'Mazhar bhai, I desperately need your help. I tried to hang myself from the ceiling yesterday. Please call me when you see this. I may succeed next time.'

At the end of the message was a UAE cell phone number.

I called it right away. The woman who answered the call said she was from India and her name was Zainab Fawad.

Two minutes into the conversation, I realised that she was truly in bad shape.

'I have only half a packet of biscuits left. I tried to hang myself yesterday but the thoughts of my little boys stopped me … A neighbour told me about you. She said you write stories about people needing help so I am reaching out to you,' she said.

'Where are you?'

'In a shared accommodation in Al Nahda, near Sahara Centre,' she said. 'But I don't know for how long … I haven't paid my rent for two months.'

The following day was my weekend. I asked Zainab if she could meet me at Tim Hortons in Sharjah's Al Majaz waterfront.

It wasn't far from her place.

She kept quiet.

'Could you confirm it?'

Silence.

'Zainab, are you there?'

'Yes, Mazhar bhai, it's just that I have only Dh20 with me. Will you pay the return fare?'

'Yes, I will take care of it.'

Zainab arrived dot at 10 a.m. She was a fair-complexioned woman in her mid-forties with light brown sunken eyes and a weary expression.

We ordered croissants, bagels and coffee as Zainab began talking.

An ethnic Persian member of the Zoroastrian community in Gujarat, Zainab was an arts graduate who came to Dubai in 2003 looking for a job.

Four years later, she embraced Islam and married Pakistani expat Fawad whom she met while working at a company in Jebel Ali. In 2012, the couple moved to an apartment in Al Muhaisnah but marital bliss didn't last long. It worsened after Zainab delivered twins, Mustafa and Muzammil.

'We started fighting over petty things. He became distant and started coming home late,' Zainab recalled.

Unknown to her, Fawad had opened an events management company in her name.

She found out about it when she went to a police station in late 2014 to report a missing wallet but was arrested as the events company had defaulted on payments.

Bouncing cheques was a criminal offence in the UAE before 2 January 2022.

Zainab spent nearly a month in prison. By the time she got out, her world had crashed around her.

Fawad had divorced her and remarried. He had also taken the twins—both Indian passport-holders—to Pakistan and wouldn't answer her calls.

With nowhere to go, Zainab roughed it out in airport waiting areas and survived on handouts. An elderly man offered shelter but molested her.

Between July and September 2015, she was arrested two more times for unpaid court fines and for a case filed by the landlord of their Al Muhaisnah home whose lease was also in her name.

Zainab was now an illegal resident. Her visa had long expired. She couldn't renew it as her passport was with Sharjah Court since 2013. She had pledged it as a guarantee to secure the release of her husband in a defamation case filed by an Arab.

Zainab's sole concerns were her children.

'I am going insane without my kids. Please help me,' she pleaded with folded hands as tears ran down her cheeks.

A heavy-set Arab man sitting across our table at Tim Hortons stared at me.

'Look, Zainab,' I said, 'you have nothing to eat and nowhere to live. You can't return to India as your passport is with the court. You need to straighten your life first. What will you do if you get your children back? At least they are safe in Pakistan. You need to take one thing at a time.'

A mother's love is a force like no other. It sees no reasoning.

We chatted for an hour. Zainab remained unconvinced.

As we stepped out of the cafe, she dug into her purse and pulled out two stamp size photographs. 'My darlings,' she said and broke down once again. The human side of me wanted to comfort her, the journalist side wanted to capture her anguish. Eventually, the latter prevailed. I took out my smartphone and clicked a few pictures.

When Zainab regained her composure, I walked down to a nearby ATM, drew out Dh1,000 and gave it to her. 'This will help you get by till the time we publish your story,' I said.

'Do you think your report will help me get back my sons?'

I didn't want to give her any false hope.

'Frankly, I don't know,' I said. 'My job is to report a story to the best of my ability. What happens afterwards is beyond my control.'

We published a close-up of Zainab on the cover, hoping it would tug at readers' hearts.

The response it generated was beyond our wildest imagination.

In less than twenty-four hours, hundreds of readers reached out to us from all over the world. They clogged our phone lines and inundated our emails and WhatsApp service with help offers. Scores showed up at our office. The only time I saw such a massive outpouring of support was in 2013 when I ran a story about a man who turned up at Bur Dubai station with his wife and two minor kids and begged the duty incharge to put them in jail so that they don't starve.

The man's wife was eight months pregnant. Her name was also Zainab. The similarities don't end here. She was also from India and had embraced Islam to marry a Pakistani.

The family had fallen on bad times and had been sleeping on pavements on empty stomachs.

As a last resort, they borrowed Dh30 from a friend and took a cab to our office. Our story changed their fortune overnight.

In less than a week, Zainab Fawad's life had taken a dramatic turn.

Readers reached out to us from as far as the UK, the US, Saudi Arabia, Bahrain, Kuwait, India, Canada, Pakistan and Oman.

In the UAE, many drove down to Zainab's shared accommodation in Sharjah from Abu Dhabi and Al Ain. An Emirati man gave her Dh30,000. An Egyptian settled her dues with the landlord.

People gave not just food and money but also moral and legal assistance.

I stayed up several nights to respond to thousands of messages that came on email and the newspaper's WhatsApp number.

Social worker Juhi Yasmeen Khan, lawyer Farhat Khan and a group of women from a local NGO contacted the India and Pakistan embassies to help Zainab complete the complex paperwork that could pave the way for her boys to be flown to Dubai.

The time finally came at 7.45 a.m. on Friday, 30 December 2016.

As the electronic bulletin board at Terminal 3 of Dubai International Airport flashed the arrival of Emirates Flight EK 605 from Karachi, Zainab pinched herself to make sure it was all real.

I had picked her on my way to the airport where Juhi and Farhat were already waiting with goodie bags.

A few minutes later I captured the moment when Mustafa and Muzammil showed up at the airport's meet-and-greet area and Zainab dashed down the hallway carrying balloons in her outstretched arms.

'My darlings, my darlings, oh how I missed you!' she exclaimed as she kneeled down and hugged the children in a tight embrace, bursting into tears.

The kids smiled coyly and soon busied themselves with Superman and Spiderman toys that Zainab had brought with her.

As journalists, we do many stories but nothing is more endearing than seeing a mother reunite with her children.

The story of their reunion made headlines as far as India and Pakistan. It also reached listeners in their cars and homes after popular local radio jockey Kritika Rawat put Zainab and me on air.

Zainab said her story was an encouragement to every woman never to lose hope.

Her dogged determination inspired another Dubai-based divorcee to resume her fight against her ex-husband who had kidnapped their daughters and flown with them to Pakistan never to return.

I first wrote about Maimouna Liskauskaite from Lithuania, in 2011, shortly after her husband of seven years took their daughters out on the pretext of taking them to Safa Park but instead bundled them onto a plane to his homeland and disappeared.

The girls Mariam, seven, Aisha, five, and Amna, three, were all Lithuanian passport holders.

Maimouna was still reeling from the shock when she was couriered divorce papers from Pakistan and her in-laws asked her to vacate their Jumeirah villa.

It would take seven years of relentless torment and heartache before Maimouna would see her daughters again.

Maimouna, formerly known as Edita, met Dubai-born Jamshed Siddique in the mid-1990s when he came to Lithuania to study medicine. In January 2003, she embraced Islam and married Jamshed who gave her a new name, Maimouna.

Betrayed and homeless, Maimouna was a wreck when I met her in April 2011, shortly after her daughters were taken away.

Thankfully she got a job at a preschool. In her spare time, she used to make cute bracelets. She gifted a few to my daughters when she came home on Eid. We tried to offer her money but she graciously refused.

Maimouna applied for a visit visa to Pakistan many times but each time it was rejected.

The setbacks didn't waver her resolve.

My story on Zainab gave her new vigour. 'I am going to get a Pakistan visa no matter what it takes and knock on the door of the Supreme Court of Pakistan for justice,' she told me.

Initially, Maimouna had approached the Lahore High Court. But when the court dismissed her petition, she appealed to the Supreme Court in Islamabad.

Pakistan's highest court heard her plea after office hours and ordered the police to present her daughters, then thirteen, eleven and nine years, before the court.

Maimouna was subsequently granted interim custody of her children.

She called me from Pakistan to break the news.

'I am the happiest woman in the world today. Praise be to Allah who made this possible,' she shouted.

Hordes of media gathered outside the court building as a three-judge bench headed by the Chief Justice of Pakistan, Saqib Nisar, heard the petition.

Justice Nisar asked the girls if they had met their mother. The eldest, Mariam, responded: 'I don't even know her.'

When the bench directed court officials to arrange a meeting between the children and their mother, Mariam insisted her father be present.

'This is your upbringing?' asked Justice Nisar. He then turned towards Jamshed. 'You have poisoned their minds,' he said.

The court said that they had no sympathy for Siddique.

'Why should we not lodge an FIR against the man?' Justice Nisar asked.

'It is an established fact that the father kidnapped his daughters from Dubai,' the bench said.

The court also ordered to lodge a police complaint against Siddique but retracted the order after his counsel pleaded for mercy.

I called Maimouna after she shared a picture of herself enjoying a meal with her daughters.

'Alhamdolillah, my prayers have been finally answered. I am rediscovering the joy of motherhood all over again. Like Zainab, I also went through hell but never lost hope. Our stories are similar. We were both abandoned by our husbands and separated from our children. So I thought if an Indian woman can get her kids back from Pakistan then why can't I?

'For seven long years, my daughters have been living away from me, completely devoid of motherly love, so it's going to take a while before they feel for me the way I feel for them.'

Back in Dubai, Zainab was preparing to return to India with her boys on a one-way ticket. Her life was back on track but one last hurdle remained. Her passport remained stuck in Sharjah.

The Consulate General of India in Dubai wrote to the Ministry of Foreign Affairs' Sharjah office, requesting them to repatriate Zainab and her children to India. However, nothing came of it. Undaunted, Zainab filed an appeal before a Sharjah court requesting them to release her passport on humanitarian grounds. This time, the court considered her appeal and released her passport.

Eram and I went to the airport to see off the family.

'Thank you, Mazhar bhai, for everything,' she said, flashing their boarding passes. 'I had many ups and downs in life but as they say all's well that ends well.'

But not all stories of parental child abduction have ended happily in Dubai.

Hasan was still being breastfed when he and his four-year-old brother were snatched away from their Pakistani mother and flown to India by their estranged dad.

'I am living a nightmare,' the young woman told me when I met her after the incident in early 2011.

Similarly, Chinara Kassymova, a Kazakh mother in Dubai, kept agonising over the fate of daughter Mariam and son Mohammad for four years when her Syrian husband bundled them away to the northern Syrian city of Aleppo, without her knowledge in 2016.

Mariam was seven years old at that time while Mohammad had just turned three.

Chinara found out about them only in 2020 when her husband was arrested in Sudan following an Interpol alert.

Parental child abduction is a huge concern in the UAE because of the country's large expat community. A parent or grandparent could face legal action if they abduct their own child or grandchild from the person who has legal guardianship or custody as established by a UAE judicial decision. But since the UAE is not a signatory to the Hague Convention on the Civil Aspects of International Child Abduction, foreign governments cannot enforce their laws here. Figures on parental child abduction in the UAE are hard to come by but local lawyers reckon they could be in the hundreds. But dry statistics alone don't quite tell the story as they are unable to capture a mother's pain or portray the horror and tragedies such incidents leave in their wake.

The King and I: My Showdown with Michael Jackson

This is easily my favourite story. No matter how many times I tell it, I still feel excited about it. It's been over a decade and a half and yet it hasn't lost any of its appeal. Understandably so, whether I am delivering a talk to journalism students or out at a party, the conversation invariably veers to my encounter with Michael Jackson.

To say that I met the King of Pop would be an understatement because mine was no ordinary meeting. I had a full-blown showdown with Michael Jackson. I said a few nasty things, and he held nothing back.

My bizarre story dates back to the year 2005, 12 November to be precise.

Still new to Dubai, I was window-shopping at the Ibn Battuta Mall with my wife and daughters, Unaiza and Shazia, aged eight and four then, when a strange scene caught our attention.

Just outside Magrudy's bookstore at the mall's Egypt Court, we saw a young woman chasing an abaya-clad figure, hurling expletives as she ran.

The fleeting figure couldn't go far, losing balance and tripping over, as I arrived on the scene.

It was 7.15 p.m.

'Catch him, catch him, there's a man inside that abaya,' the woman shrieked, pointing an accusing finger at the cornered figure.

'A man? Are you sure?' I asked.

'Absolutely, and he was in the women's toilet,' she replied. 'He was applying make-up and he tried to sneak away when I saw him. When I tried to stop him, he attacked me. Don't let him go, please, I am calling the police.'

The young woman, later identified as a Tunisian teacher, was hysterical.

Gingerly, I approached the figure, who was now joined by three children. 'Hey, you, is that true … I mean that you're a man and not a woman?' I asked. There was no reply. I thought I hadn't been heard, so I stepped closer and repeated the question. Silence.

'Well, if what the woman there is saying is true, then you're in serious trouble,' I explained. 'She's called the police and they will be here any minute,' I said.

'All right, we'll see,' the figure snapped back in a male voice.

'You're a man, of course,' I said, 'and she tells me you were in the women's loo?'

He seemed unperturbed.

'I was. I can go wherever I want to,' he replied.

'Even to the women's loo?'

'Yeah, anywhere.'

I don't remember what he said next, but there was some mention about 'respecting' his 'privacy' and him being at the 'wrong place at the wrong time'.

He must be high, I thought.

'Respect your privacy!' I shot back. 'You've violated the privacy of women by going into their toilet and now you talk about your privacy. Who do you think you are?'

'And who are you? Go away, you freaking son of a bitch,' he retorted.

Just then, the young woman took out a cell phone and started clicking pictures. The figure shouted something unintelligible and darted into Magrudy's.

The children followed him.

By now, a small crowd of onlookers was beginning to mill around the place. Among them was a black woman wearing a long coat and an oversized hat.

'Please let him go,' she pleaded with the young woman, who was now joined by two male friends, one of whom wore a grey suit.

There had already been enough action for a news report.

So, at 7.45 p.m, I called my editor Nirmala Jansen. Since *XPRESS* had not yet been launched then, she alerted the news desk at *Gulf News*, our sister publication.

A man wearing an abaya caught in the women's loo! It was an interesting story, all right. But it wasn't a major story yet.

In the next few hours, it would be one of the biggest celebrity-sighting stories ever reported.

At Ibn Battuta, events were unfolding fast.

At 8.30 p.m., a visibly alarmed European man, who apparently represented the mall management, came running with security guards and ordered the crowd to disperse.

I found this strange, because the guards did nothing to the man in the abaya, who was now sauntering around the bookstore, picking up books at random and casually flipping through them with insouciant indifference.

I went up to the mall management's representative, identified myself and demanded to know what was happening.

He looked at my business card.

'So, the press is already here. That was quick. I am sorry I cannot comment on the situation,' he said, looking very flustered.

At that point, I made my second call to Nirmala. 'Hey, this abaya guy must be someone important because they aren't doing anything to him; instead they are shooing us away.'

I had a cheap cell phone with a terrible camera.

I took out my analogue camera to capture the scene, but the guards wouldn't let me do so.

Around 9.30 p.m., the black woman in the oversized hat came up to me and said politely: 'I believe you're from the media. There has been a misunderstanding. It's being sorted out. We don't want any bad press, please.'

'That's fine, ma'am, but I need to know who he is.'

'Give me your number. I will check with him. If he deems it fit he will call you,' she said.

Now when I see photographs of Michael Jackson's long-time nanny Grace Rwaramba, I realise that it was her.

'All right,' I said, handing her my business card. She looked at it intently and rushed into Magrudy's. Minutes later my phone rang. It was an Etisalat number. I answered the call but the person on the other end kept quiet.

'Hello, hello,' I shouted into the receiver. 'You want to say something … hello …'

There was no response. A few seconds later the line went dead. What prompted Michael Jackson to call me and then hang up, I will never know.

Quickly, I scrolled down to my received calls list and dialled the last number. In the cordoned-off Magrudy's store, barely fifteen metres from where I stood, I saw the man in the abaya take out the ringing cell phone from his pocket and place it on a bookshelf. It was a Vertu, the most expensive phone in the world with prices starting at $6,000 for the basic model and $50,000 for the signature version.

Rich bloke. Probably the spoiled son of a rich sheikh, I thought.

Cops were now swarming around Egypt Court. There were many of them. No one was allowed inside the bookshop. The only people I saw being let in were a middle-aged Indian couple carrying some clothes. I suspect they might have been for Michael Jackson.

'Everything okay, ma'am?' I made an effort to strike up a conversation with the woman.

'Yes, yes,' she said smilingly before hurrying away. My wife and kids were getting impatient, but I wasn't moving until I had cracked the mystery.

An imprudent Bangladeshi guard eased my misery. 'Would you know who he is?' I asked him.

'No, sir, he looks like someone important. They are saying he is Mikil Jai Kishen. Have you heard of him?'

I froze.

'Michael Jackson? Did they say he was Michael Jackson?'

'Yes, sir, that is who they said he is, you know him?'

'Jesus Christ,' I muttered under my breath. All this while I had been talking to Michael Jackson without knowing it was him. And he even called me on my phone! My mind went blank.

From inside the bookshop, Michael Jackson watched the colour drain from my face. He knew I knew.

I rang up Nirmala. 'It's Michael Jackson! It's Michael Jackson,' I shouted excitedly as the enormity of the situation dawned on me.

I was still on the phone when Michael Jackson pointed me out to some policemen.

'That man is from the media and he knows who I am,' he must have told the cops, because in the next instant they were all over me.

I was whisked away to a corner where the cops took my cell phone, noted my personal details, and warned me not to report the incident.

'Michael Jackson is a guest,' a uniformed officer said. 'You write one word about it and there could be a big problem for you. Is that clear?'

'Yes, if I write about this, there could be problems for me,' I replied. 'I get that. Now, can I leave?'

'Not yet.'

I knew my family would be worried sick about me, but all I could do was wait. My cell phone rang incessantly in an officer's pocket.

I wondered if it was my wife or my editor or both.

The cops let me go at 11 p.m. They also returned my phone. It had eight missed calls from the news desk.

I rushed to the office of *Gulf News* on Sheikh Zayed Road. While my wife and children waited in our deserted canteen, I banged in some words, just before the deadline. My story appeared on the front page, without my byline, of course.

The following day, our report was picked up by several media entities.

I had Michael Jackson's Dubai number for two years. Before my phone book got accidentally deleted, I tried calling him many times.

His phone was usually off, and when it did ring occasionally, nobody answered.

After the incident, Michael Jackson's publicist issued a statement, saying the singer entered the women's restroom by mistake as he did not understand the Arabic sign on the door.

The statement didn't hold much water as the toilet signs at the Ibn Battuta Mall—as just about everywhere else in Dubai—are also in English. What's more, the restrooms have clear visuals indicating 'men' and 'women'. Michael Jackson went to the women's loo because he was wearing an abaya and in that dress he couldn't have possibly gone to the men's toilet!

I revisited the story in June 2009, shortly after Michael Jackson's death.

A salesman at Magrudy's told me that Michael Jackson and his children were in a small staff pantry at the bookstore before being escorted out through the fire exit.

Numerous exaggerated versions of the story have spread, including one where I supposedly knocked Michael Jackson with a single punch. It was during an Eid gathering in Dubai when the gracious host rose to his feet, catching everyone's attention with an unexpected announcement, 'We have among us a famous journalist who once rescued a woman from Michael Jackson by delivering a left jab to his face.' The man, enthusiastic to recreate the scene, positioned himself in the centre of the living room, hunched his shoulders like a boxer, and threw an uppercut into the air. 'Whoosh,' he exclaimed dramatically, 'and Michael Jackson found himself on all fours. Maz, could you share the real story?'

Salman, Shah Rukh, Amitabh

Shah Rukh Khan, Salman Khan, Amitabh Bachchan—each of these Bollywood superstars have been a subject of my stories but for all the wrong reasons.

Let me start with Salman. I never quite liked him as an actor so when my editor Nirmala Jansen asked me if I could cover an event where Salman was the chief guest, I tried to think of an excuse. I had covered showbiz for long enough in India to not be excited by Bollywood stars.

Bollywood stars are routinely invited to ribbon-cutting ceremonies in Dubai. They make for great photo-opportunities, not sit-in interviews.

Salman is a big star, yes, but he wasn't hot property back then. Remember, this was in 2005, long before the days of *Dabangg*, *Ek Tha Tiger* and *Bajrangi Bhaijaan*. Khan was out of favour, having delivered a series of duds like *Dil Ne Jise Apna Kaha*, *Lucky* and *Phir Milenge*.

His last solo hit was *Tere Naam* in 2003.

'What's the event about?' I asked, mildly interested.

'It's the launch of a new Belhasa centre.'

I nearly fell off my chair.

'You mean Belhasa, the driving institute?'

'Yes, that's what it says,' said Nirmala as she handed me the invite.

I rubbed my eyes in disbelief.

It was indeed the launch of Belhasa Driving School's new complex that Salman was to inaugurate. As PR disasters go I don't remember anything close to it.

Salman was the prime accused in a hit-and-run case and had spent seventeen days in jail.

He had run over four pavement dwellers in their sleep after a row with his then girlfriend and Bollywood diva Aishwarya Rai in 2003. One of the men died. Salman was reportedly drunk.

'Of course, I will cover the event,' I said.

The next day I found myself sitting diagonally behind Salman and his brother Arbaaz in a first floor hall at Belhasa Driving Centre where a press conference had been convened to announce Salman as the face of their safe driving campaign.

I reached out and gently tapped the actor's shoulder. He turned around with a quizzical look.

'Salman bhai,' I whispered in his ear, 'I don't quite get it.'

'Get what?'

'You and safe driving.'

'Shhh,' he said, putting his index finger on his lips.

I leaned forward. 'I will ask that question when you take the stage. Keep your answer ready.'

Salman was not amused. He turned back and gave me a murderous glare.

When he was called to the dais, Salman tried to pre-empt me by thanking the organisers and saying that he couldn't have dreamt of inaugurating a driving school in India after what happened.

'Sir, you have been made brand ambassador for safe driving. Do you think that's right?' I asked.

It was like announcing Bill Cosby as the face of child protection.

A hush fell over the room.

Salman baulked for a moment. Before he could respond, a woman jumped to his rescue. She was Sarah Belhasa, the host of the event and vice-chairman of the Belhasa Group.

Sarah was originally from India. It was rumoured that she joined Belhasa's Driving School as an instructor but rose through the ranks after marrying the company's Emirati CEO to become the conglomerate's vice chairman. 'Salman made a mistake; that doesn't mean that he doesn't deserve a second chance,' she said.

Fifteen years later, Sarah Belhasa would also make a grave mistake. She would never get a second chance. But that's another story for another day.

We published the Salman Khan story on the front page of *Gulf News*. The headline read: Actor Who Ran over Four, Inaugurates Driving School.

The story did not go down well with the Belhasas. The following morning, I got a call from the company's marketing manager followed by an angry call from Sarah herself.

'Salman is extremely angry,' she said. 'I am also deeply upset. Please do something to fix it.'

The story was already out. I couldn't have done anything to fix it even if I had wanted to.

In May 2015, Salman was found guilty of all charges of culpable homicide in the hit-and-run case. The Bombay Sessions Court concluded that he was driving under the influence of alcohol.

A few months later Salman was mysteriously acquitted of all charges due to lack of evidence.

The previous year he had visited Narendra Modi in Ahmedabad. The two shared lunch and then flew a kite together.

Salman also, uncharacteristically, lavished praises on Modi who was then the chief minister of Gujarat.

In 2014, Modi became the prime minister of India, riding on popular sentiments and BJP's evocative slogan '*Abki Baar Modi Sarkar*'.

Talking of sarkar, I am reminded of *Sarkar*, a Bollywood action thriller starring Amitabh Bachchan. In this film, which is inspired by *The Godfather*, Subhash Nagre (Amitabh Bachchan) is a mafia don who runs a parallel government in Mumbai where he has a huge following. When his enemies plot to kill him, his son Shankar Nagre (Abhishek Bachchan) takes charge.

Sarkar was released in Dubai but was pulled out of theatres after my story kicked up a row.

In the movie, a rival gang hires an Olympic gold medallist shooter from Dubai to kill Subhash Nagre but misses the target. Now, the Olympic gold for shooting was won by a member of Dubai's royal family in the double trap shooting event.

Sheikh Ahmed al-Maktoum had just become the first Olympic medallist from the UAE with his win in Athens in 2004. It was the UAE's biggest sporting achievement.

The portrayal of a hitman as an Olympic gold medallist was an insult to the shooting champion, I wrote. The movie was immediately taken out of theatres.

The matter was resolved only after Ravi Prakash, the spokesman for the film's director Ram Gopal Varma, tendered an apology.

'It was pure coincidence. In an attempt to make the script more interesting, the writer added this angle and we were completely unaware of the real-life context. We had absolutely no idea (Sheikh al-Maktoum) was also an Olympic gold medallist in shooting,' he said in the statement.

In 2011, national award-winning Bollywood director Madhur Bhandarkar had to also issue a statement when I called out the teaser of his movie *Heroine*.

The promotional clip showed protagonist Kareena Kapoor rebuking journalists saying: 'You people should be writing scripts. If a heroine buys a car, it's given to her by a businessman, if she goes to LA, she's getting plastic surgery done and, God forbid, if she goes to Dubai, you people make her a rate card.'

The suggestion that Bollywood female actors who visit Dubai end up as sex workers with price tags was sickening. Many felt it tarnished the image of Dubai by typecasting it as the hub of illegal and immoral activities.

Ironically, Bhandarkar had been honoured in Dubai for his contribution to Indian cinema the previous year.

Following my story, Bhandarkar got the reference to Dubai removed and issued a statement saying he did not mean to demean the Emirate.

Dubai is indeed very image-conscious and attempts to portray the city in a bad light are not taken kindly. Top celebs are routinely hired to promote Dubai. One such prominent name is actor Shah Rukh Khan who was named as the face of Dubai Tourism in 2022.

The actor is a part of Dubai tourism's Be My Guest campaign. He is the first Indian celebrity to be given the UAE ten-year golden visa. But long before that he was given a sprawling villa at The Palm Jumeirah by developer Nakheel.

So when Shah Rukh got embroiled in a dispute with Indian tax authorities for not declaring the house as a taxable property, we decided to show readers what his much talked about Dubai house looked like.

Until then, there had been no picture of the beachfront property in the public domain.

It would be a scoop if we got it first.

Our photographer Pankaj alias Paaji and I decided to give it a shot. All that we knew was that Shah Rukh's villa was on the K Frond, one of seventeen fronds on the palm-shaped archipelago's crown.

But getting inside the elite gated community on the manmade island was not easy. An African security guard cast an angry look at our Toyota Corolla and shooed us away dismissively even before we could reach the vehicle access control point (VACP).

As we drove back dejectedly, a question popped into my head. Would the guard have stopped us if we were driving a sports car?

'Certainly not,' said Paaji when I picked his brain.

'So let's do that,' I said.

A sly glint came to Paaji's eyes.

I used to do car reviews during those days and would get the latest models of top luxury cars to test drive.

I asked for a BMW sports convertible. It arrived two days later. Now we needed someone to sit in the front passenger seat, preferably an attractive woman who looked like she belonged to Palm Jumeirah. We didn't have to look beyond our glamorous colleague Muby Asger. She readily agreed. The next morning, we headed back to K Frond: me at the steering wheel, Muby on my side in an oversized Panama hat and Paaji in the back.

As the BMW approached the security booth, the African guard stiffened to attention. For a moment, I thought he would stop us. Instead, he flashed a salute and then opened the barrier using a remote device.

Soon, we were driving down the nearly empty K Frond streets looking for Shah Rukh's villa. It stood at the tail end of the road—a palatial white building numbered K39 with tiled rooftops and black metal fencing.

Small bushes ran along the perimeter of the backyard, with an open walkway onto the beach.

We parked the car and sneaked onto the private beach. I spotted a stray cleaner taking some laundry off the clothes rack. Black cane patio furniture surrounded a pool.

Paaji snapped a few pictures while Muby and I lazed around. Suddenly I saw two Indian security men striding towards us. 'Paaji, we have to get out of here,' I said. There was no way we could have outrun the guards. So I waved at them. 'Hello there,' I shouted, walking purposely in their direction. 'We seem to be a bit lost here. Can you help us?'

The guards hesitated. 'How did you come here?' asked one of them. 'Did I not tell you? We are lost,' I said helplessly.

'Where do you want to go?'

'To Frond J, we are already late. We have to deliver an invitation …'

'But this is Frond K.'

'Is it?' I said looking bewildered.

As the guards exchanged bemused glances, I shouted after Paaji and Muby. 'Hey guys, we are on the wrong frond, hurry up, let's go.'

We published exclusive pictures of Shah Rukh's villa the following week. We had trespassed into his house. It was a criminal offence punishable with a maximum of one year in jail or a fine of up to Dh5,000. Thankfully, Shah Rukh never pressed charges.

'Do you know why Shah Rukh's villa is on K Frond and is numbered 93?' Paaji asked as we sat in the office canteen days after the story.

'Humour me.'

'The K stands for Khan. King Khan.'

'And 93?'

'9 plus 3 equals 12. That's the sum of all the letters in the name Shah Rukh Khan.'

Secret Interview with Benazir Bhutto

In 1999, when General Pervez Musharraf took over Pakistan in a peaceful military coup, the country's biggest political parties, the Pakistan People's Party (PPP) and the Pakistan Muslim League (N), united to push for the return of civilian rule. At first, it seemed like they were making little progress. But in early 2006, things changed dramatically when the fifty-three–nation Commonwealth stepped in and applied pressure on Musharraf, putting PPP leader Benazir Bhutto back in the spotlight on Pakistan's political stage.

I decided to reach out to Benazir. At the time, the two-time former prime minister was living in self-imposed exile in Dubai. The rumours of a covert deal with General Pervez Musharraf had piqued my curiosity, and I was eager to hear her perspective firsthand. Securing the interview wasn't a straightforward task, but I persisted. Then, one day, I received a call from PPP spokesperson Farhatullah Babar—Benazir had agreed.

Benazir had just one condition for the interview: she insisted that we present it as if it took place in London, not Dubai, as she wasn't allowed to make political statements while living in the UAE. I sought approval from my editor. He gave the green light without hesitation.

Soon, I found myself in the vast living room of Benazir's 'Blessings' villa in Al Safa. Our chief photographer, Sankha Kar, sat beside me. Benazir, clad in a striking yellow and black geometric print shalwar suit with a loosely draped white dupatta, welcomed me with a warm smile.

'Are you 6'2"?' she inquired. 'You should be a fast bowler.'

I chuckled, 'Yes, close enough, and I did play some cricket. I was more of a batter.'

Our conversation quickly transcended the typical journalist–subject relationship, evolving into a captivating three-hour dialogue that even took Farhatullah Babar by surprise. He confessed it was the longest she'd ever spoken to a journalist. As we talked, I couldn't help but be charmed by Benazir's disarmingly candid demeanour.

Recording our conversation on a Dictaphone, we went through several cassettes. Unfortunately, they became corrupted. If I could somehow repair them and release the audio tapes, it had the potential to ignite political turmoil in Pakistan. Benazir revealed her innermost thoughts and fears during our exchange, occasionally marking certain parts as off the record. When I brought up the reconciliation deal with Musharraf, she vehemently dismissed it as nonsense.

'Not once has anyone approached me,' she stated firmly. 'I am willing to negotiate, but it depends on what the plan is. So far, the offer is that I should remain out of the country, that I should not even return to campaign for my party, that I should not contest the next election. If I don't agree to these things, they will ruin me and my family, they will take away my liberty and property … that's not a plan, that's a threat. Musharraf tells our party leaders to remove Benazir and we will talk to you. Do we ever say, remove Musharraf and we will talk to you?'

Amid our conversation, her son Bilawal, now the chairman of the PPP, made an appearance, sporting long hair that drew an amused comment from Benazir. She quipped, 'Look at his hair; I have been telling him to get a haircut, but he doesn't listen.' Bilawal responded with a sheepish grin as Benazir continued to discuss her concerns about Musharraf's impact on the judiciary and civil society. What Benazir told me during that February 2006 interview still rings true for Pakistan. 'The military always manages to sabotage the democratic system,' Benazir had said. 'It wants to continue its grip on power. The military regime wants to be seen as the bulwark against chaos and anarchy, but tragically it ends up creating these very conditions. Some people say that democracy should come in phases. But I don't believe that because the military governs by controlling the judiciary and civil society, you cannot have gradual democratisation.'

Indeed, it was a critical time for Benazir. The reconciliation plan with Musharraf hung in the balance, an Interpol red corner notice loomed over her, and her husband, Asif Zaradari, was undergoing treatment for a heart ailment in the US. On the first floor, her mother, Nusrat Bhutto, battled severe Alzheimer's disease.

Yet, Benazir's true strength came from her love for her children—Asifa, Bakhtawar and Bilawal. She was determined to shield them from her own challenges, saying, 'I want to keep their happiness intact.' In our conversation, she shared the hardships her family had endured over the years. Earlier that day, Asifa had innocently inquired if her mother was going to jail. Benazir replied with a reassuring laugh. 'No, dear. Don't believe what you read in the newspaper. Nothing is going to happen to your mamma.'

As Sankha clicked pictures, Benazir opened up about how her entire life had been upended. 'It's been very hard on the children,' she said. 'For ten years, we suffered. My husband was tortured and put into solitary confinement. He spent the best years of his life in jail. I raised my children alone. It was awful—a nightmare for ten long years … Asif had suffered a heart attack, and I was in the USA with him when I first heard about the red corner notice. But my daughter, who was at school in Dubai, got the news from her teacher. The teacher told her, "I'm surprised you came to school. Don't you know what's happened to your parents?"'

Benazir sought solace in life's simpler pleasures. She often took her children to Dubai's cineplexes, disguising herself with an abaya to avoid recognition. She even regaled me with an anecdote of hosting actor Salman Khan, much to her children's excitement. To cope with the weight of exile and legal battles, Benazir found refuge in the soothing melodies of Wolfgang Amadeus Mozart's string quartets. 'I like new age classical also, but Mozart is my favourite.' As our meeting neared its end, Benazir gifted me Swiss chocolates and signed copies of her autobiographies: *Daughter of the East* for me and *Daughter of Destiny* for my mother. It was a gracious gesture that would forever remind me of this extraordinary encounter.

Our conversations continued over the phone. Then, on one late September day in 2007, she called me with startling news. 'I'm going back to Pakistan.' Concerned, I asked, 'Are you sure? I mean, there are death threats against you.'

'Yes,' she responded. 'I've made up my mind. It's time.' It would be the last time we spoke.

Benazir's homecoming rally, after eight years in exile, was marred by a suicide attack that claimed the lives of 136 people. She narrowly escaped when she ducked behind her armoured vehicle at the moment of impact. Luck did not favour her the next time. A few months later, on 27 December, she held a rally at Liaquat Bagh in Rawalpindi, a venue named after the country's first prime minister, Liaquat Ali Khan, who had been assassinated at the same location in 1951.

After delivering an emotionally charged speech, Benazir prepared to leave. She emerged from her bomb-proof vehicle to wave to her supporters when a blast and gunfire pierced the air. Benazir was struck. She was rushed to the hospital. It was too late. No autopsy was performed, and even today, the mystery surrounding her assassination remains unresolved.

Four inquiries were conducted, by the police joint investigation team, the Federal Investigation Agency, the United Nations and Scotland Yard, all working to uncover the truth. However, despite these inquiries and investigations, the Bhutto family chose not to pursue the matter in the special anti-terrorism court, and no significant progress was made in bringing the case to a conclusion.

My Friend, M.F. Husain

Other than our initials, there wasn't anything common between me and the legendary M.F. Husain. He was the most celebrated and recognised Indian artist of the twentieth century. I was an ordinary journalist. Yet we shared an extraordinary bond.

Hounded out of India, Husain had made Dubai his new home, but his heart remained in India much like my other celebrity friend, musical director Nadeem Saifi of Nadeem–Shravan fame, who also lives in self-exile in Dubai.

Husain, then in his mid-nineties, had seven homes in Dubai and perhaps as many cars, including a couple of Ferraris, Bentley, Aston Martin and a customised Bugatti Veyron.

However, he mostly lived in the Deira Twin Tower. I was often invited to his fourteenth-floor apartment for dinner. The meal invariably consisted of bland kadhi–chaawal prepared by a team of uniformed butlers and served on a giant trunk coffee table around which we sat cross-legged.

The Daefi Lounge at the Jumeirah Emirates Tower Hotel (the place where Sridevi mysteriously died) was his favourite haunt. Every few days we would meet up there and chat for hours. Husain was almost childlike. He told me about his deepest fears and darkest secrets. Of course, it will be disrespectful to reveal them.

He was very unpredictable. One evening, we were sitting at Daefi when he began raving about the Bollywood romantic comedy movie *Band Baaja Baaraat* which had released a few days earlier.

He said he had watched it ten times already and asked me what I thought of the movie and its lead actors Ranveer Singh and Anushka Sharma. I hadn't even heard about them.

'I don't know. I haven't watched the movie yet,' I said.

Suddenly, he jumped to his feet. 'What a shame!' he exclaimed. 'Come,' he said, grabbing my arm, 'let's go and watch it together.'

I'd had a long day at work. I wasn't going to watch a movie I didn't know much about. So I tried to wriggle out of the situation.

'Thanks, Husain sahib,' I said. 'But right now it will be difficult, as I have plans with my wife.'

Husain would have none of it.

'Call your wife,' he said. 'Let me hear what these plans are.'

I reluctantly dialled Eram's number. As soon as she answered, Husain snatched the cell phone and put it on speaker. 'This is M.F. Husain,' he said. 'I believe you have some plans with my friend, Mazhar. I am taking him for a movie. Do you have any objections?'

'Of course not,' Eram stammered.

'Good,' said Husain. 'And now since I have ruined your plans, why don't you join us as well?'

I smiled. I knew where this was heading.

'But I am in Sharjah,' said Eram.

'*Chaand per to nahin hai?* (You are not on the moon, are you?),' he laughed. 'Come, we are waiting.'

You couldn't say no to Husain.

So Eram took a cab to the Jumeirah Emirates Hotel, from where we drove to Ibn Battuta in Husain's chauffeur-driven Bentley (he famously bought it with his credit card) where Eram and I watched *Band Baaja Baaraat* for the first time and Husain for the eleventh.

When the playful 'Ainvay Ainvay' track came on screen, Husain pursed his lips and let out a loud whistle, much to the amusement of the people sitting around us. Many recognised him and mobbed him for autographs.

Just before the interval, Husain disappeared. He returned with a popcorn bucket.

'How can one possibly enjoy a movie without popcorn,' he reasoned.

The movie ended around midnight. But Husain wasn't done yet. He took us to the Raavi Restaurant in Satwa where we gorged on lip-smacking mutton chops.

His other favourite restaurant was Ashrafi in Garhoud.

We reached home at 2 a.m. I had barely dozed off when I was woken by a phone call. It was Husain. 'Did I wake you up?' he asked politely. 'Actually it was something very urgent.'

My first thought was that this was a medical emergency and the old man needed help.

'Yes, yes, tell me what happened?'

'Do you have Anushka's cell phone number by any chance? I want it urgently. I called Yash Chopra but it appears that he's sleeping.'

I wish I could have obliged him.

Years after his death in 2011, Husain remains India's most sought-after artist. In 2020, his work *Voices* (1958) fetched $6 million. But the prolific artist, who was feted all over the world and called the Indian Picasso, found himself out of favour in his own country.

Some of Husain's paintings depicted revered Hindu gods and goddesses in the nude, sparking criticism. A decade ago, radicals had attacked his Mumbai home.

In 2011, it was a nude painting, *Mother India*, that had led him to seek refuge in Dubai away from his motherland.

'Hitler cracked down on artists when he came to power in Germany. And this is precisely what the right-wing forces are doing in India. These people are worse than Nazis and should be prosecuted,' he said when I first interviewed him about the controversial drawings.

At that time, hardliners were baying for his blood and filing lawsuits demanding his arrest. But his peace was short-lived. A district court in India had declared him absconding and ordered the police to attach his property when he failed to respond to summons.

A higher court stayed the proceedings and several moderate groups came out in his support. Husain felt more needed to be done.

'More than the brutality of the bad people, it's the ominous silence of the good that's got me worried. How long will the Indian government continue to remain a mute spectator to this witch hunting? It seems that it doesn't have the political will to take action against these belligerent blimps who know nothing about art,' said Husain.

'I have never meant to offend anyone. In any case, an artist's imagination is open to interpretation but it must remain unfettered,' he said.

I asked him if he was being victimised because he was a Muslim.

'Possibly. If my name was not M.F. Husain, things would have certainly been different.'

Husain said he had donated the contentious *Mother India* painting to Mumbai Police. It was to be auctioned to raise money for the families of policemen who died in Mumbai's train bombings.

Two of Husain's sons, Mustapha and Owais, lived in Dubai because of business interests but despite the warmth of family and friends, the maverick maestro missed India and longed for the good times he'd had there.

'I want to go back, but I don't see that happening anytime soon. So I keep myself busy,' he said.

Husain told me he was doing a series of ninety-nine paintings on the history of Arab civilisation.

'I met a member of the Qatari royal family a few days back. She has shown a keen interest in it and offered me a villa. She has also offered me Qatari nationality.'

I thought he was joking. He was not. In February 2010, he was indeed conferred the Qatar nationality—an honour that is rarely given to anyone.

One day, Husain called me to his Deira Twin Tower apartment to show what he said was his most treasured collection.

It was over fifty years old and it was dedicated to a Czech woman that he had lost his heart to. The year was 1956. Husain was holding an exhibition in Prague when he met Czech interpreter Maria Zurkova.

'We developed an instant liking for each other. There was a unique chemistry between us. I didn't have anything to give to her, so I gave her all thirty-four paintings that I displayed at my exhibition. Over the next five or six years, I travelled to Czechoslovakia several times and each time I would give her some of my paintings as a gesture of my love for her.

'Then we lost touch. For over forty years, I didn't hear from Maria until last year when we were reunited through a common friend.

'It was an emotional moment as we tried to fill the gaps. Maria had married but not forgotten me. She had lovingly treasured each of my eighty paintings all these years. Her financial condition was not good. She could have made a fortune by selling them, but she returned all the paintings, except one—a portrait that I made of her in the late Fifties.'

Throughout his life, Hussain created magic with a paintbrush. Just before his death in June 2011, he recreated the same magic with a pen.

The result: a brilliant and thought-provoking satirical poem entitled '*Kya Ek Din Kya Sau Baras* (What's one day, what's [one] hundred years)' to mark his hundredth birthday in the lunar calendar.

Handwritten in free verse by the master himself, the poem is in Urdu and runs into three full A4-size pages, encapsulating his incredible life journey and works.

Using simple yet meaningful rhyming words, the artist talks about his resolve, his rise to the pinnacle of fame and the storms he weathered along the way.

'I always wanted to dabble in writing—it's just that I was so preoccupied with my first love that I never got the time for writing. This is my first attempt,' Husain told me, reading aloud some verses from the poem over coffee. Here is an excerpt:

Kya sau baras, kya ek din
Kya kahney Allah Mian key
Unhein kaun beat kar sakta hai
Who yakta hai
Dekhiye yeh Maqbool naam ke putley ko
Na maloom kis mitti se banaya
Purey sau baras ho chalein hain
Ab tak toota nahi
Badal ne bijliya girain
Upar suraj aag babloola hua
Hawaein rukh badalti rahin
Lekin is mitti ke putley ke hawa bakta nahi huey

That was my last meeting with Husain. It was also the most memorable.

As I readied to take his leave, he handed over the A4 sheets to me.

'This is for you. There is no other copy of this poem, so keep it safely,' he said, patting my arms.

Why Husain chose to gift me with his only poem, I don't know, although he often said he got 'good vibes' from me.

On a Lion Hunt

Every time I run out of story ideas, I look up the wonderful world of classified advertisements. Whether it's a reward for a missing talking parrot or a listing for a gold-plated car, there are stories that are just waiting to be done.

It was a slow news day sometime in mid-2008. As usual, I was flipping through the classifieds section when an advert grabbed my attention: 'Lion cub for sale in Sharjah'.

The private possession of wild animals like tigers, lions and cheetahs wasn't outlawed in the country until 2017, but the UAE was still a signatory to the Convention on International Trade on Endangered Species of Wild Flora and Fauna (CITES).

I wondered how the advertisement made it to our newspaper. I promptly called the cell phone number mentioned in the advertisement. Lest suspicion be aroused I didn't make the call from the newspaper's landline.

I used my cell phone.

The phone was answered by a man who spoke in a Sudanese dialect.

'This is about the ad—' I began. He cut me mid-sentence.

'Where are you from and what do you do?'

I got the drift. He didn't want time wasters. There were more chances of the monsoon changing course and heading to the UAE than an Indian expatriate buying a lion cub in Dubai.

I quickly thought of a plausible story.

'I work for the private office of His Highness Sheikh Abdul Al Majeedullah,' I said. 'His secretary has asked me to contact you and …'

It worked.

'The lion cub will be for Dh80,000 and I would like to talk to the sheikh directly,' he interrupted me again.

'That's not a problem, but the sheikh wants to see the cub before we close the deal.'

'Certainly,' he said. 'Let him call me.'

We had just the right person for the job.

He was our new Emirati reporter Mohammad Al Khan, a tall, massively built man, who looked every bit a rich sheikh, complete with a well-groomed beard and an air of elegance about him.

I got Al Khan to call the animal seller.

They spoke in Arabic for about five minutes.

'All good,' Al Khan said, disconnecting the call. 'He has asked us to come to the Eppco Gas Station in Al Nasseriya at 1 p.m. tomorrow.'

'The lion is at the fuel station?'.

'No,' he laughed, 'the gas station is where we will meet first.'

The next day, Al Khan turned up in his crispiest kandoura and we headed to Sharjah in his full-black tinted Land Cruiser.

As soon as we reached the Eppco Gas Station, we called the man.

'Is that you in the white SUV?' he asked.

'Yes, where are you?'

'In the black Nissan Sunny to your right. Follow me.'

Soon, we were lumbering behind the car down a narrow dirty road. After a short ride, the Nissan stopped near a grocery store.

A man jumped out of the driver's seat and disappeared inside a lane.

We waited in our car as seconds ticked by. What do we do? Should we wait or step out?

Suddenly my phone rang.

It was our man. I put the phone on speaker. 'Do you see a mud-coloured villa with a small iron gate ahead of you?'

'Yes.'

'Leave your car and come inside. We are here.'

My heart was bursting with anticipation as we walked towards the house.

I had told Nirmala about our sting operation. She was excited about it. 'It will make a great cover,' she had gushed in our editorial meeting while discussing the story line-up.

Everything was happening the way I wanted. I was just about to nail another cracking story.

But my joy was short-lived. It dissipated like fleecy clouds across summer skies as we stepped into the house and came face-to-face with the man who held the lion cub in the crook of his arm.

He was our office telephone operator, an affable Sudanese guy in his mid-forties whom I had known for years. We bumped into each other in the smoking room daily. In fact, we had met that very morning. I don't know who was more shocked, him or us.

For a long moment, Al Khan and I just stood there, transfixed, unable to process the scene that had just unfolded before our eyes.

The wildlife trafficker we were hoping to expose was one of our own.

I was so deeply engrossed in the situation that I didn't notice when he let go of the animal.

It was only when the little thing tottered towards us, whimpering and crying that I realised its presence. It was a scrawny animal, the size of a house cat, with hip bones sticking out of the skin. The telephone operator broke the silence.

'What are you doing here,' he asked, offering me a Marlboro White.

'Well, that's the question we should be asking you,' I responded.

As it turned out, the lion cub belonged to his friend who was struggling to sell it and our telephone operator had placed an advertisement in our newspaper, hoping to make a cut from the sale of the animal.

'Was it you who was on the phone with us?' Al Khan asked.

The telephone operator nodded sheepishly.

'You are not going to tell anyone about it, right?' he asked fearfully.

Al Khan and I looked at each other.

There was no way we would rat out a colleague. The decision was made without a word being uttered.

'What will we tell Nirmala? She has slotted this for the cover!' Al Khan asked on the way back.

'We will tell her the man never turned up.'

'Looks like your lion seller had the heart of a chicken,' Nirmala said to me as she lit up a Rothmans Blue in the office smoking room hours later.

Standing within earshot and still looking frazzled was our telephone operator.

A slow smile worked across his face and into his eyes as I responded to Nirmala.

'Yes, a chicken's heart, that's what it looks like.'

A Night in Jail

One US Independence Day, fate led me to a place I never expected to visit: jail. The memories of that day still cling to me, as vivid as if it happened just yesterday. What haunts me most, though, is not my own imprisonment but the fact that my editor shared a similar fate that night, albeit in a different cell and for a separate case.

I couldn't help but feel a twinge at the injustice—I didn't deserve to be in a cell, he did.

He killed his wife. Struck the sixty-two-year-old woman's skull with a hammer twice. Death was instantaneous. Me? I had a clean slate. Not even a parking ticket.

In fact, on 4 July 2017, the day *Gulf News*'s editor-at-large Francis Matthew faked a burglary at his Jumeirah home to cover up the murder of his wife, Jane, I was out on a leisurely stroll with my wife Eram.

The evening started innocuously enough, with us walking around our new apartment complex in Al Majaz 3. Having recently moved to Sara Tower, we were keen to explore our surroundings.

We had barely gone a few metres when three young Arab men appeared out of nowhere. They wore tracksuits and baseball caps.

'ID, show me your ID,' one of them barked.

'Yes, but who are you?'

'Sharjah Police, CID department.'

'Can I see some IDs?' I asked.

'You think we're fake policemen?' the man sneered.

He was a brawny guy in his thirties with a hint of a moustache over a hawk-like face.

'I need to be sure,' I said, trying to keep my voice calm.

His eyes narrowed.

'Sure,' he said, flashing a card and then quickly putting it back.

Now, it's not uncommon in Sharjah for criminals to rob people posing as policemen. Sharjah Police have repeatedly issued warnings about these imposters.

In March 2014, a four-member gang was arrested for posing as CID officers, kidnapping a Bangladeshi and robbing him of Dh1,00,000. The victim said the gang leader showed a police identity card and forced him into a car.

This crime was so rampant in 2017 that Sharjah Police had to set up a special team to hunt down those behind it.

'Our control room was flooded with calls from victims,' police said.

So my fears weren't quite unfounded when I asked to see the ID again.

As a law-abiding citizen I was well within my rights, but my request did not go down well.

'ID?' he growled. 'You want to see my ID. You will see now.' He turned around and muttered inaudibly in Arabic. It was a cue for the other two men.

Suddenly, they grabbed my arms violently and the brawny guy dug into my pocket, rifling my wallet until he found my Emirates ID card.

He rattled off the fifteen-digit social security number to someone through an earpiece.

Seconds later, an evil grin plastered his face and his eyes widened in amazement. 'Matlub,' he said to the men who held me in a vice-like grip. 'He is matlub,' he repeated, almost jumping in joy. 'Take him away.'

I knew what matlub meant. It's the Arabic word for 'wanted'.

'I can't be wanted. There must be some misunderstanding,' I said as the men snatched my phone, handcuffed me behind my back and dragged me towards a civilian Nissan Pathfinder with tinted glasses.

A small crowd had milled around us. I spotted my grocer. Then my daughter Unaiza, and her friend Saima.

My eyes searched for Eram. She stood aghast, rooted to the ground.

'Look,' I said to the men. 'You seem to have got the wrong guy. Your Crown Prince has given me the highest government award for investigative journalism. He knows me. Google my name. Else, check my phone gallery. There's a picture of me receiving a trophy from him. It came with $7,000. That's about Dh25,000.'

'Really, you think we are jokers,' my captors laughed, ignoring my plea as they shoved me into the car and sat on either side.

Brawny slammed the rear door shut and took the steering wheel.

Soon we were driving away from the scene.

I was still not sure about the identity of the men. My mind wanted me to believe they were from the police; my heart thought otherwise.

I have always thought from the heart. It has cost me a lot. Will I change? Hell, no.

Could these men be part of a hit squad, I wondered. They must be very bold to abduct me from a busy street.

'Brother,' I said to the driver, edging closer, 'where are you taking me?'

He didn't reply. Instead he turned around and slammed his fist into my chest. 'Tighten his handcuffs,' he ordered the cop sitting on my right. 'And keep tightening it till he doesn't shut up.'

They had used plastic handcuffs to zip tie my wrists. At Brawny's command, the man ratcheted the cuff tighter, constricting my blood vessels.

I winced in pain. 'Aha, so it hurts. Good,' chuckled Brawny. 'Now you will shut up.'

Realising the futility of reasoning with those sadists, I kept quiet for the remainder of the journey, which concluded half an hour later at the Sharjah Police headquarters. I smiled inwardly as the familiar building loomed before me, thinking, 'At least it's not a hit squad.'

As a uniformed officer removed my handcuffs, I believed I'd speak to the person in charge, clear up the misunderstanding, and be back home within the next hour.

My optimism took a hit when an officer noted my name in a register, led me to a dingy cell, and unceremoniously threw me inside. The small, dark room reeked of urine and sweat, with around fifteen other men crammed inside.

I thought about my family, particularly my aged parents who were visiting us those days.

Barring a bunch of thieves and a drug dealer, almost everyone in the lock-up had been arrested for defaulting on a payment.

'Bounced cheque?' a young Indian man asked sympathetically.

I shook my head.

'What is it then?'

'Don't know,' I replied as I racked my brains, trying to figure out what could have possibly got me arrested.

Around midnight, an officer gave me a paper chit.

'Your wife was here,' he said. 'She asked me to give this to you.'

I recognised the cursory writing instantly. 'Stay strong,' the chit read.

It was the first good thing that happened that night.

'Would you know why I am here?' I asked the officer.

'You are wanted. There's a complaint against you in Al Barsha Police Station. We will shift you there soon.'

'Al Barsha, in Dubai?

'Yes,' said the cop. 'That is what it says in our records.'

I was at the Al Barsha Police a few weeks earlier for a story. And yes, I did get a call from them. An officer had asked me to visit them. I told our editor Abdul Hamid about it. He said I shouldn't go unless they specified why they wanted to see me. The officer never called back and the matter was soon forgotten.

A hundred questions swam in my mind as I leaned against the prison bars. Could they have arrested me for not showing up at the police station when called? Is that a crime? Assuming it is, how does it make me matlub?

I had gone to the Al Barsha Police Station only once before. It was following the arrest of the CEO of a popular American children's talent agency. He was accused of assaulting the teenage daughter of a Pakistani actor and TV presenter during an audition.

But that was two months back. In any case, it had got nothing to do with me. I tried to call the newspaper's legal head but couldn't reach him. Later, I would know he had more pressing business at hand: a premeditated murder by our editor-at-large, Francis Matthew. It would have been a befitting headline if he had chosen to flee.

At 2 a.m. an officer came to our cell and called out a few names. Mine was among them. These were people who had to be transported to the general headquarters of Dubai Police. We were bundled in a police van and taken to the imposing building in Al Qusais. Once there, we were locked up in a cell that was almost as cold as a freezer.

There were about twenty inmates there. We took turns to wrap ourselves in a prayer mat to keep warm.

Just before dawn, I was driven to Al Barsha Police Station in a police van.

An officer told me there was a police complaint against me by the CEO I had written about in a newspaper. It didn't make sense. I tried to recollect the story.

In early May, we had received a tip-off about a 'Disney' audition happening at Dubai's Ritz–Carlton hotel later that month.

'The talent agency behind the event is based out of the USA, but it has nothing to do with Disney,' said a woman over the phone. 'The fake casting call is just a ruse to get parents to shell out astronomical amounts of money on bogus acting classes. I am a victim of their scam. You've got to expose them,' she said.

The Ritz–Carlton hotel, where the audition was scheduled to take place, was located in Jumeirah Beach Residences, a stone's throw from Mrs Sara Waqar's apartment.

As an intern, she had assisted me in many investigations. This was literally right down her alley. The casting call was for boys and girls aged between seven and fifteen years. Sara's eldest child, Abaan, was seven at the time. It was the perfect cover.

I asked Sara if she was game for a possible undercover story.

She agreed.

The following afternoon, she took Abaan to the hotel and enrolled him for the audition. Since it was a weekend, hundreds of starry-eyed parents had turned up for the event. While Sara was waiting for her turn, I was catching up with my friends at Costa Café on Sheikh Zayed Road.

Around 2 p.m., my phone rang. It was Sara.

'Maz, you have to come here quickly,' she said worriedly. 'The police are here. Apparently, a girl has been assaulted during the audition and her mom has lodged a complaint. There's a lot of commotion.'

'Okay, hang in there,' I said, 'I am coming.'

I excused myself and quickly hurried out of the coffee shop. I had barely reached my car when Sara's phone rang a second time.

'The girl's mum who filed the complaint,' she began.

'What about her?'

'I just recognised her. It's Nadia Khan.'

'Nadia who?'

'Nadia Khan,' said Sara. 'She's a Pakistani actor and TV presenter. She's quite famous back home.'

This was getting interesting.

Fifteen minutes later, I was sitting with a tearful Nadia and her daughter at the hotel's lobby.

Haltingly at first, and then in a vivid rush of words, they described the sequence of events to me.

'I came here hoping it would be good for my child, but instead got the shock of my life,' Nadia said. 'When my child's turn came, the judge grabbed her roughly by the shoulder and pushed her so hard she fell on one of the parents.'

She asked her daughter to unroll her sleeves. There were multiple bruise marks on both arms. 'There were some former Disney stars at the show but they did nothing to stop the assault. I used to idolise these stars,' the teenager said.

Nadia said the incident happened in front of scores of other parents. 'I have witnesses. No one has the right to touch my child let alone subject her to public humiliation and physical abuse. I reported the matter to the police and now I am going to the hospital to get a medical report of the injuries.' I asked Nadia if she could say all of this on camera. She did not bat even an eyelid. 'Absolutely, in fact that would be brilliant,' she said, hastily pulling out a brush from her handbag. 'Let me fix my hair first.'

As a television presenter, Nadia faced the camera every day. She got rolling as soon as I pressed my phone's record button. But midway through the recording, she stopped. 'There's too much noise here. I think I will have to use a mic. Plus, the light isn't great so I will shift to the other sofa.' I waited until she had settled and recorded the interview all over again. In the nearly three-minute video, Nadia recounted the incident in detail, describing how the judge physically grabbed her child and pushed her when she began reciting her lines.

'Before my daughter, they were auditioning small children. She was the first teenager in that group. My daughter was given a two-line script, but before she could read it, she was forcefully grabbed and pushed, causing her to fall onto one of the parents. She is my daughter, and no one has the right to touch my child, let alone subject her to public humiliation and physical abuse,' Nadia said.

Nadia attempted to address the issue with the organisers, but they responded rudely and forced her to leave.

Later that evening, Nadia sent her daughter's medical reports to me via WhatsApp, confirming multiple bruise marks on both arms.

She told me that she was heading to the police station, where the CEO of the talent agency had been detained, and asked if I could accompany her.

With Nadia's version on tape, eyewitness accounts and a medical report, I needed statements from the police and the talent agency. I sent an email to the agency seeking their response and drove to Al Barsha Police Station, arriving around 10 p.m. Nadia was already there with an officer who confirmed the CEO of the talent agency had been detained for questioning. He was an American actor known for his roles in daytime soap operas. Sara also joined us at the police station and stayed until close to midnight. We grabbed some food from a nearby fuel station.

I asked Nadia for high-resolution photographs of herself for my report. Our graphic designer had tried to use screen grabs from the video I shot, but they didn't meet our quality standards.

Nadia scrolled through her phone and sent me a collection of photos, all of which were modelling shots. In one image, she posed with a bouquet of flowers, while in another, she was dressed in a gown, smiling seductively as she leaned against a pillar.

'For goodness's sake, we can't use these pictures. Your daughter has been assaulted. We can't depict you smiling and posing with lilies,' I said.

'This is all that I have,' she replied.

'Well, they won't work,' I said and asked her to come to our office for a photoshoot.

The next morning Nadia visited our office and our photographer Virendra Saklani took pictures of her looking solemn as she sat in our meeting room.

Before publishing the story, I wrote to the talent agency again. In return, I got threatened with a lawsuit. 'I find it offensive and disgusting that a news organisation and a reporter would attempt to publish information to the public without allowing the proper authorities to finish their work,' they said in an email.

Curiously, it was not the first time the CEO of the talent hunt agency had courted controversy. A YouTube video from a similar event in Singapore showed the actor spitting on a young girl.

We also found out how the talent agency used a classic 'bait and switch' sales strategy to lure parents to their events and then sought huge sums of money from them for giving acting classes to their children.

A Dubai-based mother, whose eight-year-old daughter cleared the first round, told me she had to revisit the hotel for a second evaluation and be prepared to pay if her child passed it.

'The forms of payment we accept are Visa or MasterCard. The payment is expected today if your child passes the second evaluation,' read the email sent to her.

Children passing the second evaluation were recommended one of five 'Option Levels' with fees ranging from $1,950 to $7,900.

Parents who showed up said they learnt about the talent hunt from Facebook posts calling for children to audition for their chance to meet Disney Channel stars.

'Does your child dream of becoming a Disney Channel star? We are coming to Dubai!' the post read.

Disney spokespersons repeatedly clarified that these child talent auditions were in no way associated with or endorsed by The Walt Disney Company or Disney Channel. Our news report created ripples. Pakistan media also latched on. Scores of parents called to either recount their experience or thank us for alerting them. There was only one parent who was not happy. It was Nadia. 'Why did you not mention the name of the talent agency or the man who assaulted the girl?' she demanded angrily.

I told her we couldn't publish the names for legal reasons. I thought she was convinced and moved on to another story.

But the audition saga was far from over. It came back to bite me when I was least expecting it.

Unbeknown to me, Nadia and the talent hunt agency CEO struck a deal to frame me. It was a classic case of shooting the messenger.

The talent agency boss played his cards well. He countered the legal action against him by filing a police report against Nadia. She was accused of disrupting the show and swearing at the organisers in a public place. As a result, Nadia was briefly detained at Dubai Airport while flying back from Pakistan. Her passport was also taken away by the authorities.

The lawyers representing the talent agency laid down a condition before Naida: if she wanted her passport back, she had to withdraw her complaint. She complied. Meanwhile, the American actor filed a criminal complaint against me for defamation, saying my report had damaged his reputation.

It's precisely for this reason that the Al Barsha Police Station had rung me up weeks earlier.

'You should have called me a second time before putting my name in that wanted list,' I told the officer as he uncuffed me and recorded my statement. By the time we finished it was 4 a.m.

The officer said they would have to hold my passport until the case was closed. I rang up Eram to bring it over. She answered on the first ring. She said everyone had stayed awake all night. 'Dad?' I asked hesitatingly.

'Yes, him too.'

'What did you do?'

There was silence. I thought the line had disconnected. 'Hello, Eram, are you there?'

'I lay on the floor,' she said. 'I couldn't have been in bed when you were in jail.'

The sun had not yet risen when Eram took a cab to the police station carrying my passport.

At 6 a.m., I was finally released. We didn't talk much on the way back. When we reached home, Eram broke down. My arrest had taken a toll on her.

I was exhausted and badly needed some sleep. Instead, I took a quick shower and drove down to work. A solemn mood prevailed at the office.

Word had spread about Francis Matthew's arrest. Conversations were hushed and there was an expectant uneasiness in the air as I sat down around a table in the office canteen. By now, my colleagues had also heard about my arrest but the information they had was sketchy.

A European woman sought more details, approaching our table to join us.

'Tsk, tsk, who would have thought Francis would do something like this,' she began. 'He was so gentle and soft spoken, wasn't he?'

'Yes, it's shocking,' I said as I dunked soft pillowy idli into the hot sambhar.

'I met Jane a few times, they looked like such a happy couple,' she continued.

'Oh yes, they did,' I replied.

'And you,' she hesitated. 'You are also such a nice person. And yet …'

This wasn't going anywhere. 'Stop beating around the bush, and ask what you want to ask,' I said testily.

She leaned over and whispered into my ear.

'I heard you got arrested too.'

'Yes, I was, now it's all sorted.'

'Thank God,' she exclaimed, rolling her eyes. 'I'm so glad you are out of it, but tell me, what were you doing in his house?'

I nearly spilled the sambhar on my shirt.

'Whose house?'

'Francis Matthew's house. Weren't you arrested from there?'

I was tempted to say I went there to deliver the hammer, the murder weapon.

The only reason why I didn't say that was not because it would have been insensitive but because she would have actually believed me.

'I was arrested in Sharjah in connection with a story,' I clarified. 'And it's got nothing to do with Francis.'

A few weeks later, I was summoned by the public prosecutor. He offered an out-of-court settlement. The deal was that they wouldn't press criminal charges if I admitted my guilt and apologised.

I refused. The case went to trial.

I recall standing before the judges while my lawyer Saad Salman fought for me.

Sara was an eyewitness in the case. The defence called her twice in case she had to testify. She sat on the last bench in the courtroom as the public prosecutor read the charges against me. I'm relieved that she didn't have to face the witness box.

However, I sense the existence of another witness box—one that's much bigger and more distant. There, Mrs Sara Waqar will have a lot to answer for. (The public prosecutor is not the only person I promised a book.)

'What are my winning odds?' I asked Salman as we sat in his office.

He raised both hands in the air and said, 'Inshallah'.

On 28 May 2018, exactly one year after the Ritz–Carlton incident, the court announced the verdict: not guilty.

Justice Aiman Mohammed Abdul Hakam Ashaath acquitted me of all charges, stating that there was no evidence of criminal intent or a breach of privacy.

Francis faced a different fate. He received a guilty verdict for premeditated murder and was initially sentenced to ten years in prison. However, Dubai's Court of Appeals later reduced his sentence to seven years, inciting outrage within Jane's family.

Francis confessed to the police that he had killed his wife, driven by anger when she called him a 'loser' upon hearing they had to move to a smaller home. He claimed to have experienced a 'moment of insanity', striking his wife twice in the head while she lay in bed. In October 2022, after serving his shortened sentence, Francis was released from jail and deported to Britain. One day, he reached out to me on LinkedIn. I told him about my upcoming visit to London and he suggested we meet.

Our meeting took place in September 2023 at the Botanist Restaurant in Sloane Square. Francis appeared noticeably healthier and more cheerful. He shared stories about former colleagues and his life in Dubai's prison but conspicuously avoided any mention of the murder. I refrained from broaching the subject as well, feeling it inappropriate at the time.

As our discussion continued, I revealed my plans to write a memoir. In response, he disclosed his own literary ambitions, expressing his intent to pen two books—one chronicling the rise of the UAE and the other providing insight into his life behind bars. I can't wait to read them.

On a Hit List with My Family

Throw anything at me and I will deal with it. But not death threats against my loved ones. So when some bloodthirsty hatemongers threatened to physically harm my young daughters, I was worried sick. I did not sign up for this.

For weeks on end in early 2020, I battled alone after my family and I were subjected to vicious attacks by an army of right-wingers associated with India's ruling party, the BJP.

Many of these thugs had verified accounts on X or were followed on the microblogging site by Prime Minister Narendra Modi. What they had done to deserve this honour is anyone's guess.

The threats were explicit.

'You are on our hit list. Along with your daughters,' read a post tagging me.

'Any lion ready for a small operation in Lucknow?' demanded another man.

Lucknow, the citadel of composite culture, is where my aged parents lived on their own those days.

'Mazhar is a Pakistani agent. Arrest his family. Revoke his passport.'

I was bombarded with thousands of abusive and threatening messages. They came on email, WhatsApp, Facebook Messenger and X every few minutes.

Messages were also sent to my employer and local authorities seeking my arrest and deportation.

Dubai Police were told I was a Shia and secretly worked for Iran. It was a clever ploy as the UAE and Iran were arch rivals.

For good measure, an old Facebook photograph from my trip to Taiwan was morphed to make it look like I was in Tehran, purportedly meeting Iran's military commander Qasem Soleimani who was later killed in a US airstrike in Iraq.

When none of this worked, threatening phone calls were made to me and my parents using untraceable numbers.

My crime: I had reported incidents where UAE-based Indian Hindus had been fired or deported because of their hateful social media posts.

The UAE outlaws all religious or racial discrimination under a legislation passed in 2015.

Any act that insults the divine entity, any religion, Prophet, messenger, divine book or house of worship is considered contempt of religion for which one could be jailed for years and penalised up to Dh1 million.

The law does not discriminate. There have been many occasions when Arabs, including Emiratis, have also been referred to prosecution for ridiculing someone else's religious beliefs.

So when people lost jobs or faced legal action for mocking Islam on social media, they had only themselves to blame, like this Abu Dhabi-based Indian financial manager who uploaded graphic images on Facebook depicting how a 'jihadi coronavirus suicide spitter' (sic) could 'cause 2,000 deaths compared to 20 by a jihadi bomber detonating a belt rigged with explosives'.

The post was a malicious reference to videos falsely claiming to show that members of an Islamic missionary movement in India were spitting on police during the coronavirus pandemic.

Earlier, an Indian staff member at Dubai-based Transguard Group was fired and deported for posting a Facebook comment celebrating the terror attacks in New Zealand that left fifty dead.

A rigging supervisor at an Abu Dhabi firm also lost his job after he uploaded a video in which he threatened to kill Kerala chief minister Pinarayi Vijayan and rape his family. The same month the JW Marriott Marquis Hotel in Dubai terminated its contract with Michelin-starred chef Atul Kochhar after he tweeted that followers of Islam had 'terrorised' Hindus for 2,000 years.

Sharjah-based businessman Sohan Roy had to apologise for a video depicting Islamic clerics leading blindfolded men in skull caps in an adaptation of his poem on religious bigotry.

As a journalist, I was merely reporting these stories. I was not part of them.

But yes, there were times when I did call out a few racial bigots and sex offenders.

I will gladly do that again. Any journalist will.

Which is why I did not hesitate to expose Indian expat Jayant Gokhale who lived in an Islamic country but had no qualms rejecting the application of a visiting job seeker Mohammad Abdullah because he was a Muslim. To add insult to injury, Gokhale had told Abdullah in writing that he was better off making a living by joining protests in Shaheen Bagh.

A Muslim ghetto in Delhi, Shaheen Bagh was the epicentre of a peaceful stir against India's new citizenship laws that were discriminatory to Muslims.

As the protests gained momentum, Amit Malviya, a leader of the ruling BJP and head of its IT cell, tweeted a video where claims were made that the women protesters in Shaheen Bagh were 'paid Rs 500 to 700' each.

The claims were later found to be false. But for Gokhale it was the gospel truth. His email response to Abdullah's job application read: 'Just a thought. Why u need a job? Go to Delhi and sit in Shaheen Bagh for protest. Every day you will get Rs 1000. Free food, i.e., biryani. Unlimited amount of Tea and Milk, sometimes sweets also.'

I found the email offensive on two counts. First, it ridiculed and discriminated against a job seeker on the basis of his religious identity and, second, it undermined the credibility of Shaheen Bagh protestors by suggesting that they are being paid to sit in.

I rang up Gokhale. His response left me stunned. Instead of showing any remorse, he justified his action. That's when I realised how deep-rooted the malaise was among ordinary expats.

'Yes, they are indeed getting biryani and money,' said Gokhale. 'Every day they (get) Rs 1,000. That is Rs 30,000 per month. Plus, there's free food.'

I felt sick.

'Alright,' I said. 'Let us for a moment assume what you are saying is true. Now tell me, would you have sent this email if the applicant was Ashok instead of Abdulla.

Suddenly, the very vocal Mr Gokhale became very quiet and very ill.

There was a long silence. Finally, he spoke. 'I am not feeling too well. I am undergoing dialysis every week. My email is being blown out of proportion. I didn't mean what I wrote,' he said and hung up.

A few minutes later I got an email from him.

'My message to the candidate was not intended to hurt anyone in any manner or discriminate. I have already sent an apology message to the concerned person [Abdullah],' he said in the email reproduced here ad verbatim. 'I very much value UAE's outlook, policies and culture. I do not in any way like to go against the values of the UAE. In fact, I am very thankful to the UAE for looking after my health.'

It was too little too late. I had to write the story.

Gokhale's response to Abdullah's job application was outrageous but it wasn't bad enough to warrant an action. But there was no such luck for his fellow countryman S. Bhandari who asked a visiting Indian job seeker to go to Pakistan via text message.

Bhandari was referred to prosecution. I also exposed an Indian head chef in Dubai who threatened to rape a law student in Delhi because of her views against the citizenship law.

In his profanity-laced Facebook post, chef Trilok Singh called Swati Khanna a prostitute. Singh also threatened to rape her and mutilate her genitals. Following my story, Trilok was sacked and his visa cancelled.

We refrained from publishing the translation of the threat as it is too explicit and contained references to the vagina, acid and sticks.

The obnoxious messages were brought to our attention by Swati herself after she tagged us on X, saying: 'He lives in Dubai. In a Muslim country. And says this to me. I am an Indian who lives in India. Report this terrorist.'

But right-wing publications in India labelled me as the 'head of operations' of a campaign 'targeting Hindus in the middle east'.

'What sadistic pleasure he derives by endangering the lives of Indians is something which normal humans will fail at comprehending,' wrote *TFI Post*. It went on to say that I had 'made it a life mission to find all "Islamophobic" handles working out of the middle east, and then report them to competent authorities.'

It also sought a probe into how I managed to share a stage with Indian Army chief General Bipin Rawat who gave me a journalism award in New Delhi.

Another publication, a rag sheet called *MyNation*, ran a story on me under the headline 'RakshaSetu: Exposing Mazhar Farooqi, the Kingpin Responsible for Doxxing Indians in the Gulf'.

Ironically, when right-wing groups were baying for my blood and defending blasphemous posts as freedom of speech, Indian envoys in the Gulf were reminding expats about the consequences of their actions.

'India and UAE share the value of non-discrimination on any grounds,' tweeted Pawan Kapoor, the Indian ambassador to the UAE. 'Discrimination is against our moral fabric and the rule of law. Indian nationals in the UAE should always remember this.'

Kapoor also tagged a tweet by Prime Minister Narendra Modi himself, underlining that COVID-19 did not see race, religion, colour, caste, creed, language or borders before striking and it should be defeated with the spirit of unity and brotherhood.

Former Indian ambassador Navdeep Suri also cautioned Indians about the UAE's hate speech laws. Similar warnings were issued by Indian missions in other Gulf Cooperation Council (GCC) states. But the damage had already been done. For the first time the Arab world woke up to the disturbing groundswell of Islamophobia among Indian expats.

Remember, this was two years before Muslim nations erupted in a fury following BJP spokesperson Nupur Sharma's remarks against Prophet Mohammad on a televised show.

Stung by a wave of Islamophobic posts unleashed by Indians living in the Gulf, many influential Arabs decided to hit back.

Saudi scholar Abidi Zahrani proposed to list all militant Hindus working in the Gulf and engaged in spreading hate against Islam.

'List all militant Hindus who are working in the GCC and spreading hate against Islam and Muslims or our beloved Prophet Mohammad,' he wrote using the hashtag #Send_Hindutva_back_home.

Mejbel Al Sharika, a Kuwaiti lawyer and director of International Human Rights, launched a team of legal experts to tackle Islamophobia and hate crimes on social media platforms for India and the Gulf.

Closer home, Emirati author Hend Qassimi, mistakenly referred to as a UAE princess, also waded into the controversy, only to be viciously trolled on X.

But it's me who took the brunt of the attack. I was confident my newspaper would have my back. That the organisation I gave seventeen years of my life to would stand by me if not speak up. It was a rude awakening when it didn't. I didn't expect them to publish an editorial showing support although it would have been in order because the Mumbai Press Club did come out with a public statement condemning the attacks and demanding action against the hatemongers. All I wanted from my office was for them to say they cared about me. Or at least try to understand what I was going through. Two of my daughters were in India those days. I started getting panic attacks when their personal details were shared on social media amid calls to kill them.

Newspapers and TV channels amplified the death threats, thrusting my face into the spotlight. Pakistani media worsened matters by portraying me as a target of fundamentalists from the ruling BJP government. To compound matters, certain Muslim organisations hailed me as a hero of the community, offering accolades for my supposed bravery. Despite my efforts to clarify that I was simply fulfilling my journalistic duty, my words fell on deaf ears. In response, I withdrew from public life and maintained radio silence on social media until the storm subsided, albeit after several harrowing weeks. 'Aah, don't worry,' said a senior editor over the phone when I shared my fears with him during the initial days of the threats. 'Barking dogs seldom bite.'

I realised I was barking up the wrong tree.

Like sustainability now, mental health was a buzzword those days, gaining huge traction in the aftermath of the COVID-19 pandemic.

Newspapers often publish laborious articles stressing the importance of mental health, yet their concern seems to wane when one of their own faces threats or lawsuits. In these situations, the management's response can be less than empathetic, often viewing you as a troublemaker. I've frequently found myself navigating these challenges alone, but I've managed to endure thanks to a valuable lesson I learnt.

At the Global Investigative Journalists Network (GIJN) conference in Johannesburg, I crossed paths with an elderly European reporter. Though his name and affiliation escape me, the wisdom he imparted has remained indelible. He shared a golden rule with me: hold the aces.

Over 1,200 media professionals from 130 countries had gathered at the sprawling Wits University for the five-day event, which featured a rich array of workshops, seminars and networking sessions. Stepping out of one such workshop for a smoke, I found myself in conversation with a man in his mid-sixties. Our discussion naturally gravitated towards the challenges posed by lawsuits. In the UAE, people throw around lawsuits as casually as confetti at a celebration. I even got one thrown at me by a notorious Antwerp drug lord, linked to several violent attacks that included hurling grenades at his rivals. I had merely reported on his arrest following requests from the Belgian government. We won the initial case. But he appealed. We won in the higher court too. However, the legal battles came at a high cost, a price that the drug lord's substantial financial resources allowed him to pay.

As we talked, the elderly reporter said something that would change my perspective about investigative journalism: 'Learn to hold the aces.'

While I had a rudimentary grasp of card games, his analogy remained unclear until he clarified. 'Imagine you've gathered all the evidence for an investigative story. What's your next move?' Intrigued by the question, I responded, 'Naturally, we publish it.'

'But do you lay all your cards on the table?' His question left me perplexed. 'Why wouldn't we?' I asked. His smile widened. 'Next time, consider the art of withholding. Ideally, keep your most damning evidence—your aces—hidden. Use them as leverage. So, when they brandish legal threats, you can reveal the aces from your sleeves and hint at what might come next.'

'Wouldn't that amount to blackmailing?' I protested. He shook his white-haired head. 'It's protection, son. It's your neck that's on the line there. Wouldn't you want to protect it?' At that moment, it didn't make much sense to me. However, as lawsuits began mounting against me, his advice became increasingly clear. I changed my approach. Every time I did a major exposé, I held back some information, and it invariably proved useful. For instance, when the fake University of Atlanta threatened to sue me for tarnishing their image, I sent them the address of their purported sprawling physical campus. It was a rented postbox. Similarly, when a dodgy real estate developer stormed into our office with a team of lawyers, fuming over my report, I pulled out a sheet showing the list of shell companies where their ill-gotten wealth was hidden. Their arrogance deflated, and they skulked away.

Going Undercover with a Fake Pot Belly

Undercover sting operations often require me to use a fake identity. Once it saw me using a fake pot belly too.

I never had a six pack of abs, but I was never fat either. In May 2012, I was still a few kilograms below my ideal body when I tucked a small cushion under my shirt and hit the narrow lanes of Meena Bazaar in Bur Dubai.

My padded tummy was part of a sting operation to expose a slimming racket that targets obese people. A bizarre way to expose a bizarre scam.

Just as I had been forewarned by victims, I was approached by a young Indian who struck up a conversation with me. 'Hello brother, are you from Pakistan?' he began.

'India,' I replied.

'Really? I mistook you for my friend Adil. He's from Karachi. You aren't his brother, right?'

Soon the chat veered towards my bulging waistline.

'Brother, why don't you do something about your belly?' the young man said, looking accusingly at my protruding stomach.

'I have a cheap, magic remedy. It has benefited dozens like you. In three weeks your stomach will be as flat as mine,' he said. 'I want to help because you look like a nice man. Don't pay me anything, just remember me in your prayers.'

'And what do I need to do?' I asked.

'Not much. You have to drink a mixture of herbs. People spend so much money on gyms trying to lose, but this remedy costs only Dh50. Plus, it has no side effects. Take down the names of the secret ingredients you'll need and you can make this fat-loss potion yourself,' he said.

I took out my cell phone to key in the names, but except for black olives couldn't comprehend the gibberish-sounding names of the other items.

It was going the exact way described by the victims.

'Okay, get the olives first,' said my self-professed benefactor.

'We'll look for the other ingredients later,' he said, directing me to a nearby supermarket.

As I emerged with a Dh6 bottle of pitted olives in oil, the man led me to a shop that sold herbs and spices.

Inside, he rattled out a few names. I didn't know whether anything by those names existed, but the shopkeeper nodded knowingly and pulled out an assortment of bottles carrying what looked like crushed powder and seeds.

After a bit of haggling, my 'mentor' settled the price at Dh25 each for the two ingredients that would melt my tummy fat and make my stomach as hard as rock.

'See, I told you, it costs Dh50 only,' he said, as he took the olive bottle from my hand and asked the shopkeeper to grind the seeds and pour the ingredients inside the bottle.

As the shopkeeper went about his job, the man shook my hand and bade farewell, asking me to remember him in my prayers.

No sooner had the man disappeared around a bend than the shopkeeper handed me the 'magic' potion along with a bill for Dh200. 'But we settled for Dh50,' I protested.

'Exactly, Dh50 for the two herbs. But your friend asked me to put four spoons for better results,' he said.

Obviously, there was no way to call off the deal because by this time the finely ground mix had already been poured into the olive bottle.

It was clear he was hand-in-glove with the man who accosted me.

When the shopkeeper asked for the money, I removed the pillow from beneath my shirt with a flourish and placed it on the counter along with my identity card.

I can't forget the look on the man's face.

I didn't pay the shopkeeper, but a lot of people do.

Marginally overweight Dubai resident Adil, who fell for the scam, shelled out Dh300 for the herbal potion at a shop next door. A Sharjah resident who tipped the scales at ninety-five kilograms forked out Dh1,000 after being taken to another herbal store in the vicinity.

Dozens of victims contacted us after the story. From weight loss to baldness, fairness and acne, they had paid anything between Dh300 and Dh5,000 for the dodgy herbal remedies.

The conmen operate with impunity outside the Al Ain Centre even to this day.

Twice, they have approached me.

'Good evening, sir,' said a well-built man as I stepped out of my car when I visited the computer plaza in October 2022 to get my ageing laptop repaired. 'Are you Faisal bhai?' he began.

'No,' I said, wondering what he would try to sell me.

'You look so much like my friend's brother Faisal. He's from Lahore.'

'Well, I am not him,' I said, quickening my pace.

'Brother, your thinning hair, you want to do something about it. I have a magic remedy that will regrow it in three weeks and it costs almost nothing.'

The Case of the Misused Sperm

I have covered some bizarre lawsuits but this one from 2010 takes the cake.

It involved an Egyptian man, his Kiwi wife, their Filipina maid, a three-year-old girl and a prominent hospital. At the core of it all was a frozen male sperm.

The receptionist at *Gulf News* knew whom to call in the newsroom when people showed up at our office looking for help.

'Mr Mazhar, there is a gentleman here and he's got a very juicy story,' she said.

'What makes you think it's juicy?'

'Because,' she hesitated, 'the gentleman here says he got his sperm stolen, so I thought it was kind of juicy.'

I ignored the lame pun attempt and went down to meet the visitor. He was a big, bald and powerfully built man who wore a formal grey business suit, with matching necktie.

'I am Mohmmad Fouad,' he said, giving me a bone-crushing handshake.

As we huddled in a meeting room, Fouad pulled out a pile of papers from his handbag and held them out.

'I will cut to the chase,' he began. 'These are court documents and they show how my wife Anna secretly injected my sperm into our housemaid's womb to have a baby without my knowledge. She works at a hospital in Al Ain and has admitted to the charges.'

As a newspaper we stayed away from family conflicts. This was an exception.

The thirty-three-year-old Egyptian manager had met Anna, who was five years older than him, in the UAE. They married in Auckland, New Zealand, in 2008 after a brief courtship.

The couple wanted a baby. However, Anna could not conceive even after a fertility treatment. So they agreed to have a baby through surrogacy.

But since surrogacy is illegal in the UAE, it was decided to find a woman outside the country, preferably someone from Anna's family in New Zealand.

While the hunt for a surrogate mother was still on, Anna hired a young full-time Filipina maid, Elvie Ibanez, on her sponsorship.

A couple of years later, Elvie moved into Anna's Al Ain villa. Unknown to Fouad, she was tasked with more than just domestic chores.

Around the same time Anna asked Fouad for his sperm and took it to her hospital on the pretext of routine tests.

Fouad told me his wife took his sperm on four separate occasions before he left for Egypt for a few weeks. By the time he returned, their maid had a prominent baby bump. That is when Fouad said he found out where his sperm had ended up.

'I am aghast that my wife misused my sperm to impregnate a woman we had hired to do our dishes. And she did it behind my back. Not just that, she had even prepared an elaborate tri-party surrogacy agreement contract.'

Anna and Elvie had signed the contract way back in June 2010 and now they wanted Fouad to sign it as well.

Surrogacy agreements are invalid in the UAE. In fact, a surrogacy agreement can be treated as a criminal offence and those involved could be punished under Federal Law No. 3 of 1987 in Article 356 of the UAE's Penal Code.

'I wanted to alert the authorities, but Anna said if I did that, Elvie would be arrested for getting pregnant out of wedlock and our child would be born in jail and deported,' said Fouad.

He said Anna assured him she would circumvent the situation by ensuring the baby is born in New Zealand. Left with no choice, he signed the agreement. By this time, their relationship had turned sour. Fearing Fouad would report the maid, Anna secretly whisked her away to the Philippines. But Fouad traced her and flew her back.'

On 25 December 2010, Elvie gave birth to a baby girl, Salwa, at an Al Ain hospital. For her part, she was paid Dh15,000 by Anna.

Oddly, Glenda King, the then consular officer of the Consulate General of New Zealand in Dubai signed as a witness to the surrogacy completion agreement.

Days before she returned to the Philippines for good, Elvie also forfeited her rights to the baby and gave Anna her written consent to adopt Salwa under New Zealand laws.

But now neither Fouad nor Anna wanted to raise the baby.

Fouad got her an Egyptian passport and sent her to a third family in his home country.

Since her biological mother was unmarried, local health authorities refused to issue a birth certificate. Eventually Fouad had to prove his paternity through DNA testing and have the certificate issued through the court.

We ran a cover story headlined 'My Wife Misused My Sperm'. The accompanying photograph showed Fouad sitting in our meeting room, his head down dejectedly. Years later, I met Fouad again when he acted as a middleman for a real estate developer and offered me a million dirhams to kill a story.

Essays on Sale

Between 2020 and 2021, a US court convicted dozens of wealthy people for their involvement in the US college admissions scandal that made headlines around the world.

Prosecutors said parents paid up to $25 million to get their children into elite US schools. The investigation into the scandal was codenamed Operation Varsity Blues after a 1999 film of the same name. *Varsity Blues* was also the name of a subsequent Netflix documentary that uncovered the tactics used by the rich and the famous—including actors Lori Loughlin and Felicity Huffman—to bribe and cheat their children's way into top universities such as Stanford, the University of Southern California (USC) and the University of California, Los Angeles (UCLA). The case was the biggest of its kind prosecuted by the United States Department of Justice. Yet it is dwarfed by the global multi-billion-dollar essay mill industry that encourages students to cheat by buying essays—even PhDs—and then passing off the work as their own.

Outsourcing university assignments amounts to contract cheating—a widespread epidemic with research showing as one in six students, or an estimated 31 million, having engaged in the practice.

According to *Business Insider*, the network of companies peddling completed school work has a potentially far greater reach than the US college admissions scandal.

Before ChatGPT, the UAE was a hotbed for essay mills. For students struggling with deadlines, the temptation of outsourcing assignments was often hard to resist. And it's these vulnerable groups that the self-professed academic service providers prey on.

A simple Google search threw up over fifty such essay mills tempting students with tailor-made content.

'Do you struggle with your college coursework and it stresses you out?' said the website of one such company. 'Are you falling behind your peers and need help?' asked another.

For less than Dh150 many essay mills gladly provided a 500-word 'non plagiarised, authentic, error-free essay' on any topic.

For anything between Dh400 and Dh1,000, they were also willing to write a thesis and research paper—even a personal statement that's guaranteed to impress the admission officer and open the doors to overseas colleges.

I decided to shine the spotlight on the issue in the backdrop of the US admission scandal.

So I posed as an aspiring university applicant and randomly contacted several such UAE-based agencies with improbable assignments.

The outcome was a comical spectacle.

My first stop was an agency that prided itself as the 'most recommended research essay writing agency in the UAE'.

Shortly after I paid Dh140 via my credit card, it emailed us an argumentative essay on how 'eating dates can boost the memory of the one-humped dromedary camel'.

An extract from their submission read: 'There are numerous dates in the country and too many for the animals and for the humans too … The camels, especially the Dromedary camels are known to eat dates a lot. The other camels which are mostly in other parts of the world rarely eat date or never eat them.

'Due to this reason, the Dromedary camels are considered to have a lot of sense and memory as compared to other camels. By eating these dates, these camels are considered to have very rare chance or risk of any kind of disease. This can also be seen that these camels rarely get sick and even when they do; the disease is not too much to make a fuss about.'

Similarly, another essay mill sent us 300 words on 'why brushing teeth (not over brushing, mind you) can do more harm than good'.

'This [the act of brushing] causes the layer of the gum to recede due to its fragility and exposure which causes it to be directly affected and came in contact with the bristles of the brush which are the major element of damaging in terms of practising the conventional style of brushing.

'Modern times has done more harm to the health of the tooth and gums rather than the benefits,' reasoned the wise men at the firm, with ninety active writers working on 150 orders.

Yet another academic service provider charged us Dh140 for an essay explaining 'How the return of slavery may aid the economic structure of developing nations'.

Essay writing mills caught in our sting operation evaded our phone calls.

'We have been in the business for several years and handle dozens of orders daily,' said a representative of one such company before hanging up.

'You gave us a rubbish topic so we gave you a rubbish essay,' said a woman at the agency that enlightened us about the memory-enhancing powers of dates on camels.

When I published my investigation, I also published the outlandish essays, hoping they would make for a hilarious read, despite the seriousness of the matter. However, my report was lost amid a graver concern. On 11 March 2020, just a day after my story, the World Health Organization (WHO) declared the COVID-19 pandemic.

There was panic in the newsroom. However, our opinion editor Shyam A. Krishna had his own opinion about the looming threat.

An editorial in *Gulf News* on how the next newsbreak would kill the virus. 'A major news break on something that will have far-reaching consequences will trip up the virus coverage too,' he famously wrote. 'Soon we'll be poring over the new news: breaking it down, analysing every aspect of it. We won't have time for the virus. COVID-19 will be history.'

Krishna eventually had to eat his words. Over the next two years, he himself ended up writing on every aspect of the coronavirus, often rehashing wire stories and slapping his byline over it.

Our initial coverage of the pandemic could make a study for journalism students about the pitfalls of speculative reporting. Among the many I remember was an explainer on how rain and cloud seeding in the UAE might actually prevent the spread of the coronavirus.

Beggar Turns Mugger

I have spent a large part of my life hot on the heels of hardened criminals, but in mid-2014 I spent weeks chasing a middle-aged beggar who targeted worshippers attending Friday afternoon prayers at the Ibn Abbas Mosque in Sharjah's Al Majaz 1 area where I lived those days.

After collecting hundreds of dirhams, the clean-shaven Arab man would jump into a taxi and slip away. I followed him thrice. Each time he managed to shake me off. Once he outmanoeuvred me at a traffic signal after getting the cabbie to drive around the Sharjah Gold Souq five times. On another occasion, he abruptly got off on Immigration Road and entered a salon. He emerged an hour later after getting himself a Dh45 facial. I tried to tail him on foot but he disappeared into an alley. It was embarrassing.

'Got tricked again?' mocked the anonymous caller who had tipped me off.

'No, I got him,' I said. 'He goes to a salon. You think it's a big deal?'

Men and women begging outside mosques in Dubai have been caught living in five-star hotels with sacks full of cash. A few years back a fellow journalist posed as a beggar to show how he could make Dh1,200 in a matter of minutes.

Begging is a multi-million-dollar industry in the UAE. Planeloads of professional beggars descend on the country from South Asia every month. But it's during the month of Ramadan when their numbers really peak with 'tourist beggars' arriving here from all parts to exploit charitable sentiments.

Agents linked to criminal syndicates not only arrange their air tickets, visas and accommodation but, in some instances, even plan the itinerary of their 'clients', much like tour operators.

They pick spots where the beggars are to be deployed and for how long.

I had written extensively on the organised racket, uncovering how beggars fake disabilities to gain sympathy.

The tug at the heartstrings is aimed at the purse strings.

Dubai Police once caught a beggar posing as an amputee with Dh1,00,000 stashed in his fake artificial legs.

Creating awareness through my reports to discourage begging helped, but not always. I once wrote about a vengeful beggar who superglued a woman's car doors after she turned him away.

The woman and her young nieces remained locked out of the car for two hours before attendants from a gas station were called to prise open the jammed doors with special tools.

Now that was a story.

I wasn't interested in a beggar indulging in self-care.

'It's not what you think,' the anonymous caller said.

'Then why don't you tell me?'

'You are a journalist, go find out.'

'At least give me a hint.'

'Next time, don't follow him in your car after the Friday prayer. Instead, go to King Faisal Mosque. You will find it out yourself.'

I wanted to seek more details but the line went dead.

The next Friday I did what I was told. I drove down to the King Faisal Mosque ahead of the beggar, discreetly parked my car near the entrance and waited inside the vehicle. It was 1.15 p.m.

At 1.40 p.m. a taxi showed up and parked a short distance away from me. Its engine kept running. On the front passenger seat sat a man in grey kandoura. He was our beggar.

From my tinted Kia Mohave, I saw that his gaze was transfixed on an elderly bedraggled woman standing by the footsteps of the by-now largely empty mosque.

Suddenly, the cab door flung open and the beggar dashed down towards the woman.

As I watched, he seized her by the hair, pinned her to the ground and snatched her purse.

'This woman has been caught begging, it's illegal,' the Arab shouted as I mingled in a small crowd of curious onlookers and clicked a few pictures using my cell phone.

The Asian woman was indeed a beggar. She pleaded with the Arab to return her purse, but he refused and threatened to call the police.

'Please don't take my money, I am very poor,' the woman implored with folded hands.

But the Arab would have none of it. 'You broke the law and I will hand you over to the authorities along with your purse.' At one point he even fished out a cell phone from his pocket and pretended to speak to someone in authority.

The charade was so convincing, the woman got scared and took flight. Even bystanders were impressed. 'He's from the CID. He often cracks down on beggars here,' said one of them.

As the man tried to walk away with his daylight loot, I alerted onlookers about his real identity. His cover blown, the man handed over the purse to the bystanders and ran away.

This time I was able to track him to his house. It was a two-bedroom apartment in Al Qasimya.

We published the story headlined 'Beggar in One Mosque, Mugger in Another'.

Nobody ever saw him again.

Fraudsters Trapped in My Home

Granted, this story doesn't quite fall in the league of big exposés. But I had great fun uncovering dodgy firms who go door to door using scare tactics and fraudulent methods to sell overpriced water filters and purification systems to UAE residents.

Typically, the scam runs like this: a sales agent calls you and offers to test your water quality. Because it's free, you don't mind a little demo. The sales agent comes to your house and asks for samples of your tap and bottled drinking water.

He fishes out a device with multiple rods, plugs it into a power socket and immerses the rods into the samples.

Seconds later, the colour of both water samples turns a horrid brownish black. As the water colour changes before your disbelieving eyes, the agent warns you that your water is highly contaminated and could cause a host of diseases, including kidney failure and cancer.

The best solution, you are told, is to buy their 'breakthrough' water treatment device. To illustrate his point, the agent proceeds to do the same test with a sample of water filtered by their company's product. And guess what, the water colour remains largely unchanged.

Their water filter could cost anywhere between Dh2,000 and Dh4,000. But what the heck, it's still a small price to pay for the health and safety of your family.

At this point, you have been conned by one of the oldest tricks in the chemistry book.

To expose the lies in the high-pressure sales, I posed as a potential customer and contacted sales agents of various firms for a live demonstration much to the amusement of my children.

The agents took the bait and set out to con me. Unknown to them, I had our bottled drinking and tap water samples ready in separate glasses. Not some ordinary water, but Evian and Perrier— two of the biggest and most reputed bottled mineral water brands in the world.

'Tut-tut … so this is what you use for cooking and bathing and this is what you drink. Too bad. You may not see it with the naked eye but both contain toxins,' said the agent grimly, as he held aloft the glasses, which he thought contained our tap and drinking water. Out came the electrical device and the rods were dipped into the samples.

Almost immediately, the samples turned a yucky cola brown colour. 'See for yourself,' he said, shaking the glass. 'These chemicals and impurities can cause ulcers, kidney stones, gall bladder disease and cancer. Your water is unfit for human consumption. It's dangerous to even use it for bathing or cooking,' the agent declared before proceeding on a long lecture strewn with pseudo-scientific rubbish.

Offers for tea or water during the demo were sternly declined. 'Sir, how can I have anything in a house where water is contaminated with such dangerous chemicals? It's the same problem everywhere in the UAE, which is why I carry my own filtered water,' he said, taking out a water bottle from a bag. He poured it into a glass and ran his test on it. 'See, it's clear. No impurities.'

'What do you do when you run out of it and have no access to your filtered stuff?' I enquired.

'Evian,' he said, 'I only drink Evian water in such situations.'

Turns out it's what I gave him for the test—and he made it turn a murky brown.

The same evening, we called another agent. She was given two popular local brands in the guise of tap and bottled drinking water. The results were the same. 'You're risking your family's safety,' she said, elaborating on the virtues of their seven-stage reverse osmosis ultraviolet water filter system.

Why did well-known water brands 'fail' the test, resulting in such a drastic change in colour? The explanation lies in science—or to be precise, in the sales agent's 'magical' device. It was basically a portable electrolysis kit, also known as the precipitator. Some run on batteries while others run on electricity but they work the same way.

The sales agents use it to conduct a chemistry experiment called electrolysis.

If you ask a science student, they'll tell you that when you pass an electric current through water using electrodes, it breaks down into oxygen and hydrogen, causing decomposition. However, the electrodes are typically made of reactive iron, which can oxidise and create rust, specifically ferric hydroxide. This rust doesn't dissolve easily and results in the dark sludge you see in the test. Surprisingly, this rust isn't from your building's water tank or pipes, as you might have thought, but originates from the electrodes. The murky colour occurs due to these electrodes reacting with the minerals in the water, including safe and healthy minerals like calcium and magnesium.

It's important to note that only minerals respond to the electric current; bacteria and viruses do not. So, when sales agents tested water samples, they didn't change much during the electrolysis because these samples lacked dissolved solids or minerals. No minerals mean no electrical conductivity, and without electricity, there's no electrolysis, no reaction and, consequently, no sludge. It's a straightforward process.

I took their 'contamination-free' water with a grain of salt, quite literally. I added some salt and asked for a retest. Two of them refused, and the third stopped as his water started turning gooey black.

So what's the bottom line? The products these companies are selling are just like any other water purification system that works on the principle of reverse osmosis. The issue lies in their use of dubious tactics to uncover supposed flaws in water from bottled companies and municipalities, leveraging unfounded fears among concerned residents to promote their products.

Despite the evidence presented, water purification companies have consistently denied any wrongdoing, often claiming their actions aim to 'create awareness among residents'. However, this assertion doesn't hold true.

Your bottled water is perfectly safe to drink, and municipal water in the UAE is also safe when the building's water tank is properly maintained. If you still wish to install a water purification system, opt for a reputable brand and resist the allure of filters with claims of electromagnets, electrolytic processes, molecular oscillations and the like. There is no credible evidence to support the effectiveness of these water-conditioning methods.

Another sting operation I carried out at home exposed a gang of poachers who went door to door, peddling dubious medicines derived from the highly endangered musk deer. They claimed their concoctions could cure 101 diseases, including cancer. I was tipped off about the racket after scores bought these remedies, paying up to Dh35,000 for a bottle.

All musk deer species are protected by the CITES, of which the UAE is a signatory, and anyone found selling or buying products made from the antler could face jail, a fine or both.

Posing as a customer, I called the Abu Dhabi–based gang members home and sought cures for arthritis and blood pressure.

The middle-aged husband and wife duo introduced themselves as tribals from Karnataka. Handing out a business card with local contact details, they got down to business right away.

'Our musk-based medicines have guaranteed cure for 101 ailments where Western medicines have failed. Cancer, myasthenia gravis, diabetes, you name it,' boasted the man who gave his name as Shankar.

'Many patients in Abu Dhabi, Dubai and Sharjah have benefited from our drugs,' claimed his wife, Jyothi, as she fished out a hairy-shelled woody pod from her handbag and laid it on a table.

Within seconds, the room was filled with a strong musk fragrance. 'We hunt deer for a living and spend years collecting these,' said the man as he gave a breakdown of the treatment cost.

'One gram of musk costs Dh107; you need 35 grams for arthritis medicine in addition to 25 grams of powdered deer antlers which costs Dh40 per gram. Only one out of around a hundred deer have this special powder in their antlers. We hunt many animals to see which ones have them,' said Shankar.

How did they manage to smuggle the musk pods (around fifteen by their own admission) past the UAE customs, I asked innocently.

'It was a big risk … we could have been caught,' said Shankar.

Considered one of the most precious raw materials in perfumery for thousands of years, musk is a strong-smelling brownish substance secreted by the male musk deer found in Central Asia, China, Mongolia and the Himalayas. The stag drops these woody balls to attract females and mark its territory. Each musk pod weighs about 25 grams. It is because of this tiny pod that musk deer have become the favourite target of poachers. Just one kilo of musk could fetch around $50,000 in the black market, making it one of the most expensive natural products in the world.

To obtain just one kilogram of musk, roughly 160 deer must be hunted. While it is possible to extract the gland without killing the animal, this humane method is seldom employed, with cruel trapping and killing techniques prevailing.

Our story went online around midnight. I don't know if the poachers read it but I suspect they did because they left in a haste on an early morning flight to India.

Hacker Buba and the $3 Million Ransom

Cyber security is critical for banking today, but back in 2015, it wasn't even a blip on the radar. So when Sharjah's Invest Bank was hacked and held to ransom, I jumped on the story.

The cybercriminal behind the attack was quite a character. He went by the name of Hacker Buba and mocked the bank by using a photograph of their IT head as his DP on X as he threatened to leak the personal details of thousands of customers unless he was paid $3 million in Bitcoins.

I first got to know about the breach when Buba began posting the account statements of some government entities, UAE firms and individuals on the microblogging site.

The bank got his X account suspended but the reprieve was short-lived. Within hours Buba created a new identity and was back with vengeance, uploading account statements of 500 bank customers in just one tweet attachment.

I remember visiting the bank's elderly Pakistani general manager to get a comment. I was expecting him to be jittery but he was surprisingly dismissive about the threat.

'We won't give in to any extortion threat,' he said as he sat huddled with his aides. I recognised one of them by his Carlton Banks moustache.

He was the IT manager whose picture Buba was using as his DP. 'All that the hacker has got is some customer information. What can he do with it?'

I was appalled.

It was obvious that the enormity of the situation had not dawned upon the bank's management. But customers who had found out about the leak knew what it meant. They were horrified. I reached out to Hacker Buba via a direct X message. He responded by offering me 5 per cent of the ransom amount if I cooperated with him.

'I give u 5 % from total I get. Have many banks from UAE, Qater, ksa and etc. Will work together,' he said in a message.

I refrained from mentioning the bank's name in my report, as Buba had hoped I would. He aimed to exert pressure on the bank for payment, but I refused. Our story was published without revealing the bank's identity. Nevertheless, news circulated, leading several companies to promptly close their accounts with the institution.

But the Invest Bank didn't panic. Their management stuck to their guns: no matter what happens, we will not pay the hacker.

Hacker Buba was not amused. He waited for a couple of days and then carried out his threat, dumping the data of 50,000 credit card users, account balance of 65,000 customers and about 1,00,000 transaction histories among a slew of other information in six zip files.

He had stored the files on an East European basketball team's website that he had also hacked and was now using as a temporary storage facility.

One database analysed by us included the sensitive information of around 40,000 customers, including their names, credit card numbers and birthdays. I spotted several familiar names and randomly looked up some transactions.

They said a lot about them.

Ghostbusting in Sharjah

In April 2007, my photographer colleague, Sankha Kar, and I embarked on an interesting adventure, checking into a hotel that had gained notoriety for being haunted. Our curiosity led us to the Holiday Inn on Sharjah's King Faisal Road, intrigued by the disquieting accounts from Indian pilots, including the renowned Captain Devi Sharan.

Captain Sharan had earned the prestigious Safe Skies Award for his extraordinary bravery during the hijacking of Indian Airline flight IC-814, an ordeal that began on Christmas Eve in 1999 and stretched on till New Year's Eve. The hijackers' objective was clear: secure the release of Islamist terrorists held in Indian prisons. They directed the aircraft to a series of locations, including Amritsar, Lahore, and across the Persian Gulf to Dubai. Ultimately, they forced the airbus to land in Kandahar, Afghanistan, a city then under Taliban control. The hijackers released twenty-seven of the 176 passengers in Dubai but fatally stabbed one and wounded several others.

It was truly astonishing to think that Captain Sharan, who had faced seven harrowing days in the company of armed hijackers during that terrifying incident, could be rattled by mere ghostly rumours surrounding the hotel that was often used by airline staff during flight layovers.

Late one evening, I managed to obtain a copy of the letter Captain Sharan had written to the hotel, detailing the hauntings. I promptly contacted Anand Kumar Pande, the UAE country manager, who confirmed receiving the letter but remained tight-lipped about its contents. At this point, I faced a choice: should I run the story based solely on the letter, or should I investigate by checking into the hotel? I chose the latter.

I called Nirmala and shared my plan. Her reaction was immediate. 'You're crazy, Maz,' she exclaimed. Yet, I pressed on.

'It better be worth it,' Nirmala cautioned as she reluctantly agreed to our idea. The hotel stood directly opposite my house, and Sankha, my colleague, lived nearby as well. With minimal luggage in tow, we walked up to the Holiday Inn and checked into a sixth-floor room to unravel the mysteries that shrouded this place.

As we roamed the hotel's shadowy hallways, the oppressive weight of those ghostly accounts bore down on us. The hotel seemed to guard its secrets zealously, revealing nothing to us. We didn't hear anything go bump in the night, but I must admit, there was an unmistakable eerie vibe about the place. It made me wonder if our anticipation of encountering the supernatural was playing tricks on my mind.

Sankha captured moments of me, Sherlock Holmes–style, inspecting every nook and cranny, even peering under the bed for a glimpse of paranormal activity. Meanwhile, back home, Eram launched a relentless assault on my phone, bombarding me with calls.

But the real showdown had happened a few hours earlier when she had discovered my covert mission. She was not pleased and didn't hold back her fury. 'So, what are you now, a ghostbuster?' She was resolute. 'I'm not letting you wander off into this spooky adventure. What if the ghosts decide you're their new best friend? Those pilots didn't just imagine things.'

'Everything will be fine,' I assured her, 'and I won't be alone. There are plenty of other guests staying there.' However, her worry was relentless. She hastily muttered a prayer, waved a copy of the Quran over me, and sneakily slipped it into my luggage.

Eram called me repeatedly throughout the night. 'Are you safe? Did you see anything? What are you doing?' Each call carried an undertone of anxiety. 'Recite the Quran,' she implored.

I chuckled, trying to ease her fears. 'If I recite the Quran, I might deter the ghosts. Remember, we're here to see them, not scare them away.'

We published a story, recounting our night at the hotel that had left a hero pilot and his crew on edge, reassuring our readers that we found no unusual occurrences to report.

Little did I know that in May 2007, at the Dubai airport, fate would weave our paths with those of Indian Airlines staff members. A flight delay thwarted my urgent trip to India, but it also led me to an unforgettable conversation.

As I waited at the Indian Airlines counter, I casually asked a purser about the hotel.

'Oh, so you read the report,' he remarked.

With a wry smile, I replied, 'Well, I was the one who wrote it.'

'Oh, so it was you,' he said, the hurt in his eyes evident. 'You must have thought we made all of this up,' he continued.

'Well,' I began, 'I stayed at the hotel and found—'

'Which floor did you stay on?' he interrupted.

'Sixth,' I replied.

'Try staying on one of the higher floors,' he suggested, gesturing to some cabin crew members who had gathered around, eager to share their stories.

He called a flight attendant over.

'Could you tell this gentleman what happened to you at the Sharjah Hotel?'

The attendant hesitated. 'It is okay, don't worry,' the purser encouraged him. The attendant finally spoke up, his voice trembling with fear. 'I found myself thrown out of my bed, as if someone had hurled me.'

I turned to another young man who identified himself as an inflight staff member.

'And what was your experience like?'

The inflight staff member, hailing from South India, recounted his eerie encounter. 'I was changing my uniform when I heard a loud thud followed by the sound of a child crying in the room. I looked around, thinking there was indeed a child, but there was none. Suddenly, the crying stopped, and my shaving kit, which had been on the table, fell to the floor. Immediately, my coat slipped off the hanger, and an electric kettle switched on by itself.'

I heard in disbelief as one after the other, three airline staff recounted their experiences, including a man who said he felt like someone was choking him by the throat.

My daughter, always quick-witted, suggested a clever headline for a follow-up story: 'Holiday Djinn'.

However, my attempts to book a room on one of the higher floors were thwarted by the hotel staff, who recognised my face. Subsequently, the hotel changed hands and reopened under a new name. Unfortunately, it met the same fate as two car showrooms adjacent to it and a multi-storey outlet of the UAE's largest electronic retailer. To this day, they all remain shuttered, leaving the area with an eerie atmosphere, as if haunted by the whispers of its past.

The Last Word

Just like every other industry, journalism has evolved over time. When we started, typewriters were still in use, and handwritten stories were the norm.

Our lifeline was a teleprinter that spewed scrolls of news, business updates, sports scores, national headlines and international stories, all tangled like a complex puzzle in the form of paper rolls. Senior journalists spent hours manually deciphering this deluge, sorting and categorising before distributing them to respective desks.

Then came the seismic shift as newsrooms embraced computers. Desktop publishing made typewriters relics of the past. We navigated this change with a mix of excitement and trepidation. The adrenaline of breaking news was no longer conveyed through the teleprinter's clatter but through the ping of emails and the hum of servers.

Before cell phones and instant messaging, getting our work published was no small feat.

One vivid memory whisks me back to 1997, aboard a train bound for Allahabad, carrying the last ashes of Mahatma Gandhi for their sacred immersion in the Ganges. This historic moment unfolded during my tenure at *The Pioneer*. As the train pulled into the station one late evening, I leaped onto the platform with a single purpose: find a fax machine. I had handwritten my report on an

A4 sheet using an ink pen, seated between two burly passengers in a noisy train, and I had to send it. Time was running short: the story was bound for the front pages of both the Lucknow and Delhi editions.

Just beyond the railway station, I spotted a photocopy shop. With a quick exchange, I handed my report to the shop attendant, including the newspaper's fax number. Afterwards, I hurried across the road to a nearby grocery store and purchased a water bottle. Upon returning to the shop, I anxiously asked about the fax's progress. The attendant's nonchalant response sent a wave of panic surging through me, 'I don't know where it's gone. Maybe the wind carried it away.'

Fortunately, I managed to rescue my notes. They were tethered near the edge of a drain.

At *Lucknow City Magazine*, we copied our stories in floppy drives before taking them to a computer design shop in Hazratganj where a Sikh designer would lay out the pages using any font he fancied. By the time I joined *Newslead*, newspapers had transitioned to in-house designers.

Our editor, Mr Ajit Parmar, harboured an eccentric, childlike fondness for background tints and reverse text, both of which were entirely new to him. He inundated our pages with them, much to chief designer Satish Dhiman's chagrin. One day, Satish playfully informed him that we couldn't use any more tint as we were nearly out, reserving it for emergencies. To our surprise, Mr Parmar took it quite seriously. The next day, he summoned the tech team to his office and requested them to 'refuel the tint'.

Leapfrogging from one newspaper to another, I stood in awe as the journalism landscape transformed, ushering in the era of social media, X, TikTok, Instagram and Facebook Live. We transitioned from typewriters to embrace the digital age, and now, we confront a new beast in the newsroom: AI.

As I bring this book to a close, I'm reminded of a peculiar encounter I had not too long ago. Shopping at the Mall of the Emirates, I found myself in search of a few shirts, dressed rather inconspicuously in a hoodie for no apparent reason.

Suddenly, a relative approached me from behind, his demeanour a mix of caution and curiosity. He leaned in, whispered into my ear, 'You need to pull your hoodie closer to your face. You're out investigating, right? But they can recognise you.'

A smile played across his face, convinced he had just offered me a piece of sage advice. I couldn't resist a chuckle, knowing that sometimes, the image of an investigative journalist can precede you, even on a simple shopping expedition.

So, here's to the adventures yet to be had, the mysteries yet to be solved and, of course, the perfect shirts yet to be discovered.

Acknowledgements

I would first like to express my heartfelt appreciation to those who have played pivotal roles in the creation of this memoir.

Let me begin by extending my deepest thanks to my wife and the love of my life, Eram. Her steadfast support during the darkest hours, as I faced death threats, court cases and the cold steel bars of incarceration, was my sanctuary. Her sleepless nights filled with worry and whispered prayers were the armour that shielded me. Eram, you are my rock.

To Aniruddha Bahal, one of India's most distinguished investigative journalists, your encouragement was the spark that ignited this journey. You urged me to set aside my aspirations of writing fiction and embark on this uncharted path. For that, I am profoundly grateful.

My daughter Shazia deserves a special mention. She scrutinised my manuscript with an unfiltered honesty that only a daughter can provide. Her smiles and frowns reflected the quality of my words. 'No, Abba, this sounds very tacky,' she'd declare, and with those words, she became my guiding star.

Across the border, in Lahore, Pakistan, I found Dr Amina Mahmood, a literary soul who read every word of *The Maz Files*. Her belief in my abilities breathed life into my spirit when it faltered. Amina, though we have never met in person, our collaboration on my next book, *Myra*, is a testament to the connections forged through words.

To Amanda James, a Dubai-based Briton, your contributions to our investigations were invaluable. Your dedication and tireless efforts added layers of depth to the stories we uncovered.

Next, my gratitude extends to the countless whistleblowers and sources on the ground who entrusted me with their truths. Without your courage and willingness to share, this book would have remained a mere idea.

I cannot forget the stalwart legal teams and the editors who have walked this path with me. Your guidance and support have been instrumental in bringing these investigations to light. Abdul Hamid, the editor-in-chief of *Gulf News*, and *XPRESS* editor Bobby Naqvi deserve special recognition for their commitment to journalistic integrity. Many of these stories found their way to publication under their leadership.

This memoir, born from trials and tribulations, would not have existed without the collective efforts of all those mentioned here. Your belief in the power of truth and storytelling has made this journey worthwhile.